Scala Design Patterns
Second Edition

Design modular, clean, and scalable applications by applying proven design patterns in Scala

Ivan Nikolov

BIRMINGHAM - MUMBAI

Scala Design Patterns
Second Edition

Commissioning Editor: Aaron Lazar
Acquisition Editor: Sandeep Mishra
Content Development Editor: Akshada Iyer
Technical Editor: Abhishek Sharma
Copy Editor: Safis Editing
Project Coordinator: Prajakta Naik
Proofreader: Safis Editing
Indexer: Pratik Shirodkar
Graphics: Jisha Chirayil
Production Coordinator: Shantanu Zagade

First published: February 2016
Second edition: April 2018

Production reference: 1060418

Published by Packt Publishing Ltd.
Livery Place
35 Livery Street
Birmingham
B3 2PB, UK.

ISBN 978-1-78847-130-5

www.packtpub.com

`mapt.io`

Mapt is an online digital library that gives you full access to over 5,000 books and videos, as well as industry leading tools to help you plan your personal development and advance your career. For more information, please visit our website.

Why subscribe?

- Spend less time learning and more time coding with practical eBooks and Videos from over 4,000 industry professionals

- Improve your learning with Skill Plans built especially for you

- Get a free eBook or video every month

- Mapt is fully searchable

- Copy and paste, print, and bookmark content

PacktPub.com

Did you know that Packt offers eBook versions of every book published, with PDF and ePub files available? You can upgrade to the eBook version at `www.PacktPub.com` and as a print book customer, you are entitled to a discount on the eBook copy. Get in touch with us at `service@packtpub.com` for more details.

At `www.PacktPub.com`, you can also read a collection of free technical articles, sign up for a range of free newsletters, and receive exclusive discounts and offers on Packt books and eBooks.

Contributors

About the author

Ivan Nikolov is a technical architect based in London. He works in the ad tech industry and uses Scala in combination with libraries and technologies such as Spark, Hadoop, RabbitMQ, Kafka, SQL and NoSQL stores, and Akka. He also uses other JVM and scripting languages. Some of the projects Ivan has worked on include a large-scale real-time machine learning platform, batch processing solutions, and high load APIs. Ivan also likes getting involved with open source projects, whether it be to contribute or get inspiration and good ideas.

I would like to thank Felix and Tasia and my mother, Veronika, for their interest in this book and everything I do. Thanks to Becky for dealing with me working until late in the evenings and all of her support.

Finally, thanks to everyone involved in publishing this book—editors, technical reviewer, and people I haven't been in touch with but have invested their time in making sure that everything went smoothly.

About the reviewer

Vasilis Nicolaou is a software engineer, Linux and FOSS hobbyist and enthusiast. He began his career at CERN as a Linux developer and now works for BookingGo as a senior software engineer developing microservices and distributed system solutions with Scala and Akka.

Packt is searching for authors like you

If you're interested in becoming an author for Packt, please visit `authors.packtpub.com` and apply today. We have worked with thousands of developers and tech professionals, just like you, to help them share their insight with the global tech community. You can make a general application, apply for a specific hot topic that we are recruiting an author for, or submit your own idea.

Table of Contents

Preface

Software engineering and design has existed for many years now. We use software almost everywhere in our lives, and this makes programs distinct in terms of the problems they solve.

Regardless of the number of things that can be done with programming, there are still some specific features that repeat over and over again. Over time, people have come up with some best practices that help to tackle specific patterns that emerge in programs. These are called design patterns.

Design patterns solve not only commonly occurring problems, but also deal with language limitations. No matter what the specific design patterns are and what single issue they solve, all of them in the end aim at producing better software. This includes improved readability, simplicity, easier maintainability, testability, extendibility, and efficiency. Today, design patterns are an important part of every good software engineer's arsenal.

Together with the large number of problems that we tackle with programming, there are also many languages that we can use. Every language is different and has its strengths and weaknesses, so we also need to take this into consideration when doing something. In this book, we will look at design patterns from the point of view of Scala.

Scala has become extremely popular in the last couple of years, and the numbers using it keep growing. Many companies use it in production for various purposes—big data processing, writing APIs, machine learning, and so on. Switching to Scala from popular languages, such as Java, turns out to be quite simple because it is a hybrid of an object-oriented language and a functional programming language. Using Scala to its full potential, however, requires us to be familiar with not only the object-oriented features, but also with the functional ones. The use of Scala could improve performance and the time it takes to implement the features. One of the reasons is the really high expressivity of Scala.

The fact that Scala is close to object-oriented languages means that many of the design patterns for object-oriented programming are still applicable here. The fact that it is also functional means that some other design patterns are also applicable, and some of the object-oriented ones could be modified to better fit the paradigm of Scala. In this book, we will be focusing on all of them—we will go through some specific features of Scala and then look at the popular Gang of Four design patterns viewed from the Scala perspective. We will also become familiar with design patterns that are exclusive to Scala and understand different functional programming concepts, including monoids and monads. Having meaningful examples always makes learning and understanding easier. We will try to provide examples that you can easily map to real problems that you would potentially be solving. We will also introduce some libraries that will be useful for anyone who writes real-world applications.

Who this book is for

This book is aimed for people who already have some knowledge of Scala, but want to get a more practical understanding of how to apply it in real-world application development. This book is also useful as a reference to consult while designing applications. Having an understanding of the importance of using best practices and writing nice code is good; however, even if you don't, hopefully, you will be convinced by the time you finish reading this book. Prior knowledge of design patterns is not required, but if you are familiar with some, this book will be useful, as we will take a look at them from the point of view of Scala.

What this book covers

Chapter 1, *The Design Patterns Out There and Setting Up Your Environment*, is a brief introduction to design patterns, why they exist, and their different types. This chapter also provides you with tips on how you can set up your environment in order to easily run the examples in the book.

Chapter 2, *Traits and Mixin Compositions*, talks about traits and mixin compositions in Scala, multiple inheritance, and the rules of linearization that the Scala programming language uses when extending multiple traits.

Chapter 3, *Unification*, covers the various unifications that exist in Scala, which makes it as expressive as it is.

Chapter 4, *Abstract and Self Types*, covers the different types of polymorphism that exist in Scala, which help to make generic and extendible software.

Chapter 5, *Aspect-Oriented Programming and Components*, shows the concept of aspect-oriented programming and how it can be applied to Scala. This chapter also explains what components are and how to build applications using multiple small and simple components.

Chapter 6, *Creational Design Patterns*, covers the most popular creational design patterns from the Gang of Four. All patterns are viewed from the point of view of Scala, and alternatives are shown where applicable.

Chapter 7, *Structural Design Patterns*, goes through the most popular structural design patterns from the Gang of Four from the Scala point of view. This chapter also shows Scala alternatives where this is applicable and gives usage advice.

Chapter 8, *Behavioral Design Patterns - Part One*, covers part one of the behavioral design patterns from the Gang of Four viewed from the Scala perspective. This chapter also provides examples and usage advice.

Chapter 9, *Behavioral Design Patterns - Part Two*, covers part two of the behavioral design patterns from the Gang of Four viewed from the Scala perspective. This chapter also provides examples and usage advice.

Chapter 10, *Functional Design Patterns - the Deep Theory*, delves into pure functional programming concepts, such as monoids, functors, and monads. This chapter also explains these concepts in an understandable way, along with some examples.

Chapter 11, *Applying What We Have Learned*, presents design patterns that are specific to Scala. It is loaded with examples along with theory and usage advice.

Chapter 12, *Real-Life Applications*, introduces you to the Scalaz library. You will write a complete application that applies many of the concepts learned in the book, and this chapter will finish off with a summary.

To get the most out of this book

This book assumes that the reader is already familiar with Scala. We have provided examples for each chapter in projects using Maven and SBT. You should have some knowledge of either one of these tools and have it installed on your machine. You are also recommended to have a modern and up-to-date IDE installed on your computer, for example, IntelliJ. You are encouraged to open the actual projects, as the examples in this book focus on the design patterns and, in some cases, imports are omitted in favor of space.

The examples in the book were written and tested on a Unix-based operating system; however, they should also successfully compile and run on Windows.

Download the example code files

You can download the example code files for this book from your account at `www.packtpub.com`. If you purchased this book elsewhere, you can visit `www.packtpub.com/support` and register to have the files emailed directly to you.

You can download the code files by following these steps:

1. Log in or register at `www.packtpub.com`.
2. Select the **SUPPORT** tab.
3. Click on **Code Downloads & Errata**.
4. Enter the name of the book in the **Search** box and follow the onscreen instructions.

Once the file is downloaded, please make sure that you unzip or extract the folder using the latest version of:

- WinRAR/7-Zip for Windows
- Zipeg/iZip/UnRarX for Mac
- 7-Zip/PeaZip for Linux

The code bundle for the book is also hosted on GitHub at `https://github.com/PacktPublishing/Scala-Design-Patterns-Second-Edition`. In case there's an update to the code, it will be updated on the existing GitHub repository.

We also have other code bundles from our rich catalog of books and videos available at `https://github.com/PacktPublishing/`. Check them out!

Conventions used

There are a number of text conventions used throughout this book.

`CodeInText`: Indicates code words in text, database table names, folder names, filenames, file extensions, pathnames, dummy URLs, user input, and Twitter handles. Here is an example: "The base class is specified using `extends` and then all traits are added using the `with` keyword."

A block of code is set as follows:

```
class MultiplierIdentity {
  def identity: Int = 1
}
```

When we wish to draw your attention to a particular part of a code block, the relevant lines or items are set in bold:

```
Error:(11, 8) object Clashing inherits conflicting members:
  method hello in trait A of type ()String and
  method hello in trait B of type ()String
(Note: this can be resolved by declaring an override in object Clashing.)
object Clashing extends A with B {
       ^
```

Any command-line input or output is written as follows:

```
Result 1: 6
Result 2: 2
Result 3: 6
Result 4: 6
Result 5: 6
Result 6: 3
```

Bold: Indicates a new term, an important word, or words that you see onscreen.

Warnings or important notes appear like this.

Tips and tricks appear like this.

Get in touch

Feedback from our readers is always welcome.

General feedback: Email feedback@packtpub.com and mention the book title in the subject of your message. If you have questions about any aspect of this book, please email us at questions@packtpub.com.

Errata: Although we have taken every care to ensure the accuracy of our content, mistakes do happen. If you have found a mistake in this book, we would be grateful if you would report this to us. Please visit www.packtpub.com/submit-errata, selecting your book, clicking on the Errata Submission Form link, and entering the details.

Piracy: If you come across any illegal copies of our works in any form on the Internet, we would be grateful if you would provide us with the location address or website name. Please contact us at copyright@packtpub.com with a link to the material.

If you are interested in becoming an author: If there is a topic that you have expertise in and you are interested in either writing or contributing to a book, please visit authors.packtpub.com.

Reviews

Please leave a review. Once you have read and used this book, why not leave a review on the site that you purchased it from? Potential readers can then see and use your unbiased opinion to make purchase decisions, we at Packt can understand what you think about our products, and our authors can see your feedback on their book. Thank you!

For more information about Packt, please visit packtpub.com.

The Design Patterns Out There and Setting Up Your Environment

1

In the world of computer programming, there are multiple ways to create a solution to a given problem. However, some might wonder whether there is a correct way of achieving a specific task. The answer is yes; there is always a right way, but in software development, there are usually multiple right ways to achieve a task. Some factors exist that guide the programmer to the right solution and, depending on them, people tend to get the expected result. These factors could define many things—the actual language being used, the algorithm, the type of executable produced, the output format, and the code structure. In this book, the language is already chosen for us—Scala. There are, however, a number of ways to use Scala, and we will be focusing on them—the design patterns.

In this chapter, we will explain what design patterns are and why they exist. We will go through the different types of design patterns that are out there. This book aims to provide useful examples to aid you in the learning process, and being able to run them easily is key. Hence, some points on how to set up a development environment properly will be given here. The top-level topics we will go through are as follows:

- What is a design pattern and why do they exist?
- The main types of design patterns and their features
- Choosing the right design pattern
- Setting up a development environment in real life

The last point doesn't have much to do with design patterns. However, it is always a good idea to build projects properly, as this makes it much easier to work in the future.

Design patterns

Before delving into the Scala design patterns, we have to explain what they actually are, why they exist, and why it is worth being familiar with them.

Software is a broad subject, and there are innumerable examples of things people can do with it. At first glance, most of these things are completely different—games, websites, mobile phone applications, and specialized systems for different industries. There are, however, many similarities in how software is built. Many times, people have to deal with similar issues, no matter the type of software they create. For example, computer games, as well as websites, might need to access a database. And throughout time, by experience, developers learn how structuring their code differs for the various tasks that they perform.

The formal definition for design patterns

A design pattern is a reusable solution to a recurring problem in software design. It is not a finished piece of code but a template that helps to solve a particular problem or family of problems.

Design patterns are best practices at which the software community has arrived over a period of time. They are supposed to help you write efficient, readable, testable, and easily extendable code. In some cases, they can be the result of a programming language not being expressive enough to elegantly achieve a goal. This means that more feature-rich languages might not even need a design pattern, while others still do. Scala is one of those rich languages, and in some cases, it makes the use of some design patterns obsolete or simpler. We will see how exactly it does that in this book.

The lack or existence of a certain functionality within a programming language also makes it able to implement additional design patterns that others cannot. The opposite is also valid—it might not be able to implement things that others can.

Scala and design patterns

Scala is a hybrid language that combines features from object-oriented and functional languages. This not only allows it to keep some of the well-known object-oriented design patterns relevant, but also provides various other ways of exploiting its features to write code that is clean, efficient, testable, and extendable all at the same time. The hybrid nature of the language also makes some of the traditional object-oriented design patterns obsolete, or possible, using other cleaner techniques.

The need for design patterns and their benefits

Writing code without the conscious use of a design pattern is something many software engineers do. In the end, however, they either end up using one without realizing it, or they end up with code that can be improved in some way. As we mentioned earlier, design patterns help to write efficient, readable, extendable, and testable code. All these features are really important to companies in the industry.

Even though in some cases it is preferable to quickly write a prototype and get it out, it is more usually the case that a piece of software is supposed to evolve. Maybe you will have experience of extending some badly written code, but regardless, it is a challenging task and takes a really long time, and sometimes it feels that rewriting it would be easier. Moreover, this makes introducing bugs into the system much more likely.

Code readability is also something that should be appreciated. Of course, one could use a design pattern and still have their code hard to read, but generally, design patterns help. Big systems are usually worked on by many people, and everyone should be able to understand what exactly is going on. Also, people who join a team are able to integrate much more easily and quickly if they are working on a well-written piece of software.

Testability is something that prevents developers from introducing bugs when writing or extending code. In some cases, code could be created so badly that it is not even testable. Design patterns are supposed to eliminate these problems as well.

While efficiency is often connected with algorithms, design patterns could also affect it. A simple example could be an object that takes a long time to instantiate, and instances are used in many places in an application, but could be made a singleton instead. You will see more concrete examples in the later chapters of this book.

Design pattern categories

The fact that software development is an extremely broad topic leads to a number of things that can be done with programming. Requirements can vary greatly between different industries and engineering teams. These facts have caused many different design patterns to be invented. This is further contributed to by the existence of various programming languages with different features and levels of expressiveness.

This book focuses on the design patterns from the point of view of Scala. As we mentioned previously, Scala is a hybrid language. This leads us to a few famous design patterns that are not needed anymore—one example is the null object design pattern, which can simply be replaced by Scala's `Option`. Other design patterns become possible using different approaches—the decorator design pattern can be implemented using stackable traits. Finally, some new design patterns become available that are applicable specifically to the Scala programming language—the cake design pattern, pimp my library, and so on. We will focus on all of these and make it clear where the richness of Scala helps us to make our code even cleaner and simpler.

Even if there are many different design patterns, they can all be grouped in the following:

- Creational
- Structural
- Behavioral
- Functional
- Scala-specific design patterns

Some of the design patterns that are specific to Scala can be assigned to the previous groups. They can either be additions or replacements of the already existing ones. They are typical to Scala and take advantage of some advanced language features or simply features not available in other languages.

The first three groups contain the famous *Gang of Four* design patterns. Every design pattern book covers them and so will we. The rest, even if they can be assigned to one of the first three groups, will be specific to Scala and functional programming languages. In the next few subsections, we will explain the main characteristics of the listed groups and briefly present the actual design patterns that fall under them.

Creational design patterns

The creational design patterns deal with object creation mechanisms. Their purpose is to create objects in a way that is suitable to the current situation, which could lead to unnecessary complexity and the need for extra knowledge if they were not there. The main ideas behind the creational design patterns are as follows:

- Knowledge encapsulation about the concrete classes
- Hiding details about the actual creation and how objects are combined

We will be focusing on the following creational design patterns in this book:

- The abstract factory design pattern
- The factory method design pattern
- The lazy initialization design pattern
- The singleton design pattern
- The object pool design pattern
- The builder design pattern
- The prototype design pattern

The following few sections give a brief definition of what these patterns are. They will be looked at in depth individually later in this book.

The abstract factory design pattern

This is used to encapsulate a group of individual factories that have a common theme. When used, the developer creates a specific implementation of the abstract factory and uses its methods in the same way as in the factory design pattern to create objects. It can be thought of as another layer of abstraction that helps to instantiate classes.

The factory method design pattern

This design pattern deals with the creation of objects without explicitly specifying the actual class that the instance will have—it could be something that is decided at runtime based on many factors. Some of these factors can include operating systems, different data types, or input parameters. It gives developers the peace of mind of just calling a method rather than invoking a concrete constructor.

The lazy initialization design pattern

This design pattern is an approach to delay the creation of an object or the evaluation of a value until the first time it is needed. It is much more simplified in Scala than it is in an object-oriented language such as Java.

The singleton design pattern

This design pattern restricts the creation of a specific class to just one object. If more than one class in the application tries to use such an instance, then this same instance is returned for everyone. This is another design pattern that can be easily achieved with the use of basic Scala features.

The object pool design pattern

This design pattern uses a pool of objects that are already instantiated and ready for use. Whenever someone requires an object from the pool, it is returned, and after the user is finished with it, it puts it back into the pool manually or automatically. A common use for pools are database connections, which generally are expensive to create; hence, they are created once and then served to the application on request.

The builder design pattern

The builder design pattern is extremely useful for objects with many possible constructor parameters that would otherwise require developers to create many overrides for the different scenarios an object could be created in. This is different to the factory design pattern, which aims to enable polymorphism. Many of the modern libraries today employ this design pattern. As we will see later, Scala can achieve this pattern really easily.

The prototype design pattern

This design pattern allows object creation using a `clone()` method from an already created instance. It can be used in cases when a specific resource is expensive to create or when the abstract factory pattern is not desired.

Structural design patterns

Structural design patterns exist in order to help establish the relationships between different entities in order to form larger structures. They define how each component should be structured so that it has very flexible interconnecting modules that can work together in a larger system. The main features of structural design patterns include the following:

- The use of composition to combine the implementations of multiple objects
- Help build a large system made of various components by maintaining a high level of flexibility

In this book, we will focus on the following structural design patterns:

- The adapter design pattern
- The decorator design pattern
- The bridge design pattern
- The composite design pattern
- The facade design pattern
- The flyweight design pattern
- The proxy design pattern

The next subsections will put some light on what these patterns are about before we delve into them later in this book.

The adapter design pattern

The adapter design pattern allows the interface of an existing class to be used from another interface. Imagine that there is a client who expects your class to expose a `doWork()` method. You might have the implementation ready in another class, but the method is called differently and is incompatible. It might require extra parameters too. This could also be a library that the developer doesn't have access to for modifications. This is where the adapter can help by wrapping the functionality and exposing the required methods. The adapter is useful for integrating the existing components. In Scala, the adapter design pattern can be easily achieved using implicit classes.

The decorator design pattern

Decorators are a flexible alternative to sub classing. They allow developers to extend the functionality of an object without affecting other instances of the same class. This is achieved by wrapping an object of the extended class into one that extends the same class and overrides the methods whose functionality is supposed to be changed. Decorators in Scala can be built much more easily using another design pattern called **stackable traits**.

The bridge design pattern

The purpose of the bridge design pattern is to decouple an abstraction from its implementation so that the two can vary independently. It is useful when the class and its functionality vary a lot. The bridge reminds us of the adapter pattern, but the difference is that the adapter pattern is used when something is already there and you cannot change it, while the bridge design pattern is used when things are being built. It helps us to avoid ending up with multiple concrete classes that will be exposed to the client. You will get a clearer understanding when we delve deeper in the topic, but for now, let's imagine that we want to have a `FileReader` class that supports multiple different platforms. The bridge will help us end up with `FileReader`, which will use a different implementation, depending on the platform. In Scala, we can use self-types in order to implement a bridge design pattern.

The composite design pattern

The composite is a partitioning design pattern that represents a group of objects that are to be treated as only one object. It allows developers to treat individual objects and compositions uniformly and to build complex hierarchies without complicating the source code. An example of composite could be a tree structure where a node can contain other nodes, and so on.

The facade design pattern

The purpose of the facade design pattern is to hide the complexity of a system and its implementation details by providing the client with a simpler interface to use. This also helps to make the code more readable and to reduce the dependencies of the outside code. It works as a wrapper around the system that is being simplified and, of course, it can be used in conjunction with some of the other design patterns mentioned previously.

The flyweight design pattern

The flyweight design pattern provides an object that is used to minimize memory usage by sharing it throughout the application. This object should contain as much data as possible. A common example given is a word processor, where each character's graphical representation is shared with the other same characters. The local information then is only the position of the character, which is stored internally.

The proxy design pattern

The proxy design pattern allows developers to provide an interface to other objects by wrapping them. They can also provide additional functionality, for example, security or thread-safety. Proxies can be used together with the flyweight pattern, where the references to shared objects are wrapped inside proxy objects.

Behavioral design patterns

Behavioral design patterns increase communication flexibility between objects based on the specific ways they interact with each other. Here, creational patterns mostly describe a moment in time during creation, structural patterns describe a more or less static structure, and behavioral patterns describe a process or flow. They simplify this flow and make it more understandable.

The main features of behavioral design patterns are as follows:

- What is being described is a process or flow
- The flows are simplified and made understandable
- They accomplish tasks that would be difficult or impossible to achieve with objects

In this book, we will focus our attention on the following behavioral design patterns:

- The value object design pattern
- The null object design pattern
- The strategy design pattern
- The command design pattern
- The chain of responsibility design pattern
- The interpreter design pattern
- The iterator design pattern
- The mediator design pattern
- The memento design pattern
- The observer design pattern
- The state design pattern
- The template method design pattern
- The visitor design pattern

The following subsections will give brief definitions of the aforementioned behavioral design patterns.

The value object design pattern

Value objects are immutable and their equality is based not on their identity, but on their fields being equal. They can be used as data transfer objects, and they can represent dates, colors, money amounts, numbers, and more. Their immutability makes them really useful in multithreaded programming. The Scala programming language promotes immutability, and value objects are something that naturally occur there.

The null object design pattern

Null objects represent the absence of a value and they define a neutral behavior. This approach removes the need to check for `null` references and makes the code much more concise. Scala adds the concept of optional values, which can replace this pattern completely.

The strategy design pattern

The strategy design pattern allows algorithms to be selected at runtime. It defines a family of interchangeable encapsulated algorithms and exposes a common interface to the client. Which algorithm is chosen could depend on various factors that are determined while the application runs. In Scala, we can simply pass a function as a parameter to a method, and depending on the function, a different action will be performed.

The command design pattern

This design pattern represents an object that is used to store information about an action that needs to be triggered at a later time. The information includes the following:

- The method name
- The owner of the method
- Parameter values

The client then decides which commands need to be executed and when by the invoker. This design pattern can easily be implemented in Scala using the by-name parameters feature of the language.

The chain of responsibility design pattern

The chain of responsibility is a design pattern where the sender of a request is decoupled from its receiver. This way, it makes it possible for multiple objects to handle the request and to keep logic nicely separated. The receivers form a chain where they pass the request and, if possible, they process it, and if not, they pass it to the next receiver. There are variations where a handler might dispatch the request to multiple other handlers at the same time. This somehow reminds us of function composition, which in Scala can be achieved using the stackable traits design pattern.

The interpreter design pattern

The interpreter design pattern is based on the ability to characterize a well-known domain with a language with a strict grammar. It defines classes for each grammar rule in order to interpret sentences in the given language. These classes are likely to represent hierarchies as grammar is usually hierarchical as well. Interpreters can be used in different parsers, for example, SQL or other languages.

The iterator design pattern

The iterator design pattern is when an iterator is used to traverse a container and access its elements. It helps to decouple containers from the algorithms performed on them. What an iterator should provide is sequential access to the elements of an aggregate object without exposing the internal representation of the iterated collection.

The mediator design pattern

This pattern encapsulates the communication between different classes in an application. Instead of interacting directly with each other, objects communicate through the mediator, which reduces the dependencies between them, lowers the coupling, and makes the overall application easier to read and maintain.

The memento design pattern

This pattern provides the ability to roll back an object to its previous state. It is implemented with three objects—**originator**, **caretaker**, and **memento**. The originator is the object with the internal state; the caretaker will modify the originator, and a memento is an object that contains the state that the originator returns. The originator knows how to handle a memento in order to restore its previous state.

The observer design pattern

This design pattern allows the creation of publish/subscribe systems. There is a special object called subject that automatically notifies all the observers when there are any changes in the state. This design pattern is popular in various GUI toolkits and generally where event handling is needed. It is also related to reactive programming, which is enabled by libraries such as Akka. We will see an example of this towards the end of this book.

The state design pattern

This design pattern is similar to the strategy design pattern, and it uses a state object to encapsulate different behavior for the same object. It improves the code's readability and maintainability by avoiding the use of large conditional statements.

The template method design pattern

This design pattern defines the skeleton of an algorithm in a method and then passes some of the actual steps to the subclasses. It allows developers to alter some of the steps of an algorithm without having to modify its structure. An example of this could be a method in an abstract class that calls other abstract methods, which will be defined in the children.

The visitor design pattern

The visitor design pattern represents an operation to be performed on the elements of an object structure. It allows developers to define a new operation without changing the original classes. Scala can minimize the verbosity of this pattern compared to the pure object-oriented way of implementing it by passing functions to methods.

Functional design patterns

We will be looking into all of the preceding design patterns from the point of view of Scala. This means that they will look different than in other languages, but they still haven't been designed specifically for functional programming. Functional programming is much more expressive than object-oriented programming. It has its own design patterns that help to make the life of a programmer easier. We will focus on:

- Monoids
- Monads
- Functors

After we've looked at some Scala functional programming concepts, and we've been through these, we will mention some interesting design patterns from the Scala world.

A brief explanation of the preceding listed patterns will follow in the next few subsections.

Monoids

Monoid is a concept that comes from mathematics. We will take a look at it in more detail with all the theory needed to understand it later in this book. For now, it will be enough to remember that a monoid is an algebraic structure with a single associative binary operation and an identity element. Here are the keywords that you should remember:

- The associative binary operation. This means `(a+b)+c = a+(b+c)`.
- The identity element. This means `a+i = i+a = a`. Here, the identity is `i`.

What is important about monoids is that they give us the possibility to work with many different types of values in a common way. They allow us to convert pairwise operations to work with sequences; the associativity gives us the possibility for parallelization, and the identity element allows us to know what to do with empty lists. Monoids are great to easily describe and implement aggregations.

Monads

In functional programming, monads are structures that represent computations as sequences of steps. Monads are useful for building pipelines, adding operations with side effects cleanly to a language where everything is immutable, and implementing compositions. This definition might sound vague and unclear, but explaining monads in a few sentences seems to be something hard to achieve. Later in this book, we will focus on them and try and clear things up without the use of a complex mathematical theory. We will try to show why monads are useful and what they can help with, as long as developers understand them well.

Functors

Functors come from category theory, and as for monads, it takes time to explain them properly. We will look at functors later in this book. For now, you could remember that functors are things that can allow us to lift a function of the type A => B to a function of the type F[A] => F[B].

Scala-specific design patterns

The design patterns in this group could be assigned to some of the previous groups. However, they are specific to Scala and exploit some of the language features that we will focus on in this book, and so we've decided to place them in their own group.

We will focus our attention on the following:

- The lens design pattern
- The cake design pattern
- Pimp my library
- Stackable traits
- The type class design pattern
- Lazy evaluation
- Partial functions
- Implicit injection
- Duck typing
- Memoization

The next subsections will give you some brief information about these patterns before we properly study them later in this book.

The lens design pattern

The Scala programming language promotes immutability. Having objects immutable makes it harder to make mistakes. However, sometimes mutability is required and the lens design pattern helps us to achieve this nicely.

The cake design pattern

The cake design pattern is the Scala way to implement dependency injection. It is something that is used quite a lot in real-life applications, and there are numerous libraries that help developers achieve it. Scala has a way of doing this using language features, and this is what the cake design pattern is all about.

Pimp my library

Many times, engineers need to work with libraries, which are made to be as generic as possible. Sometimes, we need to do something more specific to our use case, though. The pimp my library design pattern provides a way to write extension methods for libraries, which we cannot modify. We can also use it for our own libraries as well. This design pattern also helps to achieve better code readability.

Stackable traits

Stackable traits is the Scala way to implement the decorator design pattern. It can also be used to compose functions, and it's based on a few advanced Scala features.

The type class design pattern

This design pattern allows us to write generic code by defining a behavior that must be supported by all members of a specific type class. For example, all numbers must support the addition and subtraction operations.

Lazy evaluation

Often, engineers have to deal with operations that are slow and/or expensive. Sometimes, the result of these operations might not even be needed. Lazy evaluation is a technique that postpones the operation execution until it is actually needed. It could be used for application optimization.

Partial functions

Mathematics and functional programming are really close together. As a consequence, some functions exist that are only defined for a subset of all the possible input values they can get. A popular example is the square root function, which only works for non-negative numbers. In Scala, such functions can be used to efficiently perform multiple operations at the same time or to compose functions.

Implicit injection

Implicit injection is based on the implicit functionality of the Scala programming language. It automatically injects objects whenever they are needed, as long as they exist in a specific scope. It can be used for many things, including dependency injection.

Duck typing

This is a feature that is available in Scala and is similar to what some dynamic languages provide. It allows developers to write code that requires the callers to have some specific methods (but not implement an interface). When someone uses a method with a duck type, it is actually checked during compile time whether the parameters are valid.

Memoization

This design pattern helps with optimization by remembering function results, based on the inputs. This means that as long as the function is stable and will return the same result when the same parameters are passed, one can remember its results and simply return them for every consecutive identical call.

Choosing a design pattern

As we already saw, there are a huge number of design patterns. In many cases, they are suitable to be used in combinations as well. Unfortunately, there is no definite answer regarding how to choose the concept of designing our code. There are many factors that could affect the final decision, and you should ask yourselves the following questions:

- Is this piece of code going to be fairly static or will it change in the future?
- Do we have to dynamically decide what algorithms to use?
- Is our code going to be used by others?
- Do we have an agreed interface?
- What libraries are we planning to use, if any?
- Are there any special performance requirements or limitations?

This is by no means an exhaustive list of questions. There is a huge amount of factors that could dictate our decision in how we build our systems. It is, however, really important to have a clear *specification*, and if something seems missing, it should always be checked first.

In the rest of the chapters, we will try to give specific recommendations about when a design pattern should and should not be used. They should help you ask the right questions and take the right decision before going on and writing code.

Setting up the development environment

This book will aim to give real code examples for you to run and experiment with. As well as showing the most important code snippets in the pages of the book, you will have access to the code both from Packt Publishing as well as through GitHub for your convenience. The repository can be found at `https://github.com/nikolovivan/scala-design-patterns-v2`.

Having code examples means that it is important to be able to easily run any examples we have provided here and not to fight with the code. We will do our best to have the code tested and properly packaged, but you should also make sure that you have everything needed to run the examples.

Installing Scala

Of course, you will need the Scala programming language. It does require Java to be installed, it evolves quickly, and the newest version can be found at `https://www.scala-lang.org/download/`. There are different ways of installing the language and you can choose whichever is the most comfortable for you. There are a few tips about how to install the language in your operating system at `https://www.scala-lang.org/download/install.html`. As the official Scala website suggests, the easiest way to get started is to download an IDE (IntelliJ, for example), get the Scala plugin, and it will set things up for you. I will provide a couple of tips that have proven useful in my career that have enabled me to be very flexible while experimenting and learning.

Tips for installing Scala manually

You can always download multiple versions of Scala and experiment with them. I use Linux and my tips will be applicable to Mac OS users, too. Windows users can also do a similar setup. Here are the steps:

1. Install Scala under `/opt/scala-{version}/` or any other path you prefer.
2. Create a symlink using this command: `sudo ln -s /opt/scala-{version} scala-current`. This can make switching versions much easier, if you decide to experiment.
3. Add the path to the Scala `bin` folder to your `.bashrc` (or equivalent) file using the following lines:

   - `export SCALA_HOME=/opt/scala-current`
   - `export PATH=$PATH:$SCALA_HOME/bin`

Now if you had defined a symlink and you decide to install another version of Scala, you could simply redefine the existing symlink and you can go on with your real work.

 If you don't want to go through the hassle of installing Scala manually or you find that you often switch to different versions of the language, SBT might be a more comfortable option.

Tips for installing Scala using SBT

You can also experiment with any Scala version using SBT. To do this, you should:

1. Download and install SBT: `https://www.scala-sbt.org/download.html`.
2. Open a Terminal and run `sbt`.
3. In the SBT shell, type `++ 2.12.4` or any version you want to try. Please note that if the currently used Scala version is not binary compatible with the one you want to use, you will have to modify the command to the following—`++ 2.12.4!`. Binary compatibility is very important in Scala and you should try and make sure they use libraries written in the same version of Scala as they use. Otherwise, you might get into trouble.
4. Issue the `console` command and you will be in a Scala shell running the version of your choice.

 All the examples in this book use SBT or Maven (depending on your preferences). They are build and dependency management tools, which means that you might not even need to do anything extra to install Scala. You can just import an example project and everything will be taken care of automatically.

Scala IDEs

There are multiple IDEs out there that support development in Scala. There is absolutely no preference about which one to use to work with the code. Some of the most popular ones are as follows:

- IntelliJ
- Eclipse
- NetBeans

IntelliJ is currently the one recommended on the Scala website and probably the most used one at the time of writing. All of those IDEs use plugins to work with Scala, and downloading and using them should be straightforward.

Dependency management

Running most of the examples in this book will not require any additional dependencies in terms of special libraries. In some cases, though, we might need to show how a Scala code is unit tested, which will require us to use a testing framework. Also, we will later present some real-life use cases in which an additional library is used. Dealing with dependencies nowadays is done using specialized tools. They usually are interchangeable, and which one to use is a personal choice. The most popular tool used with Scala projects is SBT, but Maven is also an option, and there are many others out there as well. The former is normally used when a project is started from scratch and Scala is the main programming language. The latter could be useful in cases when the main language used is Java, for example, and we want to add modules written in Scala.

Modern IDEs provide the functionality to generate the required build configuration files, but we will give some generic examples that could be useful not only here, but in future projects. Depending on the IDE you prefer, you might need to install some extra plugins to have things up and running, and a quick Google search should help.

SBT

SBT stands for **Simple Build Tool** and it uses the Scala syntax to define how a project is built, managing dependencies, and so on. It uses `.sbt` files for this purpose. It also supports a setup based on Scala code in `.scala` files, as well as a mix of both.

To download SBT, go to `http://www.scala-sbt.org/1.0/docs/Setup.html` and follow the instructions. If you wish to obtain the newest version, then simply Google it and use the result you get back.

The following screenshot shows the structure of a skeleton SBT project:

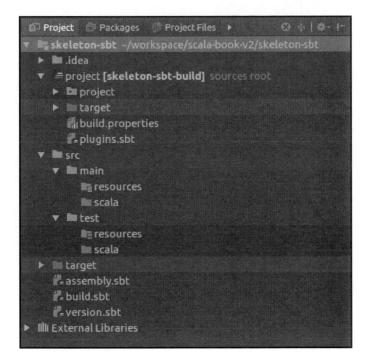

It is important to show the contents of the main .sbt files.

The version.sbt file looks as follows:

```
version in ThisBuild := "1.0.0-SNAPSHOT"
```

It contains the current version that is automatically incremented if a release is made.

The assembly.sbt file has the following content:

```
assemblyMergeStrategy in assembly := {
    case PathList("javax", "servlet", xs @ _*)          =>
MergeStrategy.first
    case PathList(ps @ _*) if ps.last endsWith ".html" =>
MergeStrategy.first
    case "application.conf"                             =>
MergeStrategy.concat
    case "unwanted.txt"                                 =>
MergeStrategy.discard
    case x =>
        val oldStrategy = (assemblyMergeStrategy in assembly).value
```

```
        oldStrategy(x)
    }

    assemblyJarName in assembly := { s"${name.value}_${scalaVersion.value}-
    ${version.value}-assembly.jar" }

    artifact in (Compile, assembly) := {
      val art = (artifact in (Compile, assembly)).value
      art.withClassifier(Some("assembly"))
    }

    addArtifact(artifact in (Compile, assembly), assembly)
```

It contains information about how to build the assembly JAR—a merge strategy, final JAR name, and so on. It uses a plugin called `sbtassembly` (`https://github.com/sbt/sbt-assembly`).

The `build.sbt` file is the file that contains the dependencies of the project, some extra information about the compiler, and metadata. The skeleton file looks as follows:

```
organization := "com.ivan.nikolov"

name := "skeleton-sbt"

scalaVersion := "2.12.4"

scalacOptions := Seq("-unchecked", "-deprecation", "-encoding", "utf8")

javaOptions ++= Seq("-target", "1.8", "-source", "1.8")

publishMavenStyle := true

libraryDependencies ++= {
  val sparkVersion = "2.2.0"
  Seq(
    "org.apache.spark" % "spark-core_2.11" % sparkVersion % "provided",
    "com.datastax.spark" % "spark-cassandra-connector_2.11" % "2.0.5",
    "org.scalatest" %% "scalatest" % "3.0.4" % "test",
    "org.mockito" % "mockito-all" % "1.10.19" % "test" // mockito for
tests
  )
}
```

As you can see, here we define the Java version against which we compile some manifest information and the library dependencies.

The dependencies for our project are defined in the `libraryDependencies` section of our SBT file. They have the following format:

```
"groupId" %[%] "artifactId" % "version" [% "scope"]
```

If we decide to separate `groupId` and `artifactId` with `%%` instead of `%`, SBT will automatically use `scalaVersion` and append `_2.12` (for Scala 2.12.*) to `artifactId`. This syntax is usually used when we include dependencies written in Scala, as the convention there requires us to have the Scala version added as part of `artifactId`. We can, of course, manually append the Scala version to `artifactId` and use `%`. This is also done in cases when we import libraries written in a different major version of Scala. In the latter case, however, we need to be careful with binary compatibility. Of course, not all libraries will be written in the version we use, so we either have to thoroughly test them and make sure they won't break our application, change our Scala version, or look for alternatives.

> The dependencies shown will not be needed at any point in this book (the one for Spark and the Datastax one). They are here just for illustration purposes, and you can safely remove them if not needed.
>
> SBT requires each statement to be on a new line and to be separated with a blank line from the previous one if we work with `.sbt` files. When using `.scala` files, we just write code in Scala.
>
> The `%%` syntax in the dependencies is a syntactic sugar, which, using `scalaVersion`, will replace the name of the library, for example, `scalatest` will become `scalatest_2.12` in our case.
>
> SBT allows the engineer to express the same things differently. One example is the preceding dependencies—instead of adding a sequence of dependencies, we can add them one by one. The final result will be the same. There is also a lot of flexibility with other parts of SBT. For more information on SBT, refer to the documentation.

The `project/build.properties` defines the `sbt` version to be used when building and interacting with the application under `sbt`. It is as simple as the following:

```
sbt.version = 1.1.0
```

Finally, there is the `project/plugins.sbt` file that defines different plugins used to get things up and running. We already mentioned `sbt assembly`:

```
addSbtPlugin("com.eed3si9n" % "sbt-assembly" % "0.14.5")
```

There are different plugins online that provide useful functionalities. Here are some common `sbt` commands that can be run from the root folder in the Terminal of this skeleton project:

- `sbt`: This opens the sbt console for the current project. All of the commands that will follow can be issued from here by omitting the `sbt` keyword.
- `sbt test`: This runs the application unit tests.
- `sbt compile`: This compiles the application.
- `sbt assembly`: This creates an assembly of the application (a fat JAR) that can be used to run as any other Java JAR.

Maven

Maven holds its configuration in files named `pom.xml`. It supports multimodule projects easily, while for `sbt`, there needs to be some extra work done. In Maven, each module simply has its own child `pom.xml` file.

To download Maven, go to `https://maven.apache.org/download.cgi`.

The following screenshot shows the structure of a skeleton Maven project:

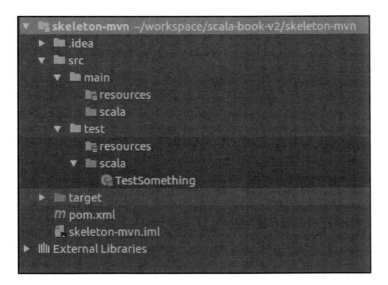

The main `pom.xml` file is much longer than the preceding SBT solution. Let's have a look at its parts separately.

There is usually some metadata about the project and different properties that can be used in the POM files in the beginning:

```
<modelVersion>4.0.0</modelVersion>
<groupId>com.ivan.nikolov</groupId>
<artifactId>skeleton-mvn</artifactId>
<version>1.0.0-SNAPSHOT</version>
<properties>
    <scala.version>2.12.4</scala.version>
    <scalatest.version>3.0.4</scalatest.version>
    <spark.version>2.2.0</spark.version>
</properties>
```

Then, there are the dependencies:

```
<dependencies>
    <dependency>
        <groupId>org.apache.spark</groupId>
        <artifactId>spark-core_2.11</artifactId>
        <version>${spark.version}</version>
        <scope>provided</scope>
    </dependency>
    <dependency>
        <groupId>com.datastax.spark</groupId>
        <artifactId>spark-cassandra-connector_2.11</artifactId>
        <version>2.0.5</version>
    </dependency>
    <dependency>
        <groupId>org.scala-lang</groupId>
        <artifactId>scala-library</artifactId>
        <version>${scala.version}</version>
    </dependency>
    <dependency>
        <groupId>org.scalatest</groupId>
        <artifactId>scalatest_2.12</artifactId>
        <version>${scalatest.version}</version>
        <scope>test</scope>
    </dependency>
    <dependency>
        <groupId>org.mockito</groupId>
        <artifactId>mockito-all</artifactId>
        <version>1.10.19</version>
        <scope>test</scope>
    </dependency>
</dependency>
```

```xml
    <dependency>
        <groupId>junit</groupId>
        <artifactId>junit</artifactId>
        <version>4.12</version>
        <scope>test</scope>
    </dependency>
</dependencies>
```

Finally, there are the build definitions. Here, we can use various plugins to do different things with our project and give hints to the compiler. The build definitions are enclosed in the <build> tags.

First, we specify some resources:

```xml
<sourceDirectory>src/main/scala</sourceDirectory>
<testSourceDirectory>src/test/scala</testSourceDirectory>
<resources>
    <resource>
        <directory>${basedir}/src/main/resources</directory>
    </resource>
</resources>
```

The first plugin we have used is scala-maven-plugin, which is used when working with Scala and Maven:

```xml
<plugin>
    <groupId>net.alchim31.maven</groupId>
    <artifactId>scala-maven-plugin</artifactId>
    <version>3.3.1</version>
    <executions>
        <execution>
            <goals>
                <goal>compile</goal>
                <goal>testCompile</goal>
            </goals>
        </execution>
    </executions>
    <configuration>
        <scalaVersion>${scala.version}</scalaVersion>
    </configuration>
</plugin>
```

Another plugin we use is `maven-assembly-plugin`, which is used for building the fat JAR of the application:

```
<plugin>
    <artifactId>maven-assembly-plugin</artifactId>
    <version>3.1.0</version>
    <configuration>
        <appendAssemblyId>false</appendAssemblyId>
        <descriptorRefs>
            <descriptorRef>jar-with-dependencies</descriptorRef>
        </descriptorRefs>
    </configuration>
    <executions>
        <execution>
            <id>make-assembly</id>
            <phase>package</phase>
            <goals>
                <goal>single</goal>
            </goals>
        </execution>
    </executions>
</plugin>
```

The complete `pom.xml` file is equivalent to the preceding `sbt` files that we presented.

As before, the Spark and Datastax dependencies are here just for illustration purposes.

The use of JUnit to run unit tests in Scala 2.12

If you look into the dependencies in more depth, you will see that we have imported `junit`, which is a Java testing framework. At first glance, someone might think that we don't actually need it. However, there is a catch. A quick Google search about how to run Scalatest unit tests with Maven would point to resources recommending the use of `scalatest-maven-plugin`. If we followed those instructions and tried running some tests from the command line, we would get a strange error. This is due to the fact that we used Scala 2.12 and the `scalatest-maven-plugin` at its current version is not binary compatible with this version of the language.

Like many things in software engineering, we have to find workarounds. Here, we could do two things:

- Use an older version of Scala.
- Force Maven to run our tests.
  Of course, the second option is the more desirable. This means that the only thing we need to do in each Scalatest we write is to add the following annotation to each test class: `@RunWith(classOf[JUnitRunner])` and make sure our test classes contain the word `Test` in their name.

Similarly to SBT, you can use Maven from the command line. Some of the commands you might find most useful with the example projects in this book are shown in the next tip.

Useful Maven commands:

- `mvn clean test`: This runs the application unit tests
- `mvn clean compile`: This compiles the application
- `mvn clean package`: This creates an assembly of the application (a fat JAR) that can be used to run as any other Java JAR

SBT versus Maven

In this book, we will be using both SBT and Maven for dependency management and creating our projects. They are interchangeable, and our source code will not depend on which build system we choose. You can easily translate the `.pom` files to `.sbt` files using the skeleton that we've provided. The only difference will really be the dependencies and how they are expressed.

Summary

By now, we have a fair idea about what a design pattern means and how it can affect the way we write our code. We've iterated through the most famous design patterns out there, and we have outlined the main differences between them. We saw that in many cases, we could use Scala's features in order to make a pattern obsolete, simpler, or different to implement compared to the classical case for pure object-oriented languages. This book will show you how Scala makes it easier to write high-quality code.

Knowing what to look for when picking a design pattern is important, and you should already know what specific details to watch out for and how important specifications are.

Last but not least, we advise you to run the examples in this book, and we have provided some pointers that should make this really easy. In some cases, creating a complete solution using SBT or Maven might be too much hassle and somewhat unnecessary, but we believe it is a good practice to follow. Additionally, the approaches we explained are used throughout the industry and will be beneficial outside the scope of this book.

In the next chapter, we will get straight to the practical part of this book, where we will look at traits and mixing compositions, what they are useful for, and how and when to use them.

Traits and Mixin Compositions

2

Before digging into some actual design patterns, we have to make sure that many of the Scala language concepts are clear to the reader. Many of those concepts will later be used in implementing the actual design patterns, and being aware of the possibilities, limitations, and pitfalls are key factors that enable us to correctly and efficiently write code. Even though those concepts are not considered *official* design patterns, they could still be used to write good software. In some cases, due to the richness of Scala, some concepts could replace a design pattern by just using language features. After all, as we have already said before, design patterns are there because a programming language lacks features and is not rich enough to complete certain tasks.

The first topic that we will look into is about traits and mixin compositions. They provide the developer with a possibility to share already implemented functionality or to define interfaces for classes in an application. Many of the possibilities, which are provided by traits and mixin compositions for developers, are useful to implement some of the design patterns that we will focus on later in this book. We will go through the following main topics in this chapter:

- Traits
- Mixin compositions
- Multiple inheritance
- Linearization
- Testing traits
- Traits versus classes

Traits

Many of you might have different perspectives of traits in Scala. They can be viewed not only as interfaces in other languages, but also as classes with only parameter-less constructors.

Trait parameters

The Scala programming language is quite dynamic and has evolved quickly throughout the years. According to the language creators, the Dotty project is the future of Scala and it is a place where passing parameters to traits and many other features are being tested and implemented. The main idea behind it is language simplification, and more information can be found at `http://dotty.epfl.ch` and `https://scala-lang.org/blog/2017/05/31/first-dotty-milestone-release.html`.

In the following few sections, we will see the traits from different points of view and try to give you some ideas about how they can be used.

Traits as interfaces

Traits can be viewed as interfaces in other languages, for example, Java. However they, allow the developers to implement some or all of their methods. Whenever there is some code in a trait, the trait is called a **mixin**. Let's have a look at the following example:

```
trait Alarm {
  def trigger(): String
}
```

Here, `Alarm` is an interface. Its only method, `trigger`, does not have any implementation and if mixed in a non-abstract class, an implementation of the method will be required.

Let's see another trait example:

```
trait Notifier {
  val notificationMessage: String

  def printNotification(): Unit = {
    System.out.println(notificationMessage)
  }

  def clear()
}
```

The `Notifier` interface shown previously has one of its methods implemented, and `clear` and the value of `notificationMessage` have to be handled by the classes that will mix with the `Notifier` interface. Moreover, the traits can require a class to have a specific variable inside it. This is somewhat similar to abstract classes in other languages.

Mixing in traits with variables

As we just pointed out, traits might require a class to have a specific variable. An interesting use case would be when we pass a variable to the constructor of a class. This will cover the trait requirements:

```
class NotifierImpl(val notificationMessage: String) extends Notifier {
  override def clear(): Unit = System.out.println("cleared")
}
```

The only requirement here is for the variable to have the same name and to be preceded by the `val` keyword in the class definition. If we don't use `val` in front of the parameter in the preceding code, the compiler would still ask us to implement the trait. In this case, we would have to use a different name for the class parameter and would have an `override val notificationMessage` assignment in the class body. The reason for this behavior is simple: if we explicitly use `val` (or `var`), the compiler will create a field with a getter with the same scope as the parameter. If we just have the parameter, a field and internal getter will be created only if the parameter is used outside the constructor scope, for example, in a method. For completeness, case classes automatically have the `val` keyword *prepended* to parameters. After what we said it means that when using `val`, we actually have a field with the given name and the right scope, and it will automatically override whatever the trait requires us to do.

Traits as classes

Traits can also be seen from the perspective of classes. In this case, they have to implement all their methods and have only one constructor that does not accept any parameters. Consider the following:

```
trait Beeper {
  def beep(times: Int): Unit = {
    1 to times foreach(i => System.out.println(s"Beep number: $i"))
  }
}
```

Now, we can actually instantiate `Beeper` and call its method. The following is a console application that does just this:

```
object BeeperRunner {
  val TIMES = 10
  def main (args: Array[String]): Unit = {
    val beeper = new Beeper {}
    beeper.beep(TIMES)
```

```
    }
  }
```

As expected, after running the application, we will see the following output in our Terminal:

```
Beep number: 1
Beep number: 2
Beep number: 3
Beep number: 4
Beep number: 5
Beep number: 6
Beep number: 7
Beep number: 8
Beep number: 9
Beep number: 10
```

Extending classes

It is possible for traits to extend classes. Let's have a look at the following example:

```
abstract class Connector {
  def connect()
  def close()
}

trait ConnectorWithHelper extends Connector {
  def findDriver(): Unit = {
    System.out.println("Find driver called.")
  }
}

class PgSqlConnector extends ConnectorWithHelper {
  override def connect(): Unit = {
    System.out.println("Connected...")
  }

  override def close(): Unit = {
    System.out.println("Closed...")
  }
}
```

Here, as expected, `PgSqlConnector` will be obliged to implement the abstract class methods. As you can guess, we could have other traits that extend other classes and then we might want to mix them in. Scala, however, will put a limit in some cases, and we will see how it will affect us later in this chapter when we look at compositions.

Extending traits

Traits can also extend each other. Have a look at the following example:

```
trait Ping {
  def ping(): Unit = {
    System.out.println("ping")
  }
}

trait Pong {
  def pong(): Unit = {
    System.out.println("pong")
  }
}

trait PingPong extends Ping with Pong {
  def pingPong(): Unit = {
    ping()
    pong()
  }
}

object Runner extends PingPong {
  def main(args: Array[String]): Unit = {
    pingPong()
  }
}
```

The preceding example is simple and it should really just make the Runner object mix the two traits separately. Extending traits is useful in a design pattern called **Stackable Traits**, which we will be looking into later in this book.

Mixin compositions

Scala allows developers to extend many traits in a single class. This adds the possibility of achieving multiple inheritance and saves a lot of effort in code writing, which has to be performed in languages where extending many classes is not allowed. In this subtopic, we will show how traits can be mixed in a specific class or used to create anonymous classes with some specific functionality while writing our code.

Mixing traits in

First of all, let's modify the code from the previous example. It is a really simple change and it will also show exactly how traits can be mixed in:

```
object MixinRunner extends Ping with Pong {
  def main(args: Array[String]): Unit = {
    ping()
    pong()
  }
}
```

As can be seen from the preceding code, we can add multiple traits to a class. We've used objects in the example just because of the main method. This would be similar to creating a class with no constructor parameters (objects in Scala are singleton classes).

How to mix traits in?
Mixing traits into a class is done with the following syntax:
`extends T1 with T2 with ... with Tn`.
If a class already extends another class, we just keep on adding the traits using the `with` keyword.
If a trait method is not implemented inside the trait body and the class we are mixing it into is not abstract, the class will have to implement the trait. Otherwise, a compilation error will occur.

Composing

Composing at creation time gives us an opportunity to create anonymous classes without the need to explicitly define them. Also, if there are many different traits that we might want to combine, creating all the possibilities would involve too much work, so this helps make things easier for us.

Composing simple traits

Let's see an example where we compose simple traits, which do not extend other traits or classes:

```
class Watch(brand: String, initialTime: Long) {
  def getTime(): Long = System.currentTimeMillis() - initialTime
}

object WatchUser {
  def main(args: Array[String]): Unit = {
    val expensiveWatch = new Watch("expensive brand", 1000L) with Alarm
with Notifier {
      override def trigger(): String = "The alarm was triggered."
      override def clear(): Unit = {
        System.out.println("Alarm cleared.")
      }
      override val notificationMessage: String = "Alarm is running!"
    }
    val cheapWatch = new Watch("cheap brand", 1000L) with Alarm {
      override def trigger(): String = "The alarm was triggered."
    }
    // show some watch usage.
    System.out.println(expensiveWatch.trigger())
    expensiveWatch.printNotification()
    System.out.println(s"The time is ${expensiveWatch.getTime()}.")
    expensiveWatch.clear()

    System.out.println(cheapWatch.trigger())
    System.out.println("Cheap watches cannot manually stop the alarm...")
  }
}
```

In the preceding example, we used the `Alarm` and `Notifier` traits from before. We created two watch instances—one is expensive that has more functionality and is more useful, and the other one is a cheap one that does not give too much control. Essentially, they are anonymous classes, which are defined during instantiation. Another thing to note is that, as expected, we have to implement the abstract methods from the traits we include. I hope this gives you an idea of how many combinations there might be in the cases where we have more traits.

Just for the sake of completeness, here is an example output of the preceding program:

```
The alarm was triggered.
Alarm is running!
The time is 1234567890562.
Alarm cleared.
The alarm was triggered.
Cheap watches cannot manually stop the alarm...
```

As expected, the highlighted time value will be different in the different runs.

Composing complex traits

It is possible that in some cases, we would have to compose more complex traits, which extend other traits or classes. If a trait and no other trait up the inheritance chain extends a specific class explicitly, then things will be pretty simple and they don't change much. In this case, we would simply have access to the methods from the super traits. However, let's see what happens if any of the traits in the hierarchy extend a specific class. For the next example, we will be using the `ConnectorWithHelper` trait defined previously. This trait extends the abstract `Connector` class. Imagine that we want to have another really expensive smart watch, which can also connect to a database:

```scala
object ReallyExpensiveWatchUser {
  def main(args: Array[String]): Unit = {
    val reallyExpensiveWatch = new Watch("really expensive brand", 1000L)
with ConnectorWithHelper {
      override def connect(): Unit = {
        System.out.println("Connected with another connector.")
      }
      override def close(): Unit = {
        System.out.println("Closed with another connector.")
      }
    }

    System.out.println("Using the really expensive watch.")
    reallyExpensiveWatch.findDriver()
    reallyExpensiveWatch.connect()
    reallyExpensiveWatch.close()
  }
}
```

It seems that everything is fine; however, when we compile, we get the following error message:

```
Error:(36, 80) illegal inheritance; superclass Watch
  is not a subclass of the superclass Connector
  of the mixin trait ConnectorWithHelper
    val reallyExpensiveWatch = new Watch("really expensive brand", 1000L)
with ConnectorWithHelper {
  ^
```

This error message tells us that since the `ConnectorWithHelper` trait extends the `Connector` class, all the classes that use this trait for composition must be subclasses of `Connector`. Let's now imagine that we wanted to mix in another trait that also extends a class, but a different one in this case. According to the preceding logic, it will be required that `Watch` should also be a subclass of the other class. This, however, wouldn't be possible, as we can only extend one class at a time and this is how Scala limits multiple inheritance in order to prevent dangerous errors from happening.

If we want to fix the compilation issue in the example, we will have to modify the original `Watch` class and make sure it is a subclass of `Connector`. This, however, might not be desired and some refactoring might be needed in such cases.

Composing with self-types

In the previous subsection, we saw how we were forced to extend `Connector` in our `Watch` class in order to properly compile our code. There are cases where we might actually want to enforce a trait to be mixed into a class that also has another trait or multiple traits mixed into it. Let's imagine that we want to have an alarm that must be able to notify us, no matter what:

```
trait AlarmNotifier {
  this: Notifier =>
  def trigger(): String
}
```

In the preceding code, we've shown a **self-type**. The highlighted piece of code brings all the methods of `Notifier` to the scope of our new trait and it also requires that any class that mixes in `AlarmNotifier` should also mix in `Notifier`. Otherwise, a compilation error will occur. Instead of this, we can use `self` and then refer to the `Notifier` methods inside `AlarmNotifier` by typing, for example, `self. printNotification()`.

The following code is an example of how to use the new trait:

```
object SelfTypeWatchUser {
  def main(args: Array[String]): Unit = {
    // uncomment to see the self-type error.
    // val watch = new Watch("alarm with notification", 1000L) with
AlarmNotifier {
    //}
    val watch = new Watch("alarm with notification", 1000L) with
AlarmNotifier with Notifier {
      override def trigger(): String = "Alarm triggered."

      override def clear(): Unit = {
        System.out.println("Alarm cleared.")
      }

      override val notificationMessage: String = "The notification."
    }

    System.out.println(watch.trigger())
    watch.printNotification()
    System.out.println(s"The time is ${watch.getTime()}.")
    watch.clear()
  }
}
```

If we comment out the `watch` variable in the preceding code and uncomment the commented bit, we will see a compilation error that is raised due to the fact that we must also mix `Notifier` in.

In this subsection, we showed a simple use of self-types. One trait can require multiple other traits to be mixed in. In such cases, they are just separated with the `with` keyword. Self-types are a key part of the **cake design pattern**, which is used for dependency injection. We will see more interesting use cases later in this book.

Clashing traits

Some of you might already have a question in your mind—what if we mix in traits that have methods with identical signatures? We will look at this in the next few sections.

Same signatures and return types

Consider an example where we want to mix two traits into a class and their declaration of a method is identical:

```
trait FormalGreeting {
  def hello(): String
}

trait InformalGreeting {
  def hello(): String
}

class Greeter extends FormalGreeting with InformalGreeting {
  override def hello(): String = "Good morning, sir/madam!"
}

object GreeterUser {
  def main(args: Array[String]): Unit = {
    val greeter = new Greeter()
    System.out.println(greeter.hello())
  }
}
```

In the preceding example, the greeter is always polite and mixes both formal and informal greetings. While implementing, it just has to implement the method once.

Same signatures and different return types traits

What if our greeting traits have more methods that have the same signatures, but a different return type? Let's add the following declaration to `FormalGreeting`:

```
def getTime(): String
```

Also, add the following to `InformalGreeting`:

```
def getTime(): Int
```

We will have to implement these in our `Greeter` class. However, the compiler will not allow us the message that `getTime` was defined twice in, which shows that Scala prevents such things from happening.

Same signatures and return types mixins

Before going further, a quick reminder that a mixin is just a trait that has some code implemented inside. This means that in the following examples, we do not have to implement the methods inside the class that uses them.

Let's have a look at the following example:

```
trait A {
  def hello(): String = "Hello, I am trait A!"
}

trait B {
  def hello(): String = "Hello, I am trait B!"
}

object Clashing extends A with B {
  def main(args: Array[String]): Unit = {
    System.out.println(hello())
  }
}
```

Probably as expected, our compilation will fail with the following message:

```
Error:(11, 8) object Clashing inherits conflicting members:
  method hello in trait A of type ()String and
  method hello in trait B of type ()String
(Note: this can be resolved by declaring an override in object Clashing.)
object Clashing extends A with B {
       ^
```

The message is useful and it even gives us a hint about how to fix the problem. Clashing methods is a problem in multiple inheritances, but as you can see, we are forced to pick one of the available methods. Here is a possible fix inside the `Clashing` object:

```
override def hello(): String = super[A].hello()
```

However, what if we want to use both the `hello` methods for some reason? In this case, we can create other methods that are named differently and call the specific traits as in the preceding example (the `super` notation). We can also directly refer to the methods with the `super` notation instead of wrapping them in a method. My personal preference, though, would be to wrap it, as the code could get messy otherwise.

The super notation

What would happen if in the preceding example, instead of `super[A].hello()`, we do the following: `override def hello(): String = super.hello()`?
Which hello method will be called and why? In the current case, it will be the one in the B trait and the output will be `Hello, I am trait B!` This depends on linearization in Scala, and we will be looking at this later in this chapter.

Same signatures and different return types mixins

As expected, the previous problem does not exist when input parameters to the methods differ either by type or by count since this is a new signature. However, the problem will still be there if we have the following two methods in our traits:

```
def value(a: Int): Int = a // in trait A
def value(a: Int): String = a.toString // in trait B
```

You will be surprised to see that the approach we used will not work here. If we decide to override only the value method in the A trait, we will get the following compilation error:

```
Error:(19, 16) overriding method value in trait B of type (a: Int)String;
  method value has incompatible type
    override def value(a: Int): Int = super[A].value(a)
               ^
```

If we override the `value` method in the B trait, the error will change respectively.

If we try and override both, then the error will be as follows:

```
Error:(20, 16) method value is defined twice
  conflicting symbols both originated in file
  '/path/to/traits/src/main/scala/com/ivan/nikolov/composition/Clashing.scala
  '
    override def value(a: Int): String = super[B].value(a)
```

This shows that Scala actually prevents us from doing some dangerous things that can occur in multiple inheritance. For the sake of completeness, if you face a similar issue, there is a workaround (by sacrificing the mix in functionality). It will look as follows:

```scala
trait C {
  def value(a: Int): Int = a
}

trait D {
  def value(a: Int): String = a.toString
}

object Example {

  val c = new C {}
  val d = new D {}

  def main (args: Array[String]): Unit = {
    System.out.println(s"c.value: ${c.value(10)}")
    System.out.println(s"d.value: ${d.value(10)}")
  }
}
```

The preceding code uses traits as collaborators, but it also loses the fact that the class that uses them is also an instance of the trait type, which can be useful for other operations as well.

Multiple inheritance

We inevitably had to mention multiple inheritance in the previous sections due to the fact that we can mix multiple traits and they can all have their own implementations of the methods. Multiple inheritance is not only a powerful technique, but also a dangerous one, and some languages such as Java have decided to not even allow it. As we already saw, Scala allows this, but with some limitations. In this subsection, we will present the problems of multiple inheritance and show how Scala deals with them.

The diamond problem

Multiple inheritance suffers from the **diamond problem**.

Let's have a look at the following diagram:

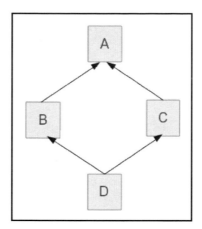

Here, both **B** and **C** extend **A**, and then **D** extends **B** and **C**. Some ambiguities might arise from this. Let's say that there was a method that was originally defined in **A**, but both **B** and **C** override it. What would happen if **D** calls this method? Which one will it exactly call?

All the preceding questions make things ambiguous and this could lead to mistakes. Let's try and reproduce this in Scala using traits:

```
trait A {
  def hello(): String = "Hello from A"
}

trait B extends A {
  override def hello(): String = "Hello from B"
}

trait C extends A {
  override def hello(): String = "Hello from C"
}

trait D extends B with C {

}

object Diamond extends D {
  def main(args: Array[String]): Unit = {
```

```
    System.out.println(hello())
  }
}
```

What would be the output of the program? Here is the output:

Hello from C

What if we just change the D trait to look as follows:

```
trait D extends C with B {

}
```

Then the output of our program will be as follows:

Hello from B

As you can see, even though the example is still ambiguous and prone to errors, we can actually tell exactly which method will be called. This is achieved using linearization, which we will look at in greater depth in the next section.

The limitations

Before focusing on linearization, let's point out the multiple inheritance limitations that Scala imposes. We already saw many of them before, so here we will simply summarize them.

Scala multiple inheritance limitations

Multiple inheritance in Scala is achieved using traits and it follows the rules of linearization.

In the inheritance hierarchy, if there is a trait that explicitly extends a class, the class that mixes in this trait must also be a subclass of the trait parent. This means that when mixing in traits that extend classes, they must all have the same parent.

It is not possible to mix traits in, which define or declare methods with the same signatures, but different return types.

Special care has to be taken when multiple traits define methods with the same signatures and return types. In cases where the methods are declared and expected to be implemented, this is not an issue and only one implementation is enough.

Linearization

As we already saw, traits offer a form of multiple inheritance. In such cases, the hierarchy is not necessarily linear, but forms an acyclic graph that needs to be flattened upon compilation. What linearization does is this—it specifies a single linear order for all of the ancestors of a class, including both the regular superclass chain and the parent chains of all of the traits.

We will not have to deal with linearization in traits that contain no code. However, if we use mixins, we will have to consider it. The following will be affected by linearization:

- Method definitions
- Variables (both mutable—`var` and immutable—`val`)

We already saw a simple example of linearization previously. Things, however, can get much more complicated and unexpected if the rules of linearization are not clear.

Rules of inheritance hierarchies

Before looking into linearization rules, we need to be clear on some inheritance rules in Scala:

- In Java, even if a class does not explicitly extend another one, its superclass will be `java.lang.Object`. The same stands for Scala, and the equivalent base is `AnyRef`.
- There is a similarity between directly extending a trait and extending the trait superclass and mixing the trait in using the `with` keyword.

 In older Scala versions, there was another type called `ScalaObject` that was implicitly added to all traits and classes.

Using those rules, we can always get to a canonical form for all traits and classes, where the base class is specified using `extends` and then all traits are added using the `with` keyword.

Linearization rules

Linearization rules in Scala are defined and exist in order to ensure well-defined behavior. The rules state the following:

- The linearization of any class must include the unmodified linearization of any *class* (but not trait) that it extends.
- The linearization of any class must include all the classes and mixin traits in the linearization of any *trait* it extends, but the mixin traits are not bound to appear in the same order as they appear in the linearization of the traits being mixed in.
- Each class or trait in the linearization can appear only once. Duplicates are ignored.

We already saw in some of the previous examples that it is not possible to mix in traits that have different base classes or to mix in a trait into a class when their base classes differ.

How linearization works

In Scala, linearizations are listed from left to right where the right-most class is the most general, for example, `AnyRef`. While doing linearization, `Any` is also added to the hierarchy list. This, combined with the rule that any class must include the linearization of its superclass, means that the superclass linearization will appear as a suffix of the class linearization.

Let's see an example with some really simple classes:

```
class Animal extends AnyRef
class Dog extends Animal
```

The linearization of these two classes will be, respectively:

```
Animal -> AnyRef -> Any
Dog -> Animal -> AnyRef -> Any
```

Now, let's try and formalize an algorithm that describes how a linearization is calculated:

1. Start with the following class declaration—`class A extends B with T1 with T2`.
2. Reverse the order of the list except the first item and drop the keywords. This way, the superclass will come as a suffix—A T2 T1 B.
3. Each item gets replaced with its linearization—A T2L T1L BL.

4. Concatenate the list elements using the right-associative concatenation operation: `A +: T2L +: T1L +: BL`.
5. Append the standard `AnyRef` and `Any` classes—`A +: T2L +: T1L +: BL +: AnyRef +: Any`.
6. Evaluate the preceding expression. Due to the right-associative concatenation, we start from the right and move to the left. In each step, we remove any element that has already appeared on the right-hand side. In our case, when we get to `BL`, we will not add `AnyRef` and `Any` that it also contains; we will just add `BL` and then we will continue. At `T1L`, we will skip the step to add anything that was added before and so on, until we reach `A`.

In the end, after the linearization finishes, we will have a list of classes and traits without duplicates.

Initialization

Now that we know what happens during linearization, we will understand how instances are being created. The rule is that the constructor code is executed in a reverse order compared to the linearization order. This means that, going from right to left, first the `Any` and `AnyRef` constructors will be invoked and then the actual class constructor will be called. Also, the superclass constructor will be called before the actual class or any of its mixins because, as we have already mentioned previously, it is added as a suffix.

Keeping in mind that we traverse the linearization from right to left also means that after the superclass constructor is called, the mixin trait constructors will be called. Here, they will be called in the order in which they appear in the original class definition (because of the right to left direction and the fact that their order is reversed when the linearization is created).

Method overriding

When overriding a method in a subclass, you may want to call the original implementation as well. This is achieved by prefixing the `super` keyword to the method name. The developer also has control to qualify the `super` keyword with a trait type, thus calling the method in the specific trait. We already saw an example of this earlier in the chapter, where we called `super[A].hello()`. In that example, we had mixins with the same methods; however, the methods themselves did not refer to `super`, but just defined their own implementations.

Let's see an example here, where we actually refer to the `super` class when overriding a method:

```
class MultiplierIdentity {
  def identity: Int = 1
}
```

Let's now define two traits that respectively double and triple the identity in our original class:

```
trait DoubledMultiplierIdentity extends MultiplierIdentity {
  override def identity: Int = 2 * super.identity
}

trait TripledMultiplierIdentity extends MultiplierIdentity {
  override def identity: Int = 3 * super.identity
}
```

As we saw in some of the previous examples, the order in which we mix in the traits matters. We will provide three implementations, where we first mix in `DoubledMultiplierIdentity` and then `TripledMultiplierIdentity`. The first one will not override the identity method, which is equivalent to using the following super notation: `super.identity`. The other two will override the method and will refer to a specific parent:

```
// first Doubled, then Tripled
class ModifiedIdentity1 extends DoubledMultiplierIdentity with
TripledMultiplierIdentity

class ModifiedIdentity2 extends DoubledMultiplierIdentity with
TripledMultiplierIdentity {
  override def identity: Int = super[DoubledMultiplierIdentity].identity
}

class ModifiedIdentity3 extends DoubledMultiplierIdentity with
TripledMultiplierIdentity {
  override def identity: Int = super[TripledMultiplierIdentity].identity
}
// first Doubled, then Tripled
```

Let's do the same thing as shown in the preceding code, but this time, we first mix in `TripledMultiplierIdentity` and then `DoubledMultiplierIdentity`. The implementations are similar to the preceding ones:

```
// first Tripled, then Doubled
class ModifiedIdentity4 extends TripledMultiplierIdentity with
DoubledMultiplierIdentity

class ModifiedIdentity5 extends TripledMultiplierIdentity with
DoubledMultiplierIdentity {
  override def identity: Int = super[DoubledMultiplierIdentity].identity
}

class ModifiedIdentity6 extends TripledMultiplierIdentity with
DoubledMultiplierIdentity {
  override def identity: Int = super[TripledMultiplierIdentity].identity
}
// first Tripled, then Doubled
```

Finally, let's use our classes:

```
object ModifiedIdentityUser {
  def main(args: Array[String]): Unit = {
    val instance1 = new ModifiedIdentity1
    val instance2 = new ModifiedIdentity2
    val instance3 = new ModifiedIdentity3
    val instance4 = new ModifiedIdentity4
    val instance5 = new ModifiedIdentity5
    val instance6 = new ModifiedIdentity6

    System.out.println(s"Result 1: ${instance1.identity}")
    System.out.println(s"Result 2: ${instance2.identity}")
    System.out.println(s"Result 3: ${instance3.identity}")
    System.out.println(s"Result 4: ${instance4.identity}")
    System.out.println(s"Result 5: ${instance5.identity}")
    System.out.println(s"Result 6: ${instance6.identity}")
  }
}
```

The example shows a multiple inheritance hierarchy, where we can see a diamond relationship exactly as in the previous figure in which we explained what it means. We have all the possibilities here in terms of the order of mixing `DoubledMultiplier` and `TripledMultiplier`, as well as how we call the identity base method.

So, what would the output of this program be? One would expect that in the cases where we don't override the identity method, it would call the identity method of the right-most trait. Since in both the cases they call the super method of the class they extend, the results should be 2 and 3. Let's see this here:

```
Result 1: 6
Result 2: 2
Result 3: 6
Result 4: 6
Result 5: 6
Result 6: 3
```

The preceding output is rather unexpected. This is, however, how the Scala type system works. In the case of linearization, where we have a multiple inheritance, the calls to the same method are chained from right to left according to the order of the appearance of the traits in the class declaration. Note that if we did not use the super notation, we would have broken the chain, as can be seen in some of the preceding examples.

The previous example is rather amusing and proves how important it is to know the rules of linearization and how linearization works. Not being aware of this feature could result in a serious pitfall, which could lead to critical mistakes in your code.

My advice would still be to try and avoid cases of diamond inheritance, even though one can argue that this way, some quite complex systems can be implemented seamlessly and without writing too much code. A case such as the preceding one could make the programs really hard to read and maintain in the future.

You should be aware that linearization exists everywhere in Scala—not just when dealing with traits. This is just how the Scala-type system works. This means that it is a good idea to be aware of the order in which constructors are called in order to avoid mistakes and generally, to try and keep the hierarchies relatively simple.

Testing traits

Testing is a really important part of software development. It ensures that changes to a certain piece of code do not end up producing errors either in the methods that were changed, or somewhere else.

There are different testing frameworks that one can use, and it really is a matter of personal preference. In this book, we have used **ScalaTest** (http://www.scalatest.org), as this is the one I use in my projects; it is understandable, readable, and easy to use.

In some cases, if a trait is mixed into a class, we could end up testing the class. However, we might want to test only a specific trait. It does not make much sense to test a trait that doesn't have all its methods implemented, so here we will look into the ones that have their code written (mixins). Also, the unit tests that we will show here are quite simple, but they are just for illustration purposes. We will be looking into more complex and meaningful tests in the following chapters of this book.

Using a class

Let's have a look at how `DoubledMultiplierIdentity`, which we saw previously, would be tested. One would try to simply mix the trait into a test class and test the methods:

```
class DoubledMultiplierIdentityTest extends FlatSpec with ShouldMatchers
with DoubledMultiplierIdentity
```

This, however, won't compile and will lead to the following error:

```
Error:(5, 79) illegal inheritance; superclass FlatSpec
 is not a subclass of the superclass MultiplierIdentity
 of the mixin trait DoubledMultiplierIdentity
class DoubledMultiplierIdentityTest extends FlatSpec with ShouldMatchers
with DoubledMultiplierIdentity {
 ^
```

We already talked about this before and the fact that a trait can only be mixed in a class that has the same super class as itself. This means that in order to test the trait, we should create a dummy class inside our test class and then use it:

```
package com.ivan.nikolov.linearization

import org.scalatest.{ShouldMatchers, FlatSpec}

class DoubledMultiplierIdentityTest extends FlatSpec with ShouldMatchers {
```

```
class DoubledMultiplierIdentityClass extends DoubledMultiplierIdentity

val instance = new DoubledMultiplierIdentityClass

"identity" should "return 2 * 1" in {
  instance.identity should equal(2)
}
}
```

Mixing the trait in

We can test a trait by mixing it in. There are a few places where we can do this—into a test class or into separate test cases.

Mixing into the test class

Mixing in a trait into a test class is only possible if the trait does not extend any other class explicitly, hence the super class of the trait and the test will be the same. Other than this, everything else is absolutely the same as done previously.

Let's test the A trait from earlier in this chapter, which says hello. We've also added an extra pass method, and now the trait looks as follows:

```
trait A {
  def hello(): String = "Hello, I am trait A!"
  def pass(a: Int): String = s"Trait A said: 'You passed $a.'"
}
```

This is what the unit test will look like:

```
package com.ivan.nikolov.composition

import org.scalatest.{FlatSpec, Matchers}

class TraitATest extends FlatSpec with Matchers with A {

  "hello" should "greet properly." in {
    hello() should equal("Hello, I am trait A!")
  }
  "pass" should "return the right string with the number." in {
    pass(10) should equal("Trait A said: 'You passed 10.'")
  }
  it should "be correct also for negative values." in {
    pass(-10) should equal("Trait A said: 'You passed -10.'")
```

```
        }
    }
```

Mixing into the test cases

We can also mix traits into the individual test cases separately. This could allow us to apply customizations specific to those test cases only. The following is just a different representation of the preceding unit test:

```
package com.ivan.nikolov.composition

import org.scalatest.{FlatSpec, Matchers}

class TraitACaseScopeTest extends FlatSpec with Matchers {
  "hello" should "greet properly." in new A {
    hello() should equal("Hello, I am trait A!")
  }

  "pass" should "return the right string with the number." in new A {
    pass(10) should equal("Trait A said: 'You passed 10.'")
  }

  it should "be correct also for negative values." in new A {
    pass(-10) should equal("Trait A said: 'You passed -10.'")
  }
}
```

As you can see in the preceding code, the test cases are identical to the previous ones. They, however, individually mix A in. This would allow us to apply different customizations in the cases where a trait requires an implementation of a method or a variable initialization. This way, we can also focus specifically on the trait being tested, rather than creating actual instances of it.

Running the tests

After the tests are written, it is useful to run them in order to see whether everything works as expected. If you're using Maven, just run the following command from the root of your project and it will execute all the tests:

```
mvn clean test
```

If you're using SBT, then the tests can be triggered using the following command:

```
sbt test
```

Traits versus classes

Traits could be similar, but also very different to classes. It could be hard for a developer to choose which one to use in various cases, but here we will try to provide some general guidelines that should help.

Use classes:

- When a behavior is not going to be reused at all or in multiple places
- When you plan to use your Scala code from another language, for example, if you are building a library that could be used in Java

Use traits:

- When a behavior is going to be reused in multiple unrelated classes.
- When you want to define interfaces and want to use them outside Scala, for example, Java. The reason is that the traits that do not have any implementations are compiled similar to interfaces.

Summary

In this chapter, we went through traits and mixin compositions in Scala. By now, you should have a good understanding of what these are and what can be achieved by using them. We also went through the examples of the different uses of traits and what to watch out for when using them. We presented the limitations of using traits for multiple inheritance. Traits are an extremely powerful concept, but they have their pitfalls as we saw with multiple inheritance, so you should use them carefully. Linearization was covered in depth and you should be familiar with what to expect when using traits for multiple inheritance and why things work exactly the way they currently do.

Testing is an essential part of every good software project, and we also presented how it should be done for traits. Last, but not least, we prepared a few guidelines that should help developers choose between working with traits or classes in Scala.

In the next chapter, we will spend some time on **unification**. We will show why it is useful and what it helps the developer to achieve in their programs.

Unification 3

Being able to understand and write good code in Scala requires developers to be familiar with the different concepts of the language. In a few places so far, we have mentioned that Scala is really expressive. To some extent, this is because there are a number of programming concepts that have been unified. In this chapter, we will focus on the following concepts:

- Functions and classes
- Algebraic data types and class hierarchies
- Modules and objects

Functions and classes

In Scala, every value is an object. Functions are first-class values, which also makes them objects of their respective classes.

The following diagram shows the Scala unified type system and how this is achieved. It is adapted from `http://www.scala-lang.org/old/sites/default/files/images/classhierarchy.png` and represents an up-to-date view of the model (some classes such as `ScalaObject` have disappeared, as we have already mentioned earlier):

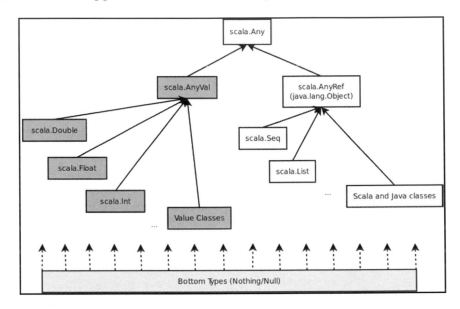

As you can see, Scala does not have the same concept of primitive types that Java has, and all types are ultimately subtypes of **Any**.

Functions as classes

The fact that functions are classes means that they can be freely passed to other methods or classes as if they were just values. This leads to improving the expressiveness of Scala and making it much easier to achieve things, such as callbacks, than in other languages such as Java.

Function literals

Let's have a look at an example:

```
class FunctionLiterals {
  val sum = (a: Int, b: Int) => a + b
}
```

```
object FunctionLiterals {

  def main(args: Array[String]): Unit = {
    val obj = new FunctionLiterals
    System.out.println(s"3 + 9 = ${obj.sum(3, 9)}")
  }
}
```

Here, we can see how the sum field of the FunctionLiterals class is actually assigned a function. We can assign any function to a variable and then call it as if it was a function (essentially invoking its apply method). Functions can also be passed as parameters to other methods. Let's add the following to our FunctionLiterals class:

```
def runOperation(f: (Int, Int) => Int, a: Int, b: Int): Int = {
  f(a, b)
}
```

We can then pass the required function to runOperation, as follows:

```
obj.runOperation(obj.sum, 10, 20)
obj.runOperation(Math.max, 10, 20)
```

Functions without syntactic sugar

In the preceding example, we just used syntactic sugar. In order to understand exactly what happens, we will show you what the function literals are converted into. They basically represent extensions to the FunctionN trait, where N is the number of parameters. The implementations of the literals are invoked using the apply method (whenever a class or an object has an apply method, it can be implicitly invoked just using parentheses after the object name or instance and passing the required parameters, if any). Let's see the equivalent implementation to our previous example:

```
class SumFunction extends Function2[Int, Int, Int] {
  override def apply(v1: Int, v2: Int): Int = v1 + v2
}

class FunctionObjects {
  val sum = new SumFunction

  def runOperation(f: (Int, Int) => Int, a: Int, b: Int): Int = f(a, b)
}

object FunctionObjects {

  def main(args: Array[String]): Unit = {
```

```
    val obj = new FunctionObjects
    System.out.println(s"3 + 9 = ${obj.sum(3, 9)}")
    System.out.println(s"Calling run operation: ${obj.
    runOperation(obj.sum, 10, 20)}")
    System.out.println(s"Using Math.max: ${obj.runOperation(Math.max,
     10, 20)}")
  }
}
```

Increased expressivity

As you can see from the examples, unifying classes and functions leads to increased expressivity and we can easily achieve various things such as callbacks, lazy parameter evaluation, centralized exception handling, and others, and without writing extra code and logic. Moreover, functions as classes mean that we can extend them to provide extra functionality.

Algebraic data types and class hierarchies

Algebraic data types (ADTs) and class hierarchies are other unifications in the Scala programming language. In other functional languages, there are special ways to create custom algebraic data types. In Scala, this is achieved using class hierarchies and namely *case classes* and *objects*. Let's see what an ADT actually is, what types there are, and how to define them.

ADTs

Algebraic data types are just composite types that combine other existing types or just represent some new ones. They only have data and do not contain any functionality on top of this data as normal classes would. Some examples can include the day of the week or a class that represents an RGB color—they have no extra functionality and they just carry information. The following few subsections will give a bit more insight on what ADTs are and what types are out there.

Sum ADTs

Sum algebraic data types are the ones in which we can simply enumerate all the possible values of a type and provide a separate constructor for each value. As an example, let's consider the months of the year. There are only 12 and they cannot change (hopefully):

```
sealed abstract trait Month
case object January extends Month
case object February extends Month
case object March extends Month
case object April extends Month
case object May extends Month
case object June extends Month
case object July extends Month
case object August extends Month
case object September extends Month
case object October extends Month
case object November extends Month
case object December extends Month

object MonthDemo {
  def main(args: Array[String]): Unit = {
    val month: Month = February
    System.out.println(s"The current month is: $month")
  }
}
```

Running this application will produce the following output:

```
The current month is: February
```

 The Month trait in the preceding code is sealed because we do not want it to be extended outside the current file. As you can see, we've defined the different months as objects, as there is no reason for them to be separate instances. The values are what they are and they do not change.

Product ADTs

In product algebraic data types, we cannot enumerate all the possible values. There are usually too many to manually write them. We cannot provide a separate constructor for each separate value.

Let's think about colors. There are different color models, but one of the most famous ones is RGB. It combines the different values of the main colors (red, green, and blue) in order to represent other colors. If we say that each of these colors can have a value between 0 and 255, this would mean that to represent all possibilities, we would need to have 256^3 different constructors. That's why we can use a product ADT:

```
sealed case class RGB(red: Int, green: Int, blue: Int)

object RGBDemo {
  def main(args: Array[String]): Unit = {
    val magenta = RGB(255, 0, 255)
    System.out.println(s"Magenta in RGB is: $magenta")
  }
}
```

 Now we can see that for the product ADTs, we have one constructor for different values.

Hybrid ADTs

Hybrid algebraic data types represent a combination of the sum and product ones we described previously. This means that we can have specific value constructors, but these value constructors also provide parameters in order to wrap other types.

Let's see an example. Imagine we are writing a drawing application:

```
sealed abstract trait Shape
case class Circle(radius: Double) extends Shape
case class Rectangle(height: Double, width: Double) extends Shape
```

We have different shapes. The preceding example shows a sum ADT because we have the specific `Circle` and `Rectangle` value constructors. Also, we have a product ADT because the constructors take extra parameters.

Let's expand our classes a bit. When drawing our shapes, we need to know their positions. This is why we can add a `Point` class that holds the x and y coordinates:

```
case class Point(x: Double, y: Double)

sealed abstract trait Shape
case class Circle(centre: Point, radius: Double) extends Shape
case class Rectangle(topLeft: Point, height: Double, width: Double) extends
Shape
```

This should hopefully clarify what ADTs are in Scala and how they can be used.

The unification

After all of the preceding examples, it is obvious that class hierarchies and ADTs are unified and look like the same thing. This adds a high level of flexibility in the language and makes modeling easier than in other functional programming languages.

Pattern matching

Pattern matching is often used with ADTs. It makes the code much clearer and more readable as well as easier to extend in comparison to using the `if...else` statements when trying to do something with ADTs based on their values. As you could imagine, these statements can get quite cumbersome in some cases, especially when there are many different possible values for a certain data type. In some cases, pattern matching can be used the same way as *enums* and the `switch` statement is used in Java.

Pattern matching with values

In the month's example stated previously, we just have the month names. We might, however, want to also get their number, as the computer will not know this otherwise. Here is how to do this:

```
object Month {
  def toInt(month: Month): Int =
    month match {
      case January => 1
      case February => 2
      case March => 3
      case April => 4
      case May => 5
```

```
        case June => 6
        case July => 7
        case August => 8
        case September => 9
        case October => 10
        case November => 11
        case December => 12
    }
}
```

You can see how we match the different values, and based on them, we return the correct values. Here is how this method can be used now:

```
System.out.println(s"The current month is: $month and it's number
${Month.toInt(month)}")
```

As expected, our application will produce the following:

The current month is: February and it's number 2

The fact that we have specified our base trait to be sealed guarantees that nobody else will extend it outside our code, and we will be able to have an exhaustive pattern match. Unexhaustive pattern matches are problematic. Just as an experiment, if we try to comment out the match rule for February and we compile, we will see the following warning:

```
Warning:(19, 5) match may not be exhaustive.
It would fail on the following input: February
    month match {
    ^
```

Running the example this way proves that the warning is true and our code has failed when we use February as a parameter. For the sake of completeness, we can add a default case:

```
case _ => 0
```

The examples shown in this subsection are what one can use in Scala, in order to achieve the functionality of *enums* in Java.

Pattern matching for product ADTs

Pattern matching shows its real power when used for product and hybrid ADTs. In such cases, we can match the actual values of the data types. Let's see how we would implement a functionality to calculate the area of a shape, as defined previously:

```
object Shape {
  def area(shape: Shape): Double =
    shape match {
      case Circle(Point(x, y), radius) => Math.PI * Math.pow(radius, 2)
      case Rectangle(_, h, w) => h * w
    }
}
```

When matching, we can ignore values we don't care about. For the area, we don't really need the position information. In the preceding code, we just showed two different ways in which a matching is possible. The _ operator can be anywhere in the match statement, and it will just ignore the value it is put for. After this, using our example is straightforward:

```
object ShapeDemo {
  def main(args: Array[String]): Unit = {
    val circle = Circle(Point(1, 2), 2.5)
    val rect = Rectangle(Point(6, 7), 5, 6)

    System.out.println(s"The circle area is: ${Shape.area(circle)}")
    System.out.println(s"The rectangle area is: ${Shape.area(rect)}")
  }
}
```

This will have an output similar to the following:

```
The circle area is: 19.634954084936208
The rectangle area is: 30.0
```

We can even put constants instead of variables for the ADT constructor parameters during pattern matching. This makes the language quite powerful and allows us to achieve even more complex logic, which will still look quite nice. You can try experimenting with the preceding examples in order to get an idea of how pattern matching actually works.

 Pattern matching is often used with ADTs and it helps to achieve clean, extendible, and exhaustive code.

Modules and objects

Modules are a way to organize programs. They are interchangeable and pluggable pieces of code that have well-defined interfaces and hidden implementations. In Java, modules are organized in packages. In Scala, modules are objects, just like everything else. This means that they can be parameterized, extended, and passed as parameters, and so on.

Scala modules can provide requirements in order to be used.

Using modules

We already established that modules and objects are also unified in Scala. This means that we can pass an entire module around our application. It would be useful, however, to show what a module actually looks like. Here is an example:

```
trait Tick {
  trait Ticker {
    def count(): Int
    def tick(): Unit
  }
  def ticker: Ticker
}
```

Here, `Tick` is just an interface to one of our modules. The following is its implementation:

```
trait TickUser extends Tick {
  class TickUserImpl extends Ticker {
    var curr = 0
    override def count(): Int = curr
    override def tick(): Unit = {
      curr = curr + 1
    }
  }
  object ticker extends TickUserImpl
}
```

The `TickUser` trait is an actual module. It implements `Tick` and contains the code hidden inside it. We create a singleton object that will carry the implementation. Note how the name in the object is the same as the method in `Tick`. This would cover the need to implement it when mixing in the trait.

Similarly, we can define another interface and an implementation as follows:

```
trait Alarm {
  trait Alarmer {
    def trigger(): Unit
  }
  def alarm: Alarmer
}
```

The implementation will be the following:

```
trait AlarmUser extends Alarm with Tick {
  class AlarmUserImpl extends Alarmer {
    override def trigger(): Unit = {
      if (ticker.count() % 10 == 0) {
        System.out.println(s"Alarm triggered at ${ticker.count()}!")
      }
    }
  }
  object alarm extends AlarmUserImpl
}
```

What is interesting here is that we extended both modules in the `AlarmUser` one. This shows how modules could be made to be dependent on each other. Finally, we can use our modules as follows:

```
object ModuleDemo extends AlarmUser with TickUser {
  def main(args: Array[String]): Unit = {
    System.out.println("Running the ticker. Should trigger the alarm
    every 10 times.")
    (1 to 100).foreach {
      case i =>
        ticker.tick()
        alarm.trigger()
    }
  }
}
```

In order for `ModuleDemo` to use the `AlarmUser` module, it is also required by the compiler to mix in `TickUser` or any module that mixes in `Tick`. This provides a possibility to plug in a different functionality.

The output of the program will be as follows:

```
Running the ticker. Should trigger the alarm every 10 times.
Alarm triggered at 10!
Alarm triggered at 20!
Alarm triggered at 30!
Alarm triggered at 40!
Alarm triggered at 50!
Alarm triggered at 60!
Alarm triggered at 70!
Alarm triggered at 80!
Alarm triggered at 90!
Alarm triggered at 100!
```

 Modules in Scala can be passed as any other object. They are extendable, interchangeable, and their implementation is hidden.

Summary

In this chapter, we focused on unification. We saw how there is a unification between functions and classes, ADTs, class hierarchies, as well as modules and objects. This allows us to be much more expressive and write cleaner and more efficient code. We also covered what pattern matching is and how it can be used in Scala to write good code.

Some of the concepts covered in this chapter will be useful in the following chapters where we will be implementing concrete design patterns. They can also be used to write good software outside the defined design patterns just because the expressivity of Scala allows it, and this defies the need to do the extra work that design patterns add.

In the next chapter, we will look at **abstract** and **self-types** and what they can be useful for.

Abstract and Self Types 4

Designing and writing high-quality code in software engineering is important in order to have applications that are easy to extend and maintain. This activity requires the domain to be well-known, correctly understood by a developer, and the requirements for the application to be well-defined. If any of these are absent, then writing good programs becomes quite challenging.

Often, engineers model the *world* using some abstractions. This helps with code extendibility and maintainability and removes duplication, which in many cases could be a reason for bugs. Good code, generally, will consist of multiple small components, that depend on and interact with each other. There are different approaches that help to achieve abstraction and interaction. We will look into the following topics in this chapter:

- Abstract types
- Polymorphism
- Self types

The topics that we will cover here will be really useful when we start looking into some of the concrete design patterns. Learning about them will also help to understand the design patterns that rely on them. Moreover, the concepts covered in this chapter are useful just by themselves for writing good code.

Abstract types

One of the most common ways to parameterize classes is by using values. This is quite simple, and it is achieved by passing different values for the constructor parameters of a class. In the following example, we can pass different values for the `name` parameter of the `Person` class, and this is how we create different instances:

```
case class Person(name: String)
```

This way, we can create different instances and distinguish them, but this is neither interesting nor rocket science. Going further, we will focus on some more interesting parameterizations that will help us improve our code.

Generics

Generics are another way of parameterizing classes. They are useful when we write a functionality whose application is the same throughout various types, and we can simply defer choosing a concrete type until later. One example every developer should be familiar with is collection classes. List, for example, can store any type of data, and we can have lists of integers, doubles, strings, custom classes, and so on. Still, the list implementation is always the same.

We can also parameterize methods. For example, if we want to implement addition, it will not change between different numerical data types. Hence, we can use generics and just write our method once instead of overloading and trying to accommodate every single type in the world.

Let's look at some examples:

```
trait Adder {
  def sum[T](a: T, b: T)(implicit numeric: Numeric[T]): T =
    numeric.plus(a, b)
}
```

The preceding code is a bit more involved and it defines a method called sum, which can be used with all numeric types. This is actually a representation of **ad hoc polymorphism**, which we will talk about later in this chapter.

The following code shows how to parameterize a class to contain any kind of data:

```
class Container[T](data: T) {
  def compare(other: T) = data.equals(other)
}
```

The following snippet shows some example uses:

```
object GenericsExamples extends Adder {
  def main(args: Array[String]): Unit = {
    System.out.println(s"1 + 3 = ${sum(1, 3)}")
    System.out.println(s"1.2 + 6.7 = ${sum(1.2, 6.7)}")
    // System.out.println(s"abc + cde = ${sum("abc", "cde")}") //
compilation fails
```

```
    val intContainer = new Container(10)
    System.out.println(s"Comparing with int: ${intContainer.compare(11)}")
    val stringContainer = new Container("some text")
    System.out.println(s"Comparing with string:
     ${stringContainer.compare("some text")}")
  }
}
```

The output of this program will be as follows:

```
1 + 3 = 4
1.2 + 6.7 = 7.9
Comparing with int: false
Comparing with string: true
```

Abstract types

Another way to parameterize classes is by using abstract types. Generics have their counterparts in other languages such as Java. Unlike them, however, abstract types do not exist in Java. Let's see how our preceding Container example will translate into one with abstract types, rather than generics:

```
trait ContainerAT {
  type T
  val data: T
  def compare(other: T) = data.equals(other)
}
```

We will use the trait in a class, as follows:

```
class StringContainer(val data: String) extends ContainerAT {
  override type T = String
}
```

After we've done this, we can have the same example as before:

```
object AbstractTypesExamples {
  def main(args: Array[String]): Unit = {
    val stringContainer = new StringContainer("some text")
    System.out.println(s"Comparing with string:
     ${stringContainer.compare("some text")}")
  }
}
```

The expected output is as follows:

```
Comparing with string: true
```

We could, of course, use it in a similar way to the generic example by creating an instance of the trait and specifying the parameters there. This means that generics and abstract types really give us the possibility of achieving the same thing in two different ways.

Generics versus abstract types

So, why are there both generics and abstract types in Scala? Are there any differences, and when should one be used over the other? We will try to give answers to these questions here.

Generics and abstract types can be interchangeable. We might have to do some extra work, but in the end, we could get what the abstract types provide using generics. Which one is chosen depends on different factors, some of which are personal preferences, such as whether someone is aiming for readability or a different kind of usage of the classes.

Let's have a look at an example and try to get an idea of when and how generics and abstract types are used. In this current example, we will talk about printers. Everyone knows that there are different types—paper printers, 3D printers, and so on. Each of these uses different materials to print with, for example toner, ink, or plastic, and they are used to print on different types of media such as paper or actually in the surrounding environment. We can represent something like this using an abstract type:

```
abstract class PrintData
abstract class PrintMaterial
abstract class PrintMedia
trait Printer {
  type Data <: PrintData
  type Material <: PrintMaterial
  type Media <: PrintMedia
  def print(data: Data, material: Material, media: Media) =
    s"Printing $data with $material material on $media media."
}
```

In order to call the `print` method, we need to have different media, types of data, and materials:

```
case class Paper() extends PrintMedia
case class Air() extends PrintMedia
case class Text() extends PrintData
case class Model() extends PrintData
case class Toner() extends PrintMaterial
case class Plastic() extends PrintMaterial
```

Let's now make two concrete printer implementations, a laser and a 3D printer:

```
class LaserPrinter extends Printer {
  type Media = Paper
  type Data = Text
  type Material = Toner
}

class ThreeDPrinter extends Printer {
  type Media = Air
  type Data = Model
  type Material = Plastic
}
```

In the preceding code, we actually gave some specifications about the kind of data, media, and materials that these printers can be used with. This way, we can't ask our 3D printer to use toner to print something or our laser printer to print in the air. This is how we will use our printers:

```
object PrinterExample {
  def main(args: Array[String]): Unit = {
    val laser = new LaserPrinter
    val threeD = new ThreeDPrinter

    System.out.println(laser.print(Text(), Toner(), Paper()))
    System.out.println(threeD.print(Model(), Plastic(), Air()))
  }
}
```

The preceding code is really readable, and it allows us to specify concrete classes easily. It makes things easier to model. It is interesting to see how the preceding code would translate to generics:

```
trait GenericPrinter[Data <: PrintData, Material <: PrintMaterial, Media <:
PrintMedia] {
  def print(data: Data, material: Material, media: Media) =
    s"Printing $data with $material material on $media media."
}
```

The trait is easily represented, and readability and logical correctness are not compromised here. However, we must represent concrete classes in this way:

```
class GenericLaserPrinter[Data <: Text, Material <: Toner, Media <: Paper]
extends GenericPrinter[Data, Material, Media]
class GenericThreeDPrinter[Data <: Model, Material <: Plastic, Media <:
Air] extends GenericPrinter[Data, Material, Media]
```

This becomes quite long, and a developer could easily make a mistake. The following snippet shows how to create instances and use the classes:

```
val genericLaser = new GenericLaserPrinter[Text, Toner, Paper]
val genericThreeD = new GenericThreeDPrinter[Model, Plastic, Air]
System.out.println(genericLaser.print(Text(), Toner(), Paper()))
System.out.println(genericThreeD.print(Model(), Plastic(), Air()))
```

Here, we can see that we must specify the types every time we create instances. Imagine if we have more than three generic types, some of which could be based on generics as well, for example collections. This could quickly get quite tedious and make the code look harder than it actually is.

On the other hand, using generics allows us to reuse `GenericPrinter` without explicitly subclassing it multiple times for each different printer representation. There is, however, the risk of making logical mistakes:

```
class GenericPrinterImpl[Data <: PrintData, Material <: PrintMaterial,
Media <: PrintMedia] extends GenericPrinter[Data, Material, Media]
```

If used as follows, there is a danger of making a mistake:

```
val wrongPrinter = new GenericPrinterImpl[Model, Toner, Air]
System.out.println(wrongPrinter.print(Model(), Toner(), Air()))
```

Usage advice

The previous examples show a relatively simple comparison between the use of generics and abstract types. Both are useful concepts; however, it is important to be aware of what exactly is being done in order to use the right one for the situation. Here are some tips that could help in making the right decision.

Use generics:

- If you need just type instantiation; a good example is the standard collection classes
- If you are creating a family of types

Use abstract types:

- If you want to allow people to mix in types using traits
- If you need better readability in scenarios where both could be interchangeable
- If you want to hide the type definition from the client code

Polymorphism

Polymorphism is something every developer who has done some object-oriented programming knows about.

> Polymorphism helps us to write generic code that can be reused and applied to a variety of types.

It is important to know that there are different types of polymorphism out there, and we will be looking at them in this section.

Subtype polymorphism

This is the polymorphism every developer knows about, and it's related to overriding methods in concrete class implementations. Consider the following simple hierarchy:

```
abstract class Item {
  def pack: String
}
```

```scala
class Fruit extends Item {
  override def pack: String = "I'm a fruit and I'm packed in a bag."
}

class Drink extends Item {
  override def pack: String = "I'm a drink and I'm packed in a bottle."
}
```

Now, let's have a shopping basket of items and call `pack` for each of them:

```scala
object SubtypePolymorphismExample {
  def main(args: Array[String]): Unit = {
    val shoppingBasket: List[Item] = List(
      new Fruit,
      new Drink
    )
    shoppingBasket.foreach(i => System.out.println(i.pack))
  }
}
```

As you can see, here we can use the abstract type and just call the `pack` method without thinking about what exactly it is. Polymorphism will take care of printing the correct value. Our output will be as follows:

```
I'm a fruit and I'm packed in a bag.
I'm a drink and I'm packed in a bottle.
```

 Subtype polymorphism is expressed using inheritance with the `extends` keyword.

Parametric polymorphism

Parametric polymorphism in functional programming is what we showed in the previous section about generics. Generics are parametric polymorphism, and as we already saw, they allow us to define methods or data structures over any type, or a subset of a given type. Concrete types can then be specified at a later stage.

Ad hoc polymorphism

Ad hoc polymorphism is similar to parametric polymorphism; however, in this case, the type of arguments is important, as the concrete implementation will depend on it. It is resolved at compile time, unlike subtype polymorphism, which is done during runtime. This is somewhat similar to function overloading.

We saw an example of it earlier in this chapter, where we created the Adder trait that can sum different types. Let's have another one but a bit more refined and step by step, and we will hopefully understand how things work. Our goal is to have a sum method that can add many different kinds of types:

```
trait Adder[T] {
  def sum(a: T, b: T): T
}
```

Next, we will create a Scala object that uses this sum method and exposes it to the outside world:

```
object Adder {
  def sum[T: Adder](a: T, b: T): T = implicitly[Adder[T]].sum(a, b)
}
```

What we saw in the preceding code is some syntactic sugar in Scala, and implicitly says that there exists an implicit conversion from the T type to Adder[T]. We can now write the following program:

```
object AdhocPolymorphismExample {
  import Adder._
  def main(args: Array[String]): Unit = {
    System.out.println(s"The sum of 1 + 2 is ${sum(1, 2)}")
    System.out.println(s"The sum of abc + def is ${sum("abc", "def")}")
  }
}
```

If we try to compile and run this, we will run into trouble and get the following errors:

```
Error:(15, 51) could not find implicit value for evidence parameter of type
com.ivan.nikolov.polymorphism.Adder[Int]
    System.out.println(s"The sum of 1 + 2 is ${sum(1, 2)}")
                                                 ^

Error:(16, 55) could not find implicit value for evidence parameter of type
com.ivan.nikolov.polymorphism.Adder[String]
    System.out.println(s"The sum of abc + def is ${sum("abc", "def")}")
                                                     ^
```

This indicates that our code does not know how to implicitly convert integers or strings to `Adder[Int]` or `Adder[String]`. What we have to do is define these conversions as well as tell our program what the `sum` method will do. Our `Adder` object will look like the following:

```
object Adder {
  def sum[T: Adder](a: T, b: T): T = implicitly[Adder[T]].sum(a, b)

  implicit val int2Adder: Adder[Int] = new Adder[Int] {
    override def sum(a: Int, b: Int): Int = a + b
  }

  // same implementation as above, but allowed when the trait has a single
method
  implicit val string2Adder: Adder[String] =
    (a: String, b: String) => s"$a concatenated with $b"
}
```

If we compile and run our application now, we will get the following output:

```
The sum of 1 + 2 is 3
The sum of abc + def is abc concatenated with def
```

Also, if you remember from the example at the beginning of the chapter, we were not able to use the `sum` method on strings. As you can see here, we can provide different implementations, and using it with anything is not a problem as long as we have defined a way to convert a type to `Adder`.

Ad hoc polymorphism allows us to extend our code without modifying the base classes. This is very useful if we are using external libraries, or if we simply are not able to change the original code for some reason. It is really powerful and is evaluated in compile time, which makes sure that our program will work as expected. Moreover, it allows us to provide function definitions for types that we have no access to (`Int` and `String`, in our case).

Adding functions for multiple types

If we look back at the beginning of this chapter, where we made `Adder` work with numeric types, we will see that our last implementation of `Adder` would require us to define an operation separately for each different numeric type. Is there a way to achieve what we showed in the beginning of the chapter here as well? Yes, there is, and this is done as follows:

```
implicit def numeric2Adder[T : Numeric]: Adder[T] = new Adder[T] {
  override def sum(a: T, b: T): T = implicitly[Numeric[T]].plus(a, b)
}
```

We just defined another implicit conversion, and it will take care of the right things for us. Now, we can also write the following code:

```
System.out.println(s"The sum of 1.2 + 6.5 is ${sum(1.2, 6.5)}")
```

 Ad hoc polymorphism is expressed using implicits to mixin behavior. It is the main building block for the **type class design pattern**, which we will look into later in this book.

Self types

One of the features of good code is the separation of concerns. Developers should aim to make classes and their methods responsible for one and only one thing. This helps in testing, maintaining, and simply understanding code better. Remember—*simple is always better*.

However, it is inevitable that when writing real software, we will need instances of some classes within other ones in order to achieve certain functionalities. In other words, once our building blocks are nicely separated, they would have dependencies in order to perform their functionality. What we are talking about here really boils down to dependency injection. Self types provide a way to handle these dependencies in an elegant way. In this section, we will see how to use them and what they are good for.

Using self types

Self types allow us to easily separate code in our applications, and then require it from other places. Everything gets clearer with an example, so let's have a look at one. Let's assume that we want to be able to persist information into a database:

```
trait Persister[T] {
  def persist(data: T)
}
```

The `persist` method will do some transformations on the data and then insert it in our database. Of course, our code is well-written, so the database implementations are separated. We have the following for our database:

```
import scala.collection.mutable

trait Database[T] {
  def save(data: T)
}

trait MemoryDatabase[T] extends Database[T] {
  val db: mutable.MutableList[T] = mutable.MutableList.empty
  override def save(data: T): Unit = {
    System.out.println("Saving to in memory database.")
    db.+=:(data)
  }
}

trait FileDatabase[T] extends Database[T] {
  override def save(data: T): Unit = {
    System.out.println("Saving to file.")
  }
}
```

We have a base trait and then some concrete database implementations. So, how do we pass our database to `Persister`? It should be able to call the `save` method defined in the database. Our possibilities include the following:

- Extend `Database` in `Persister`. This would, however, also make `Persister` an instance of `Database`, and we don't want this. We will show why later.
- Have a variable for `Database` in `Persister` and use it.
- Use self types.

We are trying to see how self types work here, so let's use this approach. Our `Persister` interface will change to the following:

```
trait Persister[T] {
  this: Database[T] =>
  def persist(data: T): Unit = {
    System.out.println("Calling persist.")
    save(data)
  }
}
```

Now, we have access to the methods in `Database` and can call the `save` method inside `Persister`.

Naming the self type

In the preceding code, we included our self type using the statement—`this: Database[T] =>`. This allows us to access the methods of our included types directly as if they were methods of the trait that includes them. Another way of doing the same here is by writing `self: Database[T] =>` instead. There are many examples out there that use the latter approach, which is useful to avoid confusion if we need to refer to `this` in some nested trait or class definitions. Calling the methods of the injected dependencies using this approach, however, would require the developer to use `self.` in order to gain access to the required methods.

The self type requires any class that mixes `Persister` in, to also mix `Database` in. Otherwise, our compilation will fail. Let's create classes to persist to memory and database:

```
class FilePersister[T] extends Persister[T] with FileDatabase[T]
class MemoryPersister[T] extends Persister[T] with MemoryDatabase[T]
```

Finally, we can use them in our application:

```
object PersisterExample {
  def main(args: Array[String]): Unit = {
    val fileStringPersister = new FilePersister[String]
    val memoryIntPersister = new MemoryPersister[Int]

    fileStringPersister.persist("Something")
    fileStringPersister.persist("Something else")

    memoryIntPersister.persist(100)
    memoryIntPersister.persist(123)
  }
}
```

Here is the output of our program:

```
Calling persist.
Saving to file.
Calling persist.
Saving to file.
Calling persist.
Saving to in memory database.
Calling persist.
Saving to in memory database.
```

What self types do is different from inheritance. They require the presence of some code, and thus allow us to split a functionality nicely. This can make a huge difference in maintaining, refactoring, and understanding a program.

Requiring multiple components

In real applications, we might require more than one component using a self type. Let's show this in our example with a `History` trait that could potentially keep track of changes to roll back at some point. Ours will just do printing:

```
trait History {
  def add(): Unit = {
    System.out.println("Action added to history.")
  }
}
```

We need to use this in our `Persister` trait, and it will look like this:

```
trait Persister[T] {
  this: Database[T] with History =>
  def persist(data: T): Unit = {
    System.out.println("Calling persist.")
    save(data)
    add()
  }
}
```

Using the `with` keyword, we can add as many requirements as we like. However, if we just leave our code changes there, it will not compile. The reason for this is that we must now mix `History` in every class that uses `Persister`:

```
class FilePersister[T] extends Persister[T] with FileDatabase[T] with
History
class MemoryPersister[T] extends Persister[T] with MemoryDatabase[T] with
History
```

That's it. If we now run our code, we will see this:

```
Calling persist.
Saving to file.
Action added to history.
Calling persist.
Saving to file.
Action added to history.
Calling persist.
Saving to in memory database.
Action added to history.
Calling persist.
Saving to in memory database.
Action added to history.
```

Conflicting components

In the preceding example, we had a requirement for the `History` trait, which has an `add()` method. What would happen if the methods in different components have the same signatures and they clash? Let's try this:

```
trait Mystery {
  def add(): Unit = {
    System.out.println("Mystery added!")
  }
}
```

We can now use this in our `Persister` trait:

```
trait Persister[T] {
  this: Database[T] with History with Mystery =>
  def persist(data: T): Unit = {
    System.out.println("Calling persist.")
    save(data)
    add()
  }
}
```

Of course, we will change all the classes that mix `Persister` in:

```
class FilePersister[T] extends Persister[T] with FileDatabase[T] with
History with Mystery
class MemoryPersister[T] extends Persister[T] with MemoryDatabase[T] with
History with Mystery
```

If we try to compile our application, we will see that it results in a failure with the following messages:

```
Error:(47, 7) class FilePersister inherits conflicting members:
  method add in trait History of type ()Unit and
  method add in trait Mystery of type ()Unit
(Note: this can be resolved by declaring an override in class
FilePersister.)
class FilePersister[T] extends Persister[T] with FileDatabase[T] with
History with Mystery
      ^


Error:(48, 7) class MemoryPersister inherits conflicting members:
  method add in trait History of type ()Unit and
  method add in trait Mystery of type ()Unit
(Note: this can be resolved by declaring an override in class
MemoryPersister.)
class MemoryPersister[T] extends Persister[T] with MemoryDatabase[T] with
History with Mystery
      ^
```

Luckily, the error messages also contain information that tells us how we can fix the problem. This is absolutely the same case that we saw earlier while using traits, and we can provide the following fix:

```
class FilePersister[T] extends Persister[T] with FileDatabase[T] with
History with Mystery {
  override def add(): Unit ={
    super[History].add()
  }
}

class MemoryPersister[T] extends Persister[T] with MemoryDatabase[T] with
History with Mystery {
  override def add(): Unit ={
    super[Mystery].add()
  }
}
```

After running the example, we will see the following output:

```
Calling persist.
Saving to file.
Action added to history.
Calling persist.
Saving to file.
Action added to history.
Calling persist.
Saving to in memory database.
Mystery added!
Calling persist.
Saving to in memory database.
Mystery added!
```

Self types and the cake design pattern

What we saw in our preceding examples was a pure example of dependency injection. We required one component to be available in another one through self types.

 Self types are often used for dependency injection. They are the main part of the **cake design pattern**, which we will become familiar with later in this book.

The cake design pattern relies completely on self types. It encourages engineers to write small and simple components, which declare and use their dependencies. After all the components in an application are programmed, they can be instantiated inside a common component registry and made available to the actual application. One of the nice advantages of the cake design pattern is that it actually checks during compile time whether all the dependencies would be satisfied. We will dedicate a complete section on the cake design pattern later in this book, where we will provide more details about how the pattern can actually be wired up, what advantages and drawbacks it has, and so on.

Self types versus inheritance

In the previous section, we said that we don't want to use inheritance in order to get access to the Database methods. Why is that? If we had made Persister extend Database, this would mean that it would become a database itself (*is-a* relationship). However, this is not correct. It uses a database in order to achieve its functionality.

Inheritance exposes a subclass to the implementation details of its parent. This, however, is not always desired. According to the authors of *Design Patterns: Elements of Reusable Object-Oriented Software*, developers should favor object composition over class inheritance.

Inheritance leaking functionality

If we use inheritance, we would also leak functionality to subclasses that we do not want. Let's look at the following code:

```
trait DB {
  def connect(): Unit = {
    System.out.println("Connected.")
  }

  def dropDatabase(): Unit = {
    System.out.println("Dropping!")
  }

  def close(): Unit = {
    System.out.println("Closed.")
  }
}

trait UserDB extends DB {
  def createUser(username: String): Unit = {
    connect()
    try {
      System.out.println(s"Creating a user: $username")
    } finally {
      close()
    }
  }

  def getUser(username: String): Unit = {
    connect()
    try {
      System.out.println(s"Getting a user: $username")
    } finally {
      close()
    }
  }
}

trait UserService extends UserDB {
  def bad(): Unit = {
    dropDatabase()
```

```
      }
   }
```

This could be a real-life scenario. Because this is how inheritance works, we would get access to `dropDatabase` in `UserService`. This is something we do not want, and we can fix it using self types. The DB trait stays the same. Everything else changes to the following:

```
trait UserDB {
  this: DB =>
  def createUser(username: String): Unit = {
    connect()
    try {
      System.out.println(s"Creating a user: $username")
    } finally {
      close()
    }
  }

  def getUser(username: String): Unit = {
    connect()
    try {
      System.out.println(s"Getting a user: $username")
    } finally {
      close()
    }
  }
}

trait UserService {
  this: UserDB =>
  // does not compile
  // def bad(): Unit = {
  // dropDatabase()
  //}
}
```

As the comments in the code show, in this last version of the code, we do not have access to the DB trait methods. We can only call the methods of the type we require, and this is exactly what we wanted to achieve.

Summary

In this chapter, we familiarized ourselves with some concepts that help us to write better, more generic, and extendible software. We focused on abstract types, polymorphism, and self types in Scala.

We looked into the differences between generics and abstract type values in classes, along with some examples and usage advice. Then, we introduced the different types of polymorphism—subtype, parametric, and ad hoc. Finally, we went through self types in Scala and how to use them. We showed that self types provide a good way to encapsulate functionality and write modular code.

In the following chapter, we will look into the importance of separating the responsibilities of software components. We will also go through aspect-oriented programming.

5
Aspect-Oriented Programming and Components

Often in programming, we see pieces of source code that are repeated in different methods. In some cases, we could refactor our code and move them to separate modules. Sometimes, however, this is not possible. Some notable examples include logging and verification. Aspect-oriented programming is helpful in such cases, and we will get an understanding of it by the end of this chapter.

Components are reusable pieces of code that provide a number of services and have some requirements. They are extremely useful for avoiding code duplication, and of course, for promoting code reuse. Here, we will see how to build components and how Scala makes the writing and use of components easier than other languages.

While getting familiar with aspect-oriented programming and components, we will go through the following top-level topics:

- Aspect-oriented programming
- Components in Scala

Aspect-oriented programming

Aspect-oriented programming (**AOP**) addresses a common functionality, that spans across an application, but cannot be otherwise abstracted in a single module using traditional object-oriented techniques. This repeated functionality is often referred to as *cross-cutting concerns*. A common example is logging—normally, loggers are created within classes and then their methods are called inside the methods of the classes. This helps with the debugging and tracing of events in an application, but it is not really related to the actual functionality in any way.

AOP recommends that cross-cutting concerns are abstracted and encapsulated in their own modules. In the next few subsections, we will look into how AOP improves code and also makes cross-cutting concerns easily extendible.

Understanding application efficiency

An important part of every program is efficiency. In many cases, we can time our methods and find bottlenecks in our applications. Let's look at an example program that we will try and time afterwards.

We will have a look at parsing. In many real-life applications, we have to read data in specific formats and parse it to the objects in our code. For this example, we will have a small database of people represented in a JSON format:

```
[
  {
    "firstName": "Ivan",
    "lastName": "Nikolov",
    "age": 26
  },
  {
    "firstName": "John",
    "lastName": "Smith",
    "age": 55
  },
  {
    "firstName": "Maria",
    "lastName": "Cooper",
    "age": 19
  }
]
```

To represent this JSON in Scala, we have to define our model. It will be simple and contain only one class—Person. Here is the code for it:

```
case class Person(firstName: String, lastName: String, age: Int)
```

Since we will be reading JSON inputs, we will have to parse them. There are many parsers out there, and everyone might have their own preferences. In the current example, we have used json4s (https://github.com/json4s/json4s). We have the following extra dependency in our build.sbt/pom.xml file:

```
<dependency>
    <groupId>org.json4s</groupId>
```

```
      <artifactId>json4s-jackson_2.12</artifactId>
      <version>3.6.0-M2</version>
</dependency>
```

The following shows the `build.sbt` equivalent of the `pom.xml` version:

```
"org.json4s" %% "json4s-jackson" % "3.6.0-M2"
```

We have written a class with two methods that parses an input file of the given preceding format and returns a list of `Person` objects. These two methods do exactly the same thing, but one of them is more efficient than the other one:

```
import org.json4s._
import org.json4s.jackson.JsonMethods._

trait DataReader {
  def readData(): List[Person]
  def readDataInefficiently(): List[Person]
}

class DataReaderImpl extends DataReader {
  implicit val formats = DefaultFormats
  private def readUntimed(): List[Person] =
parse(StreamInput(getClass.getResourceAsStream("/users.json"))).extract[Lis
t[Person]]

  override def readData(): List[Person] = readUntimed()

  override def readDataInefficiently(): List[Person] = {
    (1 to 10000).foreach {
      case num =>
        readUntimed()
    }
    readUntimed()
  }
}
```

The `DataReader` trait acts as an interface, and using the implementation is quite straightforward:

```
object DataReaderExample {
  def main(args: Array[String]): Unit = {
    val dataReader = new DataReaderImpl
    System.out.println(s"I just read the following data efficiently:
     ${dataReader.readData()}")
    System.out.println(s"I just read the following data inefficiently:
     ${dataReader.readDataInefficiently()}")
```

```
      }
   }
```

It will produce output as shown in the following screenshot:

```
volcom@volcom-Dell-System-XPS-L502X:~/workspace/scala-book/aop$ java -cp target/
aop-1.0.0-SNAPSHOT.jar com.ivan.nikolov.aop.DataReaderExample
I just read the following data efficiently: List(Person(Ivan,Nikolov,26), Person
(John,Smith,55), Person(Maria,Cooper,19))
I just read the following data inefficiently: List(Person(Ivan,Nikolov,26), Pers
on(John,Smith,55), Person(Maria,Cooper,19))
```

The preceding example is clear. However, what if we want to optimize our code and see what causes it to be slow? The previous code does not give us this possibility, so we will have to take some extra steps in order to time and see how our application performs. In the following subsections, we will show how this is done without and with AOP.

Timing our application without AOP

There is a basic way to do our timing. We could either surround the `println` statements in our application, or add the timing as a part of the methods in the `DataReaderImpl` class. Generally, adding the timing as part of the methods seems like a better choice as in some cases, these methods could be called at different places and their performance would depend on the passed parameters and other factors. Considering what we said, this is how our `DataReaderImpl` class could be refactored in order to support timing:

```
import org.json4s._
import org.json4s.jackson.JsonMethods._

class DataReaderImpl extends DataReader {
  implicit val formats = DefaultFormats

  private def readUntimed(): List[Person] =
    parse(StreamInput(getClass.getResourceAsStream("/users.json")))
    .extract[List[Person]]

  override def readData(): List[Person] = {
    val startMillis = System.currentTimeMillis()
    val result = readUntimed()
    val time = System.currentTimeMillis() - startMillis
    System.err.println(s"readData took ${time} milliseconds.")
     result
  }
```

```scala
override def readDataInefficiently(): List[Person] = {
  val startMillis = System.currentTimeMillis()
  (1 to 10000).foreach {
    case num =>
      readUntimed()
  }
  val result = readUntimed()
  val time = System.currentTimeMillis() - startMillis
  System.err.println(s"readDataInefficiently took ${time} milliseconds.")
  result
}
}
```

As you can see, the code becomes quite unreadable and the timing interferes with the actual functionality. In any case, if we run our program, the output will show us where the problem is:

```
volcom@volcom-Dell-System-XPS-L502X:~/workspace/scala-book/aop$ java -cp target/
aop-1.0.0-SNAPSHOT.jar com.ivan.nikolov.aop.DataReaderExample
readData took 254 milliseconds.
I just read the following data efficiently: List(Person(Ivan,Nikolov,26), Person
(John,Smith,55), Person(Maria,Cooper,19))
readDataInefficiently took 971 milliseconds.
I just read the following data inefficiently: List(Person(Ivan,Nikolov,26), Pers
on(John,Smith,55), Person(Maria,Cooper,19))
```

We will see how to improve our code using aspect-oriented programming in the next subsection.

 In the previous example, we used `System.err.println` to log the timing. This is just for example purposes. In practice, using loggers, for example **slf4j** (https://www.slf4j.org/), is the recommended option, as you can have different logging levels and switch logs using configuration files. Using loggers here would have added extra dependencies and it would have pulled your attention away from the important material.

Timing our application with AOP

As we saw, adding our timing code to our methods introduces code duplication and makes our code hard to follow, even for a small example. Now, imagine that we also have to do logging and other activities. Aspect-oriented programming helps in separating these concerns.

We can revert the `DataReaderImpl` class to its original state, where it does not do any logging. Then, we create another trait called `LoggingDataReader`, which extends from `DataReader` and has the following contents:

```
trait LoggingDataReader extends DataReader {

  abstract override def readData(): List[Person] = {
    val startMillis = System.currentTimeMillis()
    val result = super.readData()
    val time = System.currentTimeMillis() - startMillis
    System.err.println(s"readData took ${time} milliseconds.")
    result
  }

  abstract override def readDataInefficiently(): List[Person] = {
    val startMillis = System.currentTimeMillis()
    val result = super.readDataInefficiently()
    val time = System.currentTimeMillis() - startMillis
    System.err.println(s"readDataInefficiently took ${time} milliseconds.")
    result
  }
}
```

Something interesting here is the `abstract override` modifier. It notifies the compiler that we will be doing stackable modifications. If we do not use this modifier, our compilation will fail with the following errors:

```
Error:(9, 24) method readData in trait DataReader is accessed from super.
It may not be abstract unless it is overridden by a member declared
`abstract' and `override'
    val result = super.readData()
                 ^
Error:(17, 24) method readDataInefficiently in trait DataReader is accessed
from super. It may not be abstract unless it is overridden by a member
declared `abstract' and `override'
    val result = super.readDataInefficiently()
                 ^
```

Now, let's use our new trait using a mixin composition, which we already covered earlier in this book, in the following program:

```
object DataReaderAOPExample {
  def main(args: Array[String]): Unit = {
    val dataReader = new DataReaderImpl with LoggingDataReader
    System.out.println(s"I just read the following data efficiently:
     ${dataReader.readData()}")
    System.out.println(s"I just read the following data inefficiently:
```

```
        ${dataReader.readDataInefficiently()}")
    }
}
```

If we run this program, we will see that, as before, our output will contain the timings.

The advantage of using aspect-oriented programming is clear—the implementation is not contaminated by other code, which is irrelevant to it. Moreover, we can add extra modifications using the same approach—more logging, retry logic, rollbacks, and so on. Everything happens by just creating new traits that extend `DataReader` and mixing them in, as shown previously. Of course, we can have multiple modifications applied at the same time that will execute in order, and the order of their execution will follow the rules of linearization, which we are already familiar with.

Components in Scala

Components are parts of an application that are meant to be combined with other parts of the application. They should be reusable in order to achieve less code duplication. Components typically have interfaces, which describe the services they provide and a number of services or other components they depend on.

In large applications, we usually see multiple components that are integrated to work together. Describing the services that a component provides is usually straightforward, and it is done with the help of interfaces. Integrating other components, however, could sometimes require a developer to do extra work. This is usually done by passing the interface of the requirement as a parameter. However, imagine a large application in which we might have a lot of requirements; wiring things up could take time and effort. Moreover, every time a new requirement comes up, we would have to do quite a lot of refactoring. An alternative to parameters is multiple inheritance; however, the language needs to support it in some way.

A popular way to wire components up in languages such as Java is through dependency injection. There are libraries that exist in Java that can be used in order to inject components into each other during runtime.

Using Scala's expressive power to build components

We have already said a few times in this book that Scala is a much more expressive language than the simply object-oriented ones. We already looked into concepts such as abstract types, self types, unification, and mixin compositions. They allow us to create generic code, require specific classes, and are able to treat objects, classes, variables, and functions in the same way and achieve multiple inheritance. Using different combinations of these would allow us to write the modular code we are looking for.

Implementing components

Dependency injection is quite popular to wire components up. However, in languages such as Java, this would mean that we require someone to use the same library as we do. Having a high number of parameters in the classes throughout our applications is also not acceptable. This makes it easier to make mistakes and turns refactoring and code extension into a nightmare.

In the next subsection, we will look into how Scala self types can be used in order to create and compose components.

Self types for components

As an example, let's imagine that we are trying to build a robot that cooks food. Our robot will be able to look up recipes and cook the dishes we ask for, as well as tell us the time. We will be able to add extra functionality to our robot by simply creating new components.

We want our code to be modular, so it makes sense to split the functionality. The following diagram shows what our robot will look like and the relationships between the different components:

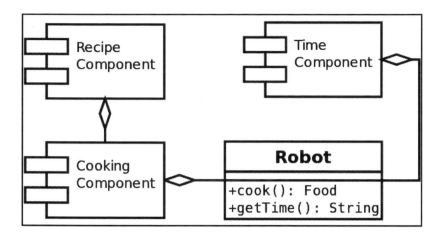

First of all, let's define the interfaces for the different components:

```
trait Time {
  def getTime(): String
}

trait RecipeFinder {
  def findRecipe(dish: String): String
}

trait Cooker {
  def cook(what: String): Food
}
```

We need our Food class to be defined, and for this example, it will be as simple as this:

```
case class Food(name: String)
```

Once this is done, we can start creating our components. First is the TimeComponent and the implementation of Time in a nested class:

```
trait TimeComponent {
  val time: Time

  class TimeImpl extends Time {
    val formatter = DateTimeFormatter.ofPattern("HH:mm:ss")
    override def getTime(): String = s"The time is:
      ${LocalDateTime.now().format(formatter)}"
  }
}
```

Now, we can implement the `RecipeComponent` in a similar way. The following is the component code and the implementation code:

```
trait RecipeComponent {
  val recipe: RecipeFinder

  class RecipeFinderImpl extends RecipeFinder {
    override def findRecipe(dish: String): String = dish match {
      case "chips" => "Fry the potatoes for 10 minutes."
      case "fish" => "Clean the fish and put in the oven for 30 minutes."
      case "sandwich" => "Put butter, ham and cheese on the bread,
       toast and add tomatoes."
      case _ => throw new RuntimeException(s"${dish} is unknown recipe.")
    }
  }
}
```

Finally, we need to implement the `CookingComponent`. It actually requires a `RecipeComponent`. Here is how this is done:

```
trait CookingComponent {
  this: RecipeComponent =>

  val cooker: Cooker

  class CookerImpl extends Cooker {
    override def cook(what: String): Food = {
      val recipeText = recipe.findRecipe(what)
      Food(s"We just cooked $what using the following recipe:
       '$recipeText'.")
    }
  }
}
```

Now, we have all the components separately implemented, and we can combine them in order to create our robot. We will create a component registry that the robot will use, as follows:

```
class RobotRegistry extends TimeComponent with RecipeComponent with
CookingComponent {
  override val time: Time = new TimeImpl
  override val recipe: RecipeFinder = new RecipeFinderImpl
  override val cooker: Cooker = new CookerImpl
}
```

Let's now create a `Robot`:

```
class Robot extends RobotRegistry {
  def cook(what: String) = cooker.cook(what)
  def getTime() = time.getTime()
}
```

An example program that uses our robot will look like the following:

```
object RobotExample {
  def main(args: Array[String]): Unit = {
    val robot = new Robot
    System.out.println(robot.getTime())
    System.out.println(robot.cook("chips"))
    System.out.println(robot.cook("sandwich"))
  }
}
```

An example output of this program is shown in the following screenshot:

```
volcom@volcom-Dell-System-XPS-L502X:~/workspace/scala-book/aop$ java -cp target/
aop-1.0.0-SNAPSHOT.jar com.ivan.nikolov.components.RobotExample
The time is: 20:36:19
Food(We just cooked chips using the following recipe: 'Fry the potatoes for 10 m
inutes.'.)
Food(We just cooked sandwich using the following recipe: 'Put butter, ham and ch
eese on the bread, toast and add tomatoes.'.)
```

In the preceding example, we saw the way Scala implements dependency injection that is easy to wire up without using extra libraries. This is really useful as it doesn't make our constructors large and we don't have to extend many classes as well. Moreover, the components we have are nicely separated, testable, and clearly define their requirements. We also saw how we can add requirements recursively using components that require other ones.

The preceding example is actually a representation of the **cake design pattern**. One of the nice features here is that the presence of dependencies is evaluated at compile time rather than at runtime, as popular Java libraries do.

The cake design pattern has its drawbacks as well, but we will be focusing on all the features—good and bad ones—later in this book. This is where we will show how the components can be tested as well.

The cake design pattern example in this chapter is really simple. In real-life applications, we might have components that depend on other components, which have their own dependencies and so on. In such cases, things can get complicated. We will aim to showcase this better and in much more detail later in this book.

Summary

In this chapter, we looked into aspect-oriented programming in Scala. We now know how to separate code that normally wouldn't be possible to move into modules. This will lead to avoiding code duplication and make our programs nice with different, specialized modules.

We also showed how to create reusable components using techniques we covered in the previous chapters of this book. Components provide interfaces and have specific requirements, which could be easily satisfied using the richness of Scala. They are really relevant to design patterns because they have the same purpose—to make the code better, avoid repetition, and be able to easily test it.

In the following chapters of this book, we will start looking at some concrete design patterns with their useful features and use cases. We will start with *creational design patterns* as they are defined by the *GoF*, but of course, from the Scala point of view.

Creational Design Patterns 6

From this chapter onward, we will be delving into the actual design patterns that are out there. We have already mentioned the importance of knowing and being able to properly make use of the different design patterns that exist.

Design patterns can be thought of as best practices or even templates that can be used in solving specific problems. The number of problems that a developer will have to tackle is endless, and in many cases, different design patterns have to be combined. However, based on the aspects of a program on which a piece of code is written to solve a problem, we can split design patterns into the following main groups:

- Creational
- Structural
- Behavioral

This chapter will focus on the **creational design patterns**, and of course, we will look at them from the point of view of the Scala programming language. We will go through the following topics:

- What are creational design patterns
- The factory method
- The abstract factory
- Other factory design patterns
- Lazy initialization
- The singleton
- The builder
- The prototype

After formally defining the creational design patterns, we will look at each one of them separately in greater detail. We will focus on when and how to use them, when to avoid some patterns, and of course, show some relevant examples.

What are creational design patterns?

Creational design patterns, as the name suggests, deal with object creation. In some cases, creating objects in a program could involve some extra complexities, and creational design patterns hide these complexities in order to make the use of software components easier. The object creation complexity could be caused by any of the following:

- The number of initialization parameters
- Required validation
- The complexity of acquiring the required parameters

The preceding list could possibly be expanded even more and in many cases, these factors are present not just individually, but in combinations.

We will be focusing on the aspects of creational design patterns in the following sections of this chapter and hopefully, you will have a good understanding of why they are needed and how to use them in real life.

The factory method design pattern

The factory method design pattern exists in order to encapsulate an actual class instantiation. It simply provides an interface to create an object, and then the subclasses of the factory decide which concrete class to instantiate. This design pattern could become useful in cases where we want to create different objects during the runtime of the application. This design pattern is also helpful when object creation would otherwise require extra parameters to be passed by the developer.

Everything will become clearer with an example, and we will provide one in the following subsections.

An example class diagram

For the factory method, we will be showing an example with databases. To keep things simple (just because the actual `java.sql.Connection` has a lot of methods), we will define our own `SimpleConnection` and it will have concrete implementations for `MySQL` and `PostgreSQL`.

The diagram for the connection classes looks like the following:

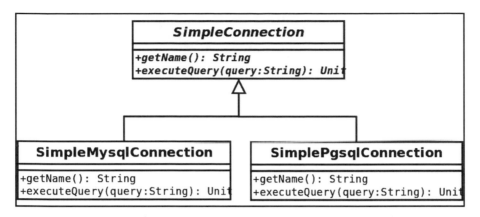

Now, creating these connections will depend on the database we want to use. However, using them will be exactly the same because of the interface they provide. The actual creation might also involve some extra computations that we want to hide from the user and which will be relevant if we're talking about a different constant for each database. That's why we use a factory method design pattern. The following diagram shows how the rest of our code will be structured:

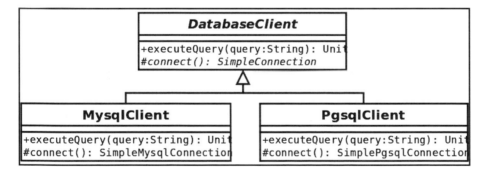

In the preceding figure, **MysqlClient** and **PgsqlClient** are the concrete implementations of the **DatabaseClient**. The factory method is **connect** and it returns a different connection in different clients. Since we override, the signature in the code still shows that the method returns a **SimpleConnection**, but the actual types are concrete. In the diagram, for clarity, we have chosen to show the actual returned type.

A code example

From the preceding diagram, it is clear that depending on the database client we use, a different connection will be used and created. Now, let's have a look at the code representation for the preceding diagrams. First is the `SimpleConnection` with its concrete implementations:

```scala
trait SimpleConnection {
  def gctName(): String

  def executeQuery(query: String): Unit
}

class SimpleMysqlConnection extends SimpleConnection {
  override def getName(): String = "SimpleMysqlConnection"

  override def executeQuery(query: String): Unit = {
    System.out.println(s"Executing the query '$query' the MySQL way.")
  }
}

class SimplePgSqlConnection extends SimpleConnection {
  override def getName(): String = "SimplePgSqlConnection"

  override def executeQuery(query: String): Unit = {
    System.out.println(s"Executing the query '$query' the PgSQL way.")
  }
}
```

We use these implementations in our factory method, called `connect`. The following code snippet shows how we can take advantage of `connect` and how we can implement it in specific database clients:

```scala
abstract class DatabaseClient {
  def executeQuery(query: String): Unit = {
    val connection = connect()
    connection.executeQuery(query)
  }

  protected def connect(): SimpleConnection
}

class MysqlClient extends DatabaseClient {
  override protected def connect(): SimpleConnection = new
SimpleMysqlConnection
}
```

```
class PgSqlClient extends DatabaseClient {
  override protected def connect(): SimpleConnection = new
SimplePgSqlConnection
}
```

Using our database clients is then straightforward, as shown here:

```
object Example {
  def main(args: Array[String]): Unit = {
    val clientMySql: DatabaseClient = new MysqlClient
    val clientPgSql: DatabaseClient = new PgSqlClient
    clientMySql.executeQuery("SELECT * FROM users")
    clientPgSql.executeQuery("SELECT * FROM employees")
  }
}
```

The preceding code example will produce the following output:

```
volcom@volcom-Dell-System-XPS-L502X:~/workspace/scala-book/creational-design-pat
terns$ java -cp target/creational-1.0.0-SNAPSHOT.jar com.ivan.nikolov.creational
.factories.factory_method.Example
Executing the query 'SELECT * FROM users' the MySQL way.
Executing the query 'SELECT * FROM employees' the PgSQL way.
```

We saw how the factory method design pattern works. If we need to add another database client, then we can just extend `DatabaseClient` and return a class that extends `SimpleConnection` when we implement the `connect` method.

 The preceding choice to use an abstract class for the `DatabaseClient` and a trait for the `SimpleConnection` was just random. We could, of course, change the abstract class with a trait.

In other cases, the objects created by the factory method might require parameters in their constructor and these parameters could depend on some specific state or functionality of the object that owns the factory method. This is where this design pattern could actually shine.

Scala alternatives

As with anything in software engineering, this design pattern could also be achieved using different approaches. Which one to use really boils down to the requirements and specific features of the application and objects being created. Some possible alternatives include the following:

- Passing the needed components to the class that needs them in the constructor (object composition). This, however, would mean that these components will be specific instances rather than new ones, every time a request for them is made.
- Passing a function that will create the objects we need.

Using the richness of Scala, we can avoid this design pattern or we can just be smarter about how we create the objects that we will be using or exposing whatever the factory method will be creating. There is no right or wrong way in the end. There is, however, a way that would make things simpler, both in terms of usage and maintenance, and it should be chosen by considering the specific requirements.

What it is good for?

As with other factories, the details of object creation are hidden. This means that if we change the way a specific instance has to be created, we would have to change only the factory methods that create it (this might involve a lot of creators though, depending on the design). The factory method allows us to use the abstract version of a class and defer the object creation to subclasses.

What it is not so good for?

In the preceding examples, we might quickly run into issues if we have more than one factory method. This would first require the programmer to implement many more methods, but more importantly, it could lead to the returned objects being incompatible. Let's see this in a short example. First, we will declare another trait called `SimpleConnectionPrinter`, which will have one method that prints something when called:

```
trait SimpleConnectionPrinter {
  def printSimpleConnection(connection: SimpleConnection): Unit
}
```

Now, we want to change our `DatabaseClient` and name it differently
(`BadDatabaseClient`). It will look like the following:

```
abstract class BadDatabaseClient {
  def executeQuery(query: String): Unit = {
    val connection = connect()
    val connectionPrinter = getConnectionPrinter()
    connectionPrinter.printSimpleConnection(connection)
    connection.executeQuery(query)
  }

  protected def connect(): SimpleConnection

  protected def getConnectionPrinter(): SimpleConnectionPrinter
}
```

The only difference here to our original example is that we have another factory method,
that we will also call when executing a query. Similar to the `SimpleConnection`
implementations, let's now create two more for MySQL and PostgreSQL for our
`SimpleConnectionPrinter`:

```
class SimpleMySqlConnectionPrinter extends SimpleConnectionPrinter {
  override def printSimpleConnection(connection: SimpleConnection): Unit =
{
    System.out.println(s"I require a MySQL connection. It is:
'${connection.getName()}'")
  }
}

class SimplePgSqlConnectionPrinter extends SimpleConnectionPrinter {
  override def printSimpleConnection(connection: SimpleConnection): Unit =
{
    System.out.println(s"I require a PgSQL connection. It is:
'${connection.getName()}'")
  }
}
```

We can now apply the factory design pattern and create MySQL and PostgreSQL clients, as
shown here:

```
class BadMySqlClient extends BadDatabaseClient {
  override protected def connect(): SimpleConnection = new
SimpleMysqlConnection

  override protected def getConnectionPrinter(): SimpleConnectionPrinter =
new SimpleMySqlConnectionPrinter
}
```

```scala
class BadPgSqlClient extends BadDatabaseClient {
  override protected def connect(): SimpleConnection = new
SimplePgSqlConnection

  override protected def getConnectionPrinter(): SimpleConnectionPrinter =
new SimpleMySqlConnectionPrinter
}
```

The preceding implementations are completely valid. We can now use them in an example:

```scala
object BadExample {
  def main(args: Array[String]): Unit = {
    val clientMySql: BadDatabaseClient = new BadMySqlClient
    val clientPgSql: BadDatabaseClient = new BadPgSqlClient
    clientMySql.executeQuery("SELECT * FROM users")
    clientPgSql.executeQuery("SELECT * FROM employees")
  }
}
```

This example will have the following output:

```
volcom@volcom-Dell-System-XPS-L502X:~/workspace/scala-book/creational-design-pat
terns$ java -cp target/creational-1.0.0-SNAPSHOT.jar com.ivan.nikolov.creational
.factories.factory_method.BadExample
I require a MySQL connection. It is: 'SimpleMysqlConnection'
Executing the query 'SELECT * FROM users' the MySQL way.
I require a MySQL connection. It is: 'SimplePgSqlConnection'
Executing the query 'SELECT * FROM employees' the PgSQL way.
```

What happened in the preceding example is that we got a logical error, and nothing notifies us about this. When the number of methods to implement grows, this could become a problem and mistakes could be easily made. For example, our code didn't throw an exception, but this pitfall could lead to runtime errors that could be really hard to discover and debug.

The abstract factory

The abstract factory is another design pattern from the family of *factory* patterns. The purpose is the same as all factory design patterns—to encapsulate the object creation logic and hide it from the user. The difference is how it is implemented.

The abstract factory design pattern relies on object composition in contrast to inheritance, which is used by the factory method. Here, we have a separate object, which provides an interface to create instances of the classes we need.

An example class diagram

Let's keep using the preceding SimpleConnection example here. The following diagram shows how the abstract factory is structured:

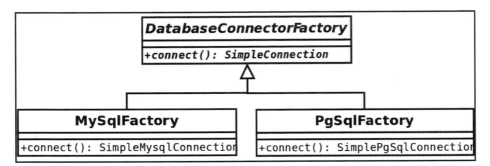

As we can see from the preceding diagram, now we have a hierarchy of factories rather than a method inside our database client. We will be using the abstract **DatabaseConnectorFactory** in our application and it will be returning the right objects, depending on the actual instance type.

A code example

Let's have a look at our example from the source point of view. The following code listing shows the factory hierarchy:

```
trait DatabaseConnectorFactory {
  def connect(): SimpleConnection
}

class MySqlFactory extends DatabaseConnectorFactory {
  override def connect(): SimpleConnection = new SimpleMysqlConnection
}

class PgSqlFactory extends DatabaseConnectorFactory {
  override def connect(): SimpleConnection = new SimplePgSqlConnection
}
```

We can then use our factory by passing it to a class, that will call the required methods. Here is an example similar to the one we showed for the factory method design pattern:

```scala
class DatabaseClient(connectorFactory: DatabaseConnectorFactory) {
  def executeQuery(query: String): Unit = {
    val connection = connectorFactory.connect()
    connection.executeQuery(query)
  }
}
```

Let's see an example that uses our database client:

```scala
object Example {
  def main(args: Array[String]): Unit = {
    val clientMySql: DatabaseClient = new DatabaseClient(new MySqlFactory)
    val clientPgSql: DatabaseClient = new DatabaseClient(new PgSqlFactory)
    clientMySql.executeQuery("SELECT * FROM users")
    clientPgSql.executeQuery("SELECT * FROM employees")
  }
}
```

The following screenshot shows the output of this program:

```
volcom@volcom-Dell-System-XPS-L502X:~/workspace/scala-book/creational-design-pat
terns$ java -cp target/creational-1.0.0-SNAPSHOT.jar com.ivan.nikolov.creational
.factories.abstract_factory.Example
Executing the query 'SELECT * FROM users' the MySQL way.
Executing the query 'SELECT * FROM employees' the PgSQL way.
```

This is how the abstract factory design pattern works. If we need to add another database client to our application, we can achieve this by adding another class that extends `DatabaseConnectionFactory`. This is nice because it makes refactoring and extending easy.

Scala alternatives

This design pattern can also be achieved using different approaches. The fact that we use object composition to pass a factory to our class indicates that we can do something else—we can simply pass a function, just because in Scala they are a part of unification and they are treated the same way as objects.

What it is good for?

As with all factories, the details of object creation are hidden. The abstract factory design pattern is particularly useful when we want to expose families of objects (for example, database connectors). The clients then become decoupled from the concrete classes. This pattern is commonly shown as an example in different UI toolkits, where elements differ for different operating systems. It is also quite testable because we can provide mocks instead of an actual factory to the clients.

Even though the incompatibility problem that we mentioned previously is still present here, it is somewhat harder to encounter now. This is mainly because here, the client will actually just pass one single factory as a parameter, and in the case where we provide the user with concrete factories, everything was already taken care of when these factories were written.

What it is not so good for?

It could be problematic if the objects and methods we are using (`SimpleConnection`, in our case) change signatures. In some cases, this pattern could also complicate our code unnecessarily and make it unreadable and hard to follow.

Other factory design patterns

There are some different variations of the factory design patterns. In all cases though, the purpose is generally the same—hide creation complexity. In the following subsections, we will briefly mention two of the other factory design patterns—**static factory** and **simple factory**.

The static factory

The static factory could be represented as a static method, which is a part of the base class. It is called to create concrete instances, which extend the base class. One of the biggest drawbacks here, however, is that if another extension of the base class is added, the base class (because of the static method) also has to be edited. Let's show a simple example from the world of animals:

```
trait Animal
class Bird extends Animal
class Mammal extends Animal
class Fish extends Animal
```

```
object Animal {
  def apply(animal: String): Animal = animal.toLowerCase match {
    case "bird" => new Bird
    case "mammal" => new Mammal
    case "fish" => new Fish
    case x: String => throw new RuntimeException(s"Unknown animal: $x")
  }
}
```

Here, every time we add a new extension of `Animal`, we would have to change the `apply` method to account for it, especially if we want to account for the new types.

 The preceding example uses the special apply method of the `Animal` companion object. We could have different versions of it and it would provide us with a syntactic sugar that allows us to simply use `Animal("mammal")`. This makes it even more convenient to use the factory, as its existence will be indicated by the good IDEs because of the base class.

The simple factory

The simple factory is better than the static factory, because the actual factory functionality is in another class. This removes the requirement for the base class to be modified every time a new extension is added. This is similar to the abstract factory, but the difference is that here we don't have a base factory class, we use a concrete one instead. Usually, one starts with a simple factory, which evolves to abstract with time and project evolution.

Factory combinations

Of course, it is possible to combine different types of factories together. This, however, needs to be done with caution and only if necessary. Otherwise, overusing the design pattern could lead to bad code.

Lazy initialization

Lazy initialization in software engineering is when we delay the instantiation of an object or a variable until the first time we need it. The idea behind this is to defer or even avoid some expensive operations.

An example class diagram

In other languages, such as Java, lazy initialization is often used in conjunction with the factory method design pattern. This method usually checks whether the object/variable we want to use is initialized; if not, it initializes the object and finally returns it. In consecutive uses, the already initialized object/variable is returned.

The Scala programming language has built-in support for lazy initialization. It makes use of the `lazy` keyword. That's why providing a class diagram in this case is pointless.

A code example

Let's see how lazy initialization works in Scala and also prove that it is indeed lazy. We will look at an example that calculates a circle area. As we know, the formula is `pi * r`^{2}. Programming languages have support for mathematical constants and this is not how we will do it in real life. However, the example is still relevant if we're talking about a different constant that is not widely known, or a constant that usually fluctuates around a value, but could be different every day.

At school, we've been taught that pi is equal to 3.14. This is true, however, there are many extra digits after that and if we really care about precision, we will need to account for them as well. For example, pi with 100 digits looks like this:

```
3.1415926535897932384626433832795028841971693993751058209749445923078164062
86208998628034825342117067
```

So, let's create a utility that will return the area when given a circle radius. We will have our basic pi as a variable in our utility class, but we will also allow the users to decide if they want a precise area or not. If they do, we will read the 100-digit pi from a configuration file:

```scala
import java.util.Properties

object CircleUtils {
  val basicPi = 3.14
  lazy val precisePi: Double = {
    System.out.println("Reading properties for the precise PI.")
    val props = new Properties()
    props.load(getClass.getResourceAsStream("pi.properties"))
    props.getProperty("pi.high").toDouble
  }

  def area(radius: Double, isPrecise: Boolean = false): Double = {
    val pi: Double = if (isPrecise) precisePi else basicPi
```

```
      pi * Math.pow(radius, 2)
    }
  }
```

The preceding code does exactly what we said. Depending on precision, we will use a different version of pi. The lazy initialization here is useful because we might never ever need a precise area, or we could need it sometimes, but not others. Moreover, reading from a configuration file is an I/O operation, which is considered to be slow and it could have a negative effect when done multiple times. Let's see how we use our utility:

```
object Example {
  def main(args: Array[String]): Unit = {
    System.out.println(s"The basic area for a circle with radius 2.5 is
${CircleUtils.area (2.5)}")
    System.out.println(s"The precise area for a circle with radius 2.5 is
${CircleUtils.area (2.5, true)}")
    System.out.println(s"The basic area for a circle with radius 6.78 is
${CircleUtils.area (6.78)}")
    System.out.println(s"The precise area for a circle with radius 6.78 is
${CircleUtils.area (6.78, true)}")
  }
}
```

The output of this program will be the following:

```
volcom@volcom-Dell-System-XPS-L502X:~/workspace/scala-book/creational-design-pat
terns$ java -cp target/creational-1.0.0-SNAPSHOT.jar com.ivan.nikolov.creational
.lazy_init.Example
The basic area for a circle with radius 2.5 is 19.625
Reading properties for the precise PI.
The precise area for a circle with radius 2.5 is 19.634954084936208
The basic area for a circle with radius 6.78 is 144.340776
The precise area for a circle with radius 6.78 is 144.41398773727704
```

We can have a few observations from our example output. First, the precision really matters and there are industries out there including financial institutions, space industry, and so on where precision is taken really seriously. Second, in the lazy initialization block, we used a `print` statement and it is printed when we used the precise implementation for the first time. Normal values get initialized when the instance is created. This shows that indeed, lazy initialization in Scala defers it until the variable is used for the first time.

What it is good for?

Lazy initialization is particularly useful when initializing an object or variable that would take too long or might not even be needed. Some might say that we can simply use methods, and this is partly true. However, imagine a case where we might need to access a lazily initialized variable/object from multiple methods in different calls to our object. In this case, it is useful to store the result somewhere and just reuse it.

What it is not so good for?

In languages other than Scala, some special care needs to be taken when lazy initialization is used in a multithreaded setting. In Java, for example, you need to do initialization in a `synchronized` block. In order to provide even better safety, *double-checked locking* is preferred. There is no such danger in Scala.

The singleton design pattern

The singleton design pattern ensures that a class has only one object instance in the entire application. It introduces a global state in the applications it is used in.

A singleton object can be initialized using different strategies—lazy initialization or eager initialization. This all depends on the intended use, the time it takes an object to be initialized, and so on.

An example class diagram

Singletons are another example of design patterns, which are supported out of the box by the Scala programming language syntax. We achieve this by using the object keyword. In this case, again, providing a class diagram is not necessary, so we will step right into the example in the next subsection.

A code example

The aim of this example is to show how to create singleton instances in Scala and have an understanding of when exactly instances are created in Scala. We will look at a class called `StringUtils`, that provides different utility methods related to strings:

```scala
object StringUtils {
  def countNumberOfSpaces(text: String): Int = text.split("\\s+").length -
1
}
```

Using this class is then straightforward. Scala takes care of creating the object, thread safety, and so on:

```scala
object UtilsExample {
  def main(args: Array[String]): Unit = {
    val sentence = "Hello there! I am a utils example."
    System.out.println(
      s"The number of spaces in '$sentence' is:
${StringUtils.countNumberOfSpaces(sentence)}"
    )
  }
}
```

The output from this program will be the following:

```
volcom@volcom-Dell-System-XPS-L502X:~/workspace/scala-book/creational-design-pat
terns$ java -cp target/creational-1.0.0-SNAPSHOT.jar com.ivan.nikolov.creational
.singleton.UtilsExample
The number of spaces in 'Hello there! I am a utils example.' is: 6
```

The preceding example is clear and even though the `StringUtils` object will be a singleton instance, it more resembles a class with static methods. This is actually how static methods are defined in Scala. It would be more interesting to add some state to a singleton class. The following example shows exactly this:

```scala
object AppRegistry {
  System.out.println("Registry initialization block called.")
  private val users: Map[String, String] = TrieMap.empty

  def addUser(id: String, name: String): Unit = {
    users.put(id, name)
  }

  def removeUser(id: String): Unit = {
    users.remove(id)
```

```
  }

  def isUserRegistered(id: String): Boolean = users.contains(id)

  def getAllUserNames(): List[String] = users.map(_._2).toList
}
```

The AppRegistry contains a concurrent map of all the users currently using the application. This is our global state and we have methods that allow us to manipulate it. We also have a println statement, which will be executed when the singleton instance is created. We can use our registry in the following application:

```
object AppRegistryExample {
  def main(args: Array[String]): Unit = {
    System.out.println("Sleeping for 5 seconds.")
    Thread.sleep(5000)
    System.out.println("I woke up.")
    AppRegistry.addUser("1", "Ivan")
    AppRegistry.addUser("2", "John")
    AppRegistry.addUser("3", "Martin")
    System.out.println(s"Is user with ID=1 registered?
${AppRegistry.isUserRegistered("1")}")
    System.out.println("Removing ID=2")
    AppRegistry.removeUser("2")
    System.out.println(s"Is user with ID=2 registered?
${AppRegistry.isUserRegistered("2")}")
    System.out.println(s"All users registered are:
${AppRegistry.getAllUserNames().mkString (",")}")
  }
}
```

```
volcom@volcom-Dell-System-XPS-L502X:~/workspace/scala-book/creational-design-pat
terns$ java -cp target/creational-1.0.0-SNAPSHOT.jar com.ivan.nikolov.creational
.singleton.AppRegistryExample
Sleeping for 5 seconds.
I woke up.
Registry initialization block called.
Is user with ID=1 registered? true
Removing ID=2
Is user with ID=2 registered? false
All users registered are: Martin,Ivan
```

Now, our example presents a proper singleton instance, which contains a global state. This state will be accessible from all the application classes while the instance runs. From the example code and our output, we can make a few conclusions:

- Singletons in Scala are lazily initialized
- While creating a singleton instance, we cannot provide dynamic parameters to the singleton class instance

What it is good for?

In Scala, the singleton design pattern and static methods are implemented the same way. That's why singletons are useful for creating utility classes that have no state. Singletons in Scala can also be used to build ADTs, which we talked about in the previous chapters.

Another thing that is strictly valid for Scala is that in Scala, singletons are created in a thread-safe way out of the box and without the need to take any special care.

What it is not so good for?

Often, the singleton design pattern is actually considered an anti-pattern. Many people say that global state should not exist the way it does with singleton classes. Some say that if you have to use singletons, you should try and refactor your code. While this is true in some cases, there is sometimes a good use for singletons. Generally, the rule of thumb is—if you can avoid them, then do.

Another thing that could be pointed out specifically for Scala singletons is that they can really have only one instance. While this is the actual definition of the pattern, with other languages, we could have a predefined number of more than just one singleton object and have some control on this using custom logic.

This does not really affect Scala but it is still worth mentioning. In the case where a singleton is initialized lazily in an application, in order to provide thread safety, you need to rely on locking mechanisms, for example, the double-checked locking mentioned in the previous section. Accessing the singletons in an application, no matter if it's Scala or not, also needs to be done in a thread-safe way or the singleton should take care of this internally.

The builder design pattern

The builder design pattern helps to create instances of classes using class methods rather than the class constructors. It is particularly useful in cases where a class might need multiple versions of its constructor in order to allow different usage scenarios.

Moreover, in some cases, it might not even be possible to define all combinations or they might not be known. The builder design pattern uses an extra object, called `builder`, in order to receive and store initialization parameters before building the final version of an object.

An example class diagram

In this subsection, we will provide a class diagram for the builder pattern the way it was classically defined and the way it looks in other languages, including Java. Later, we will present different versions of the code on the basis of them being more appropriate for Scala and of the observations and discussions we will have around them.

Let's have a `Person` class with different parameters—`firstName`, `lastName`, `age`, `departmentId`, and so on. We will show the actual code for it in the next subsection. Creating a concrete constructor, especially if those fields might not always be known or required, might take too much time. It would also make the code extremely hard to maintain in the future.

A builder pattern seems like a good idea and the class diagram for it will look like the following:

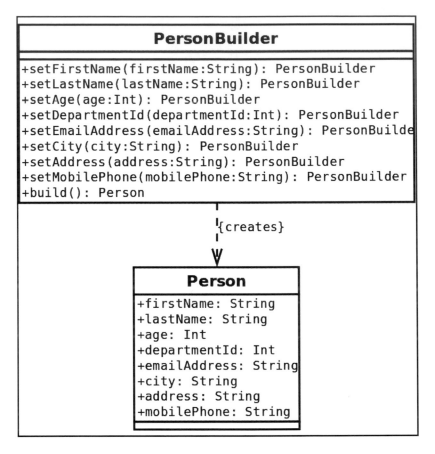

As we already mentioned, this is how the builder pattern looks in purely object-oriented languages (not Scala). There could be different representations of it where the builder is abstracted, and then there are concrete builders. The same is true for the product that is being built. In the end, they all aim to get to the same point—make object creation easier.

In the next subsection, we will provide code implementations that will show exactly how to use and write the builder design pattern in Scala.

A code example

There are actually three main ways in which we can represent the builder design pattern in Scala:

- The classical way, as shown in the preceding diagram, is like other object-oriented languages. This way is actually not recommended, even though it is possible in Scala. It uses mutability in order to work, which contradicts the immutability principle of the language. We will show it here for completeness and in order to point out how much easier it is to achieve the builder design pattern using simple features of Scala.
- Using case classes with default parameters. We will see two versions—one that validates the parameters and another one that doesn't.
- Using generalized type constraints.

We will focus on these in the next few subsections. In order to keep things short and simple, we will have fewer fields in our classes; however, it has to be noted that the builder design pattern really shines when there is a large number of fields. You can experiment by adding more fields to the code examples that are provided in this book.

A Java-like implementation

This implementation directly reflects what we have in the previous diagram. First, let's see what our `Person` class will look like:

```
class Person(builder: PersonBuilder) {
  val firstName = builder.firstName
  val lastName = builder.lastName
  val age = builder.age
}
```

As we can see in the preceding code, it takes a builder and uses the values set in the builder for initialization of its fields. The builder code will look like the following:

```
class PersonBuilder {
  var firstName = ""
  var lastName = ""
  var age = 0

  def setFirstName(firstName: String): PersonBuilder = {
    this.firstName = firstName
    this
  }
```

```
    def setLastName(lastName: String): PersonBuilder = {
      this.lastName = lastName
      this
    }

    def setAge(age: Int): PersonBuilder = {
      this.age = age
      this
    }

    def build(): Person = new Person(this)
}
```

Our builder has methods that can set each corresponding field of the `Person` class. These methods return the same instance of the builder and this allows us to chain many calls together. Here is how we can use our builder:

```
object PersonBuilderExample {
  def main(args: Array[String]): Unit = {
    val person: Person = new PersonBuilder()
      .setFirstName("Ivan")
      .setLastName("Nikolov")
      .setAge(26)
      .build()
    System.out.println(s"Person: ${person.firstName} ${person.lastName}.
Age: ${person.age}.")
  }
}
```

This is how to use the builder design pattern. Now, we can create a `Person` object and provide whatever data we have for it—even if we have a subset of all possible fields, we can specify them and the rest will have a default value. There is no need to create new constructors if other fields are being added to the `Person` class. They just need to be made available through the `PersonBuilder` class.

Implementation with a case class

The preceding builder design pattern looks nice and clear, but it requires writing some extra code and creating boilerplate. Moreover, it requires us to have mutable fields in the `PersonBuilder` class, which is against some of the principles in Scala.

Preferring immutability

Immutability is an important principle in Scala and it should be preferred. The builder design pattern with case classes uses immutable fields and this is considered a good practice.

Scala has case classes, which make the implementation of the builder pattern much simpler. Here is what it will look like:

```
case class Person(
  firstName: String = "",
  lastName: String = "",
  age: Int = 0
)
```

The use of this case class is similar to how the preceding builder design pattern is used:

```
object PersonCaseClassExample {
  def main(args: Array[String]): Unit = {
    val person1 = Person(
      firstName = "Ivan",
      lastName = "Nikolov",
      age = 26
    )
    val person2 = Person(
      firstName = "John"
    )
    System.out.println(s"Person 1: ${person1}")
    System.out.println(s"Person 2: ${person2}")
  }
}
```

The preceding code is much shorter and easier to maintain than the first version. It allows the developer to do absolutely the same as the original builder pattern, but with a shorter and cleaner syntax. It also keeps the fields of the `Person` class immutable, which is a good practice to follow in Scala.

Choosing default values

The choice of default values for the builder design pattern is entirely up to the developer. Some would prefer to use `Option` and put `None` when there is no value specified. Others might assign some different special values. This choice can be dictated by personal choice, the problem that is being solved, the style guides employed by an engineering team, and more.

One drawback of the preceding two approaches is that there is no validation. What if some components depended on each other and there are specific variables that require initialization? In the cases that use the preceding two approaches, we could run into runtime exceptions. The next subsection will show us how to make sure that validation and requirement satisfactions are implemented.

Using generalized type constraints

In many cases in which we create objects in software engineering, we have dependencies. We either need to have something initialized in order to use a third component, or we require a specific order of initialization, and so on. Both builder pattern implementations we looked at earlier lack the capability to make sure something is or isn't initialized. This way, we need to create some extra validation around the builder design pattern in order to make sure everything will work as expected, yet we will see whether it is safe to create an object only during runtime.

Using some of the techniques we already looked at earlier in this book, we can create a builder that validates whether all requirements are satisfied during compile time. This is called a **type-safe builder**, and in the next example, we will present this pattern.

Changing the Person class

First of all, we start with the same classes as we have in the example where we showed the way in which Java uses the builder pattern. Now, let's put a constraint on the example and say that every person must have at least `firstName` and `lastName` specified. In order to make the compiler aware that fields are being set, this needs to be encoded as a type. We will be using ADTs for this purpose. Let's define the following:

```
sealed trait BuildStep
sealed trait HasFirstName extends BuildStep
sealed trait HasLastName extends BuildStep
```

The preceding abstract data types define the different steps of the build progress. Now, let's make some refactoring to the builder class and the `Person` class:

```
class Person(
  val firstName: String,
  val lastName: String,
  val age: Int
)
```

We will use the full constructor for the `Person` class rather than passing a builder. This is to show another way of building instances and keeping the code simpler in the later steps. The change would require the `build` method in the `PersonBuilder` to change as well to:

```
def build(): Person = new Person(
  firstName,
  lastName,
  age
)
```

This would require all the methods we have, which returned `PersonBuilder` before, to return `PersonBuilder[PassedStep]` now. Also, this would make it impossible to create a builder using the `new` keyword because the constructor is now private. Let's add some more constructor overloads:

```
protected def this() = this("","",0)
protected def this(pb: PersonBuilder[_]) = this(
  pb.firstName,
  pb.lastName,
  pb.age
)
```

We will see how these overloads are used later. We need to allow our users to create a builder using another method, since all constructors are invisible to the outside world. That's why we should add a companion object, as shown here:

```
object PersonBuilder {
  def apply() = new PersonBuilder[BuildStep]()
}
```

The companion object uses one of the constructors we previously defined and it also makes sure the object returned is at the right build step.

Adding generalized type constraints to the required methods

What we have so far, however, is still not going to satisfy our requirements regarding what every `Person` object should have initialized. We would have to change some methods in the `PersonBuilder` class. These methods are `setFirstName`, `setLastName`, and `build`. Here are the changes to the set methods:

```
def setFirstName(firstName: String): PersonBuilder[HasFirstName] = {
  this.firstName = firstName
  new PersonBuilder[HasFirstName](this)
}
```

```
def setLastName(lastName: String): PersonBuilder[HasLastName] = {
  this.lastName = lastName
  new PersonBuilder[HasLastName](this)
}
```

The interesting part comes with the `build` method. Let's have a look at the following initial implementation:

```
def build()(implicit ev: PassedStep =:= HasLastName): Person =
  new Person(
    firstName,
    lastName,
    age
  )
```

The preceding syntax sets a generalized type constraint and says that `build` can only be called on a builder, which has passed the `HasLastName` step. It seems like we are coming close to what we wanted to achieve, but now `build` will only work if `setLastName` was the last of those four methods called on the builder, and it will still not validate the other fields. Let's use a similar approach for the `setFirstName` and `setLastName` methods and chain them up so that each one will require the previous one to be called before. Here is what the final code for our `PersonBuilder` class looks like (notice the other implicits in the set methods):

```
class PersonBuilder[PassedStep <: BuildStep] private(
  var firstName: String,
  var lastName: String,
  var age: Int
) {
  protected def this() = this("", "", 0)

  protected def this(pb: PersonBuilder[_]) = this(
    pb.firstName,
    pb.lastName,
    pb.age
  )

  def setFirstName(firstName: String): PersonBuilder[HasFirstName] = {
    this.firstName = firstName
    new PersonBuilder[HasFirstName](this)
  }

  def setLastName(lastName: String)(implicit ev: PassedStep =:=
HasFirstName): PersonBuilder[HasLastName] = {
    this.lastName = lastName
    new PersonBuilder[HasLastName](this)
```

```
  }

  def setAge(age: Int): PersonBuilder[PassedStep] = {
    this.age = age
    this
  }

  def build()(implicit ev: PassedStep =:= HasLastName): Person =
    new Person(
      firstName,
      lastName,
      age
    )
}
```

Using the type-safe builder

We can now use the builder to create a `Person` object:

```
object PersonBuilderTypeSafeExample {
  def main(args: Array[String]): Unit = {
    val person = PersonBuilder()
      .setFirstName("Ivan")
      .setLastName("Nikolov")
      .setAge(26)
      .build()
    System.out.println(s"Person: ${person.firstName} ${person.lastName}.
Age: ${person.age}.")
  }
}
```

If we omit one of our two required methods or rearrange them in some way, we will get a compilation error similar to the following (the error is for the missing first name):

```
Error:(103, 23) Cannot prove that com.ivan.nikolov.creational.builder.
type_safe.BuildStep =:=
com.ivan.nikolov.creational.builder.type_safe.HasFirstName.
    .setLastName("Nikolov")
                ^
```

The order requirement could be considered a slight drawback, especially if it's not needed.

Here are some observations about our type-safe builder:

- Using a type-safe builder, we can require a specific call order and certain fields to be initialized.
- When we require multiple fields, we have to chain them, which makes the order of calls important. This could make the library hard to use in some cases.
- Compiler messages, when the builder is not used correctly, are not really informative.
- The code looks pretty much similar to how it would be implemented in Java.
- The similarity in code with Java leads to relying on mutability, which is not recommended.

Scala allows us to have a nice and clean implementation of a builder design pattern, which also has requirements for order and what is initialized. This is a good feature, even though sometimes it could be tedious and limiting in terms of how exactly methods are being used.

Using require statements

The type-safe builder we showed previously is nice, but it has some drawbacks:

- Complexity
- Mutability
- A predefined order of initialization

However, it could be quite useful because it allows us to write code that will be checked for correct usage as soon as we compile it. Sometimes, compile-time validation is not required, though. If this is the case, we can make things extremely simple and get rid of the entire complexity using the already known case classes and the `require` statements:

```
case class Person(
  firstName: String = "",
  lastName: String = "",
  age: Int = 0
) {
  require(firstName != "", "First name is required.")
  require(lastName != "", "Last name is required.")
}
```

If the preceding Boolean conditions are not satisfied, our code will throw an `IllegalArgumentException` with the correct message. We can use our class the same way as we would normally use a case class:

```
object PersonCaseClassRequireExample {
  def main(args: Array[String]): Unit = {
    val person1 = Person(
      firstName = "Ivan",
      lastName = "Nikolov",
      age = 26
    )
    System.out.println(s"Person 1: ${person1}")
    try {
      val person2 = Person(
        firstName = "John"
      )
      System.out.println(s"Person 2: ${person2}")
    } catch {
      case e: Throwable =>
        e.printStackTrace()
    }
  }
}
```

As we can see, things here are much simpler, fields are immutable, and we don't actually have any special order of initialization. Moreover, we can put meaningful messages that could help us diagnose potential issues. As long as compile-time validation is not required, this should be the preferred method.

What it is good for?

The builder design pattern is really good for cases in which we need to create a complex object and would otherwise have to define many constructors. It makes the creation of objects easier and somewhat cleaner and more readable using a step-by-step approach.

What it is not so good for?

As we saw in our type-safe builder example, adding more advanced logic and requirements could involve quite a bit of work. Without this possibility, the developer will risk the users of their classes making more mistakes. Also, the builder contains quite a lot of seemingly duplicate code, especially when it is implemented using a Java-like code.

The prototype design pattern

The prototype design pattern is a creational design pattern that involves creating objects by cloning them from existing ones. Its purpose is related to performance and keeping it high by trying to avoid expensive calls.

An example class diagram

In languages such as Java, we usually see a class that implements an interface with a `clone` method, which returns a new instance of the class. Consider the following diagram:

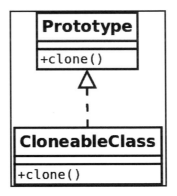

In the next section, we will provide a code example of the prototype design pattern from the point of view of Scala.

A code example

The prototype design pattern is really easy to implement in Scala. We can just use one of the language features. Since the prototype design pattern really resembles how cells in biology divide, let's use a cell as an example:

```
/**
  * Represents a bio cell
  */
case class Cell(dna: String, proteins: List[String])
```

In Scala, all case classes have a `copy` method, which returns a new instance that is cloned from the original one. It can also change some of the original properties while copying. Here is some example usage of our cell:

```
object PrototypeExample {
  def main(args: Array[String]): Unit = {
    val initialCell = Cell("abcd", List("protein1", "protein2"))
    val copy1 = initialCell.copy()
    val copy2 = initialCell.copy()
    val copy3 = initialCell.copy(dna = "1234")
    System.out.println(s"The prototype is: ${initialCell}")
    System.out.println(s"Cell 1: ${copy1}")
    System.out.println(s"Cell 2: ${copy2}")
    System.out.println(s"Cell 3: ${copy3}")
    System.out.println(s"1 and 2 are equal: ${copy1 == copy2}")
  }
}
```

The output of this example will be this:

```
volcom@volcom-Dell-System-XPS-L502X:~/workspace/scala-book/creational-design-pat
terns$ java -cp target/creational-1.0.0-SNAPSHOT.jar com.ivan.nikolov.creational
.prototype.PrototypeExample
The prototype is: Cell(abcd,List(protein1, protein2))
Cell 1: Cell(abcd,List(protein1, protein2))
Cell 2: Cell(abcd,List(protein1, protein2))
Cell 3: Cell(1234,List(protein1, protein2))
1 and 2 are equal: true
```

As you can see, using `copy`, we acquired different instances of our prototype cell.

What it is good for?

The prototype design pattern is useful when performance is important. Using the `copy` method, we can get instances that otherwise take time to create. The slowness could be caused by some calculations performed during creation, a database call that retrieves data, and so on.

What it is not so good for?

Mistakes and side effects could be caused using shallow copies of objects, where the actual references point to the original instances. Also, avoiding constructors could lead to bad code. The prototype design pattern should be really used in cases where there might be a massive performance impact without it.

Summary

This was the first chapter of this book that focused on some specific design patterns. We looked at the following creational design patterns—factory method, abstract factory, lazy initialization, singleton, builder, and prototype. Wherever relevant, we presented a diagram that visually showed class relationships. Also, we gave typical examples and went through the possible pitfalls and recommendations about when to use them.

In real-life software engineering, design patterns are usually combined together rather than being used in an isolated manner. Some examples include a prototype that is being supplied by a singleton instance, abstract factories that can store different prototypes and supply copies when objects are created, factories that can use builders to create instances, and so on. In some cases, design patterns could be interchangeable depending on the use case. For example, lazy initialization could be enough to lower the performance impact and could be chosen instead of a prototype design pattern.

In the next chapter, we will continue our journey into design patterns; this time, we will focus on the *structural design patterns* family.

7
Structural Design Patterns

The next stop of our journey through design patterns will focus on the family of **structural design patterns**. We will be doing a Scala point of view exploration of the following structural design patterns:

- Adapter
- Decorator
- Bridge
- Composite
- Facade
- Flyweight
- Proxy

This chapter will give a better understanding of what structural design patterns are and why they are useful. After familiarizing ourselves with what they are, we will be looking into each of them separately and in detail, including code examples and hints about when to use each of them and when to avoid them, as well as what to be careful with when using them.

Defining structural design patterns

Structural design patterns are concerned with composing objects and classes in our software. They use different approaches in order to obtain new functionality and larger and potentially more complex structures. These approaches include the following:

- Inheritance
- Composition

Properly identifying the relationships between objects in an application is key to simplifying the application's structure. In the following sections, we will be looking at different design patterns and provide examples, which will give us a better feel of how to use the various structural design patterns.

The adapter design pattern

In many cases, we have to make applications work by combining different components together. However, quite often, we have a problem where the component interfaces are incompatible with each other. Similarly with using public or any libraries, which we cannot modify ourselves, it is quite rare that someone else's views will be exactly the same as ours in our current settings. This is where adapters help. Their purpose is to help incompatible interfaces work together without modifying their source code.

We will be showing how adapters work using a class diagram and an example in the next few subsections.

Example class diagram

For the adapter class diagram, let's imagine that we want to switch to using a new logging library in our application. The library we are trying to use has a log method that takes the message and the severity of the log. However, throughout our whole application, we expect to have the `info`, `debug`, `warning`, and `error` methods that only take the message and automatically set the right severity. Of course, we cannot edit the original library code, so we have to use the adapter pattern. The following figure shows the class diagram that represents the adapter design pattern:

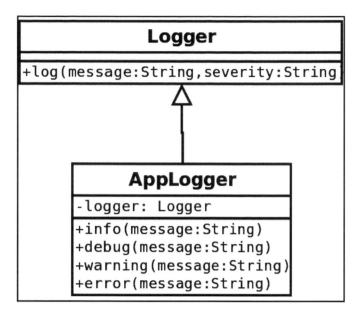

In the preceding diagram, we can see our adapter (**AppLogger**) extend and also use an instance of **Logger** as a field. While implementing the methods, we then simply call the log method with different parameters. This is the general adapter implementation and we will see the code for it in the next subsection. There are some cases where extending might not be possible and we will show how Scala can deal with this. Also, we will show some advanced usage of the language features to achieve the adapter pattern.

Code example

First of all, let's see the code for our `Logger` that we assume that we cannot change:

```
class Logger {
  def log(message: String, severity: String): Unit = {
    System.out.println(s"${severity.toUpperCase}: $message")
  }
}
```

We've tried to keep it as simple as possible in order to not distract the reader from the main purpose of this book. Next, we could either just write a class that extends `Logger` or we could provide an interface for abstraction. Let's take the second approach:

```
trait Log {
  def info(message: String)
  def debug(message: String)
  def warning(message: String)
  def error(message: String)
}
```

Finally, we can create our `AppLogger`:

```
class AppLogger extends Logger with Log {
  override def info(message: String): Unit = log(message, "info")
  override def warning(message: String): Unit = log(message, "warning")

  override def error(message: String): Unit = log(message, "error")

  override def debug(message: String): Unit = log(message, "debug")
}
```

We can then use it in the following program:

```
object AdapterExample {
  def main(args: Array[String]): Unit = {
    val logger = new AppLogger
    logger.info("This is an info message.")
    logger.debug("Debug something here.")
    logger.error("Show an error message.")
    logger.warning("About to finish.")
    logger.info("Bye!")
  }
}
```

As expected, our output will look as follows:

```
volcom@volcom-Dell-System-XPS-L502X:~/workspace/scala-book/structural-design-pat
terns$ java -cp target/structural-1.0.0-SNAPSHOT.jar com.ivan.nikolov.structural
.adapter.AdapterExample
INFO: This is an info message.
DEBUG: Debug something here.
ERROR: Show an error message.
WARNING: About to finish.
INFO: Bye!
```

You can see that we haven't implemented the class diagram exactly as shown. We don't need the `Logger` instance as a field of our class, because our class is an instance of `Logger` already and we have access to its methods anyway. If we were to expand the behavior of the original `log` method, then we would need an instance of `Logger` as well.

This is how we implement and use the basic adapter design pattern. However, there are cases where the class we want to adapt is declared as `final` and we are unable to extend it. We will show how to handle this in the next subsection.

The adapter design pattern with final classes

If we declare our original logger as final, we will see that our code will not compile. There is a different way to use the adapter pattern in this case. Here is the code:

```scala
class FinalAppLogger extends Log {
  private val logger = new FinalLogger

  override def info(message: String): Unit = logger.log(message, "info")

  override def warning(message: String): Unit = logger.log(message,
    "warning")

  override def error(message: String): Unit = logger.log(message, "error")

  override def debug(message: String): Unit = logger.log(message, "debug")
}
```

In this case, we simply wrap the final logger inside a class and then use it to call the `log` method with different parameters. The usage is absolutely the same as before. This could have a variation where the logger is passed as a constructor parameter as well. This is useful in cases where creating the logger requires some extra parameterization during creation.

The adapter design pattern the Scala way

As we have already mentioned multiple times, Scala is a rich programming language. Because of this fact, we can use implicit classes to achieve what the adapter pattern does. We will be using the same `FinalLogger` that we had in the previous example.

Implicit classes provide implicit conversions in places where possible. In order for the implicit conversions to work, we need to have the implicits imported and that's why they are often defined in objects or package objects. For this example, we will use a package object. Here is the code:

```
package object adapter {

    implicit class FinalAppLoggerImplicit(logger: FinalLogger) extends Log {
        override def info(message: String): Unit = logger.log(message, "info")

        override def warning(message: String): Unit = logger.log(message,
          "warning")

        override def error(message: String): Unit = logger.log(message,
          "error")

        override def debug(message: String): Unit = logger.log(message,
          "debug")
    }
}
```

This is a `package object` for the package where our logger examples are defined. It will automatically convert a `FinalLogger` instance to our implicit class. The following code snippet shows an example usage of our logger:

```
object AdapterImplicitExample {
  def main(args: Array[String]): Unit = {
    val logger: Log = new FinalLogger
    logger.info("This is an info message.")
    logger.debug("Debug something here.")
    logger.error("Show an error message.")
    logger.warning("About to finish.")
    logger.info("Bye!")
  }
}
```

The final output will be exactly the same as our first example.

What it is good for

The adapter design pattern is useful in cases *after* the code is designed and written. It allows us to make, otherwise incompatible, interfaces work together. It is also pretty straightforward to implement and use.

What it is not so good for

There is a problem with the last implementation mentioned in the preceding section. It is the fact that we will have to always import our package or normal object when using the logger. Also, implicit classes and conversions sometimes make the code much harder to read and understand. Implicit classes have some limitations, as described here: `http://docs.scala-lang.org/overviews/core/implicitclasses.html`.

As we already mentioned, the adapter design pattern is useful when we have code that we cannot change. If we are able to fix our source code, then this might be a better decision because using adapters throughout our program will make it difficult to maintain and hard to understand.

The decorator design pattern

There are cases where we might want to add some extra functionality to a class in an application. This could be done via inheritance; however, we might not want to do this or it may affect all the other classes in our application. This is where the decorator design pattern is useful.

 The purpose of the decorator design pattern is to add functionality to objects without extending them and without affecting the behavior of other objects from the same class.

The decorator design pattern works by wrapping the decorated object, and it can be applied during runtime. Decorators are extremely useful in the cases where there could be multiple extensions of a class and they could be combined in various ways. Instead of writing all the possible combinations, decorators can be created and they can stack the modifications on top of each other. The next few subsections will show how and when to use decorators in real-world situations.

Example class diagram

As we saw previously with the adapter design pattern, its aim is to change an interface to a different one. The decorator, on the other hand, helps us to enhance an interface by adding extra functionality to methods. For the class diagram, we will use an example with data streams. Imagine that we have a basic stream. We might want to be able to encrypt it, compress it, replace its characters, and so on. Here is the class diagram:

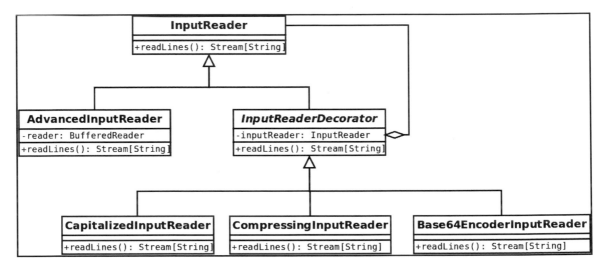

In the preceding diagram, the `AdvancedInputReader` provides a basic implementation of the `InputReader`. It wraps a standard `BufferedReader`. Then, we have an abstract `InputReaderDecorator` class that extends the `InputReader` and contains an instance of it. By extending the base decorator, we provide the possibility to have streams that capitalize, compress, or `Base64` encode the input they get. We might want to have different streams in our application and they could be able to do one or more of the preceding operations in different orders. Our code will quickly become difficult to maintain and messy if we try and provide all possibilities, especially when the number of possible operations is even more. With decorators, it is nice and clean, as we will see in the next section.

Code example

Now, let's have a look at the actual code that describes the decorator design pattern shown in the previous diagram. First of all, we define our `InputReader` interface using a trait:

```
trait InputReader {
  def readLines(): Stream[String]
}
```

Then, we provide the basic implementation of the interface in the `AdvancedInputReader` class:

```
class AdvancedInputReader(reader: BufferedReader) extends InputReader {
  override def readLines(): Stream[String] =
    reader.lines().iterator().asScala.toStream
}
```

In order to apply the decorator design pattern, we have to create different decorators. We have a base decorator that looks as follows:

```
abstract class InputReaderDecorator(inputReader: InputReader) extends
InputReader {
  override def readLines(): Stream[String] =
    inputReader.readLines()
}
```

Then, we have different implementations of our decorator. First, we implement a decorator that turns all text into upper case:

```
class CapitalizedInputReader(inputReader: InputReader) extends
InputReaderDecorator(inputReader) {
  override def readLines(): Stream[String] =
    super.readLines().map(_.toUpperCase)
}
```

Next, we implement a decorator that uses `gzip` to compress each line of our input separately:

```
class CompressingInputReader(inputReader: InputReader) extends
InputReaderDecorator(inputReader) with LazyLogging {
  override def readLines(): Stream[String] = super.readLines().map {
    case line =>
      val text = line.getBytes(Charset.forName("UTF-8"))
      logger.info("Length before compression: {}", text.length.toString)
      val output = new ByteArrayOutputStream()
      val compressor = new GZIPOutputStream(output)
      try {
        compressor.write(text, 0, text.length)
        val outputByteArray = output.toByteArray
        logger.info("Length after compression: {}",
         outputByteArray.length.toString)
        new String(outputByteArray, Charset.forName("UTF-8"))
```

```
    } finally {
      compressor.close()
      output.close()
    }
  }
}
```

Finally, a decorator that encodes each line to `Base64`:

```
class Base64EncoderInputReader(inputReader: InputReader) extends
InputReaderDecorator(inputReader) {
  override def readLines(): Stream[String] = super.readLines().map {
    case line =>
Base64.getEncoder.encodeToString(line.getBytes(Charset.forName("UTF-8")))
  }
}
```

 We have demonstrated the decorator design pattern using an intermediate abstract class that all decorators extend. We could have achieved this design pattern without the intermediate class and by just directly extending and wrapping `InputReader`. This implementation, however, adds a bit more structure to our code.

Now, we can use these decorators in our application to add extra functionality to our input stream as needed. The usage is straightforward. Here is an example:

```
object DecoratorExample {
  def main(args: Array[String]): Unit = {
    val stream = new BufferedReader(
      new InputStreamReader(
        new
BufferedInputStream(this.getClass.getResourceAsStream("data.txt"))
      )
    )
    try {
      val reader = new CapitalizedInputReader(new
AdvancedInputReader(stream))
      reader.readLines().foreach(println)
    } finally {
      stream.close()
    }
  }
}
```

In the preceding example, we used the text file part of our classpath with the following contents:

```
this is a data file
which contains lines
and those lines will be
manipulated by our stream reader.
```

As expected, the order in which we apply decorators will define the order in which their enhancements will be applied. The output of the preceding example will be the following:

```
volcom@volcom-Dell-System-XPS-L502X:~/workspace/scala-book/structural-design-pat
terns$ java -cp target/structural-1.0.0-SNAPSHOT.jar com.ivan.nikolov.structural
.decorator.DecoratorExample
THIS IS A DATA FILE
WHICH CONTAINS LINES
AND THOSE LINES WILL BE
MANIPULATED BY OUR STREAM READER.
```

Let's see another example, but this time we will apply all the decorators we have:

```
object DecoratorExampleBig {
  def main(args: Array[String]): Unit = {
    val stream = new BufferedReader(
      new InputStreamReader(
        new
BufferedInputStream(this.getClass.getResourceAsStream("data.txt"))
      )
    )
    try {
      val reader = new CompressingInputReader(
        new Base64EncoderInputReader(
          new CapitalizedInputReader(
            new AdvancedInputReader(stream)
          )
        )
      )
      reader.readLines().foreach(println)
    } finally {
      stream.close()
    }
  }
}
```

This example will read the text, capitalize it, `Base64` encode it, and finally compress it with `gzip`. The following screenshot shows the output:

```
volcom@volcom-Dell-System-XPS-L502X:~/workspace/scala-book/structural-design-pat
terns$ java -cp target/structural-1.0.0-SNAPSHOT.jar com.ivan.nikolov.structural
.decorator.DecoratorExampleBig
[main] INFO  com.ivan.nikolov.structural.decorator.CompressingInputReader  - Len
gth before compression: 28
[main] INFO  com.ivan.nikolov.structural.decorator.CompressingInputReader  - Len
gth after compression: 10

[main] INFO  com.ivan.nikolov.structural.decorator.CompressingInputReader  - Len
gth before compression: 28
[main] INFO  com.ivan.nikolov.structural.decorator.CompressingInputReader  - Len
gth after compression: 10

[main] INFO  com.ivan.nikolov.structural.decorator.CompressingInputReader  - Len
gth before compression: 32
[main] INFO  com.ivan.nikolov.structural.decorator.CompressingInputReader  - Len
gth after compression: 10

[main] INFO  com.ivan.nikolov.structural.decorator.CompressingInputReader  - Len
gth before compression: 44
[main] INFO  com.ivan.nikolov.structural.decorator.CompressingInputReader  - Len
gth after compression: 10
```

As you can see from the preceding screenshot, in the compressing decorator code, we are logging the size of the lines in bytes. The output is gzipped and this is the reason for the text showing up as unreadable characters. You can experiment and change the order of the application of the decorators or add new ones in order to see how things can differ.

The decorator design pattern the Scala way

As with the other design patterns, this one has an implementation that takes advantage of the richness of Scala and uses some of the concepts we looked at throughout the initial chapters of this book. The decorator design pattern in Scala is also called **stackable traits**. Let's see what it looks like and how to use it. The `InputReader` and `AdvancedInputReader` code will remain exactly as shown in the previous section. We are actually reusing it in both examples.

Next, instead of defining an `abstract` decorator class, we will just define the different reader modifications in new traits as follows:

```
trait CapitalizedInputReaderTrait extends InputReader {
  abstract override def readLines(): Stream[String] =
    super.readLines().map(_.toUpperCase)
}
```

Then, we define the compressing input reader:

```
trait CompressingInputReaderTrait extends InputReader with LazyLogging {
  abstract override def readLines(): Stream[String] =
    super.readLines().map {
      case line =>
        val text = line.getBytes(Charset.forName("UTF-8"))
        logger.info("Length before compression: {}", text.length.toString)
        val output = new ByteArrayOutputStream()
        val compressor = new GZIPOutputStream(output)
        try {
          compressor.write(text, 0, text.length)
          val outputByteArray = output.toByteArray
          logger.info("Length after compression: {}",
           outputByteArray.length.toString)
          new String(outputByteArray, Charset.forName("UTF-8"))
        } finally {
          compressor.close()
          output.close()
        }
    }
}
```

Finally, the `Base64` encoder reader is as follows:

```
trait Base64EncoderInputReaderTrait extends InputReader {
  abstract override def readLines(): Stream[String] =
    super.readLines().map {
      case line =>
Base64.getEncoder.encodeToString(line.getBytes(Charset.forName("UTF-8")))
    }
}
```

As you can see, the implementation here is not much different. Here, we used traits instead of classes, extended the base `InputReader` trait, and used `abstract override`.

Abstract override allows us to call `super` for a method in a trait that is declared abstract. This is permissible for traits as long as the trait is mixed in after another trait or a class that implements the preceding method. The abstract override tells the compiler that we are doing this on purpose and it will not fail our compilation—it will check later, when we use the trait, whether the requirements for using it are satisfied.

Previously, we presented two examples. We will now show you what they look like with stackable traits. The first one that only capitalizes will look as follows:

```
object StackableTraitsExample {
  def main(args: Array[String]): Unit = {
    val stream = new BufferedReader(
      new InputStreamReader(
        new
BufferedInputStream(this.getClass.getResourceAsStream("data.txt"))
      )
    )
    try {
      val reader = new AdvancedInputReader(stream) with
CapitalizedInputReaderTrait
      reader.readLines().foreach(println)
    } finally {
      stream.close()
    }
  }
}
```

The second example that capitalizes, `Base64` encodes, and compresses the stream will look as follows:

```
object StackableTraitsBigExample {
  def main(args: Array[String]): Unit = {
    val stream = new BufferedReader(
      new InputStreamReader(
        new
BufferedInputStream(this.getClass.getResourceAsStream("data.txt"))
      )
    )
    try {
      val reader = new AdvancedInputReader(stream) with
CapitalizedInputReaderTrait
        with Base64EncoderInputReaderTrait
        with CompressingInputReaderTrait
      reader.readLines().foreach(println)
    } finally {
```

```
        stream.close()
      }
    }
  }
```

The output of both the examples will be exactly the same as in the original examples. Here, however, we are using mixin composition and things look somewhat cleaner. We also have one class less, as we don't need the abstract decorator class. Understanding how modifications are applied is also easy—we just follow the order in which the stackable traits are mixed in.

Stackable traits follow the rules of linearization

The fact that in our current example the modifications are applied from left to right is deceiving. The reason this happens is because we push calls on the stack until we reach the basic implementation of readLines and then apply modifications in a reverse order. We will see more in-depth examples of stackable traits that will showcase all of their specifics in the coming chapters of this book.

What it is good for

Decorators add a lot of flexibility to our applications. They don't change the original classes, hence they don't introduce errors in the older code and can save on a lot of code writing and maintenance. Also, they could prevent us from forgetting or not foreseeing some use cases with the classes we create.

In the previous examples, we showed some static behavior modifications. However, it is also possible to dynamically decorate instances at runtime.

What it is not so good for

We have covered the positive aspects of using decorators; however, we should point out that overusing decorators could cause issues as well. We might end up with a high number of small classes and they could make our libraries much harder to use and more demanding in terms of requiring more domain knowledge. They also complicate the instantiation process, which would require other (creational) design patterns, for example, factories or builders.

The bridge design pattern

Some applications can have multiple different implementations of a specific functionality. The implementations could be in the form of different algorithms or something to do with multiple platforms. The implementations tend to vary often and they could also have new implementations throughout the life cycle of a program. Moreover, the implementations could be used in different ways for different abstractions. In cases like these, it is good to decouple things in our code, or else we are in danger of a class explosion.

 The purpose of the bridge design pattern is to decouple an abstraction from its implementation so that the two can vary independently.

The bridge design pattern is quite useful in the cases where the abstractions or the implementations could vary often and independently. If we directly implement an abstraction, variations to the abstraction or the implementations would always affect all other classes in the hierarchy. This makes it hard to extend, modify, and reuse classes independently.

The bridge design pattern eliminates a problem by directly implementing an abstraction, thus making the abstractions and implementations reusable and easier to change.

The bridge design pattern is very similar to the adapter design pattern. The difference between them is that in the former, we apply it when we design our application, and the latter is used for legacy or third-party code.

Example class diagram

For the class diagram and the code example, let's imagine that we are writing a library that hashes passwords. In practice, storing passwords in plain text is something that should be avoided. This is what our library will help our users to do. There are many different hashing algorithms that can be used. Some are **SHA-1**, **MD5**, and **SHA-256**. We want to be able to support at least these and have the possibility to add new ones easily. There are different hashing strategies—you can hash multiple times, combine different hashes, add salt to the passwords, and so on. These strategies make our passwords harder to guess using rainbow tables, for example. For this example, we will show hashing with salt and simple hashing with any of the algorithms we have.

Here is our class diagram:

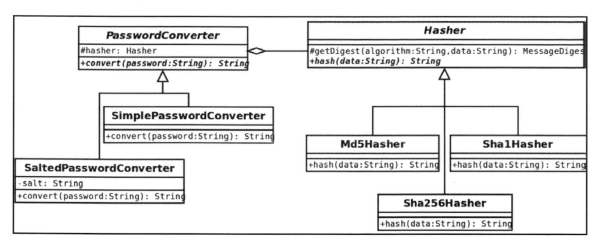

As you can see from the preceding diagram, we separated the implementation (**Hasher** and its implementations) from the abstraction (**PasswordConverter**). This allows us to easily add a new hashing implementation and then instantly use it by just providing an instance of it when creating a **PasswordConverter**. If we hadn't used the preceding builder pattern, we would probably have to create a password converter for each hashing algorithm separately—something that would make our code explode in size or become tedious to use.

Code example

Now, let's have a look at the previous class diagram from the point of view of Scala code. First, we will focus on the implementation side with the Hasher trait:

```scala
trait Hasher {
  def hash(data: String): String

  protected def getDigest(algorithm: String, data: String) = {
    val crypt = MessageDigest.getInstance(algorithm)
    crypt.reset()
    crypt.update(data.getBytes("UTF-8"))
    crypt
  }
}
```

Then, we have three classes that implement it—Md5Hasher, Sha1Hasher, and Sha256Hasher. Their code is pretty simple and similar, but yields different results:

```
class Sha1Hasher extends Hasher {
  override def hash(data: String): String =
    new String(Hex.encodeHex(getDigest("SHA-1", data).digest()))
}

class Sha256Hasher extends Hasher {
  override def hash(data: String): String =
    new String(Hex.encodeHex(getDigest("SHA-256", data).digest()))
}

class Md5Hasher extends Hasher {
  override def hash(data: String): String =
    new String(Hex.encodeHex(getDigest("MD5", data).digest()))
}
```

Now, let's take a look at the abstraction side of things. This is what our clients will use. The following listing shows the PasswordConverter:

```
abstract class PasswordConverter(hasher: Hasher) {
  def convert(password: String): String
}
```

We have chosen to provide two different implementations here—SimplePasswordConverter and SaltedPasswordConverter. The code for them is as follows:

```
class SimplePasswordConverter(hasher: Hasher) extends
PasswordConverter(hasher) {
  override def convert(password: String): String =
    hasher.hash(password)
}

class SaltedPasswordConverter(salt: String, hasher: Hasher) extends
PasswordConverter(hasher) {
  override def convert(password: String): String =
    hasher.hash(s"${salt}:${password}")
}
```

Now, if a client wanted to use our library, they could write a program similar to the following one:

```
object BridgeExample {
  def main(args: Array[String]): Unit = {
    val p1 = new SimplePasswordConverter(new Sha256Hasher)
```

```
val p2 = new SimplePasswordConverter(new Md5Hasher)
val p3 = new SaltedPasswordConverter("8jsdf32T^$%", new Sha1Hasher)
val p4 = new SaltedPasswordConverter("8jsdf32T^$%", new Sha256Hasher)
System.out.println(s"'password' in SHA-256 is:
 ${p1.convert ("password")}")
System.out.println(s"'1234567890' in MD5 is:
 ${p2.convert ("1234567890")}")
System.out.println(s"'password' in salted SHA-1 is:
 ${p3.convert ("password")}")
System.out.println(s"'password' in salted SHA-256 is:
 ${p4.convert ("password")}")
  }
}
```

The output of this example application will look like the one in the following screenshot:

```
volcom@volcom-Dell-System-XPS-L502X:~/workspace/scala-book/structural-design-pat
terns$ java -cp target/structural-1.0.0-SNAPSHOT.jar com.ivan.nikolov.structural
.bridge.BridgeExample
'password' in SHA-256 is: 5e884898da28047151d0e56f8dc6292773603d0d6aabbdd62a11ef
721d1542d8
'1234567890' in MD5 is: e807f1fcf82d132f9bb018ca6738a19f
'password' in salted SHA-1 is: 71147d2ecf154fb670e8af874b42f4cb9c60c8e3
'password' in salted SHA-256 is: 8c58a827d5329261e7e3c1c409f1ec8ee0fe8bfb4af0f8f
1ffa203e1c84993e0
```

Our library now allows us to easily add new strategies or new hashing algorithms and use them instantly. We don't have to change any of the existing classes.

The bridge design pattern the Scala way

The bridge design pattern is another example of those that can be achieved with the powerful features of the Scala programming language. Here, we will be using self types. The initial Hasher trait remains unchanged. Then, the actual implementations become traits instead of classes as follows:

```
trait Sha1Hasher extends Hasher {
  override def hash(data: String): String =
    new String(Hex.encodeHex(getDigest("SHA-1", data).digest()))
}

trait Sha256Hasher extends Hasher {
  override def hash(data: String): String =
    new String(Hex.encodeHex(getDigest("SHA-256", data).digest()))
}
```

```
trait Md5Hasher extends Hasher {
  override def hash(data: String): String =
    new String(Hex.encodeHex(getDigest("MD5", data).digest()))
}
```

Having traits would allow us to mix them in when needed later.

We've changed some names for this version of our example just to avoid confusion. The `PasswordConverter` (`PasswordConverterBase` in this case) abstraction now looks as follows:

```
abstract class PasswordConverterBase {
  self: Hasher =>
  def convert(password: String): String
}
```

This tells the compiler that when we use `PasswordConverterBase`, we also need to have a `Hasher` mixed in. Then, we change the converter implementation to the following:

```
class SimplePasswordConverterScala extends PasswordConverterBase {
  self: Hasher =>
  override def convert(password: String): String = hash(password)
}

class SaltedPasswordConverterScala(salt: String) extends
PasswordConverterBase {
  self: Hasher =>
  override def convert(password: String): String =
    hash(s"${salt}:${password}")
}
```

Finally, we can use our new implementations, as follows:

```
object ScalaBridgeExample {
  def main(args: Array[String]): Unit = {
    val p1 = new SimplePasswordConverterScala with Sha256Hasher
    val p2 = new SimplePasswordConverterScala with Md5Hasher
    val p3 = new SaltedPasswordConverterScala("8jsdf32T^$%") with
    Sha1Hasher
    val p4 = new SaltedPasswordConverterScala("8jsdf32T^$%") with
    Sha256Hasher
    System.out.println(s"'password' in SHA-256 is:
    ${p1.convert("password")}")
    System.out.println(s"'1234567890' in MD5 is:
    ${p2.convert("1234567890")}")
    System.out.println(s"'password' in salted SHA-1 is:
    ${p3.convert("password")}")
```

```
    System.out.println(s"'password' in salted SHA-256 is:
      ${p4.convert("password")}")
  }
}
```

The output of this program will be identical to the original one. However, when we use our abstractions, we can mix in the hash algorithms we want to use. The benefits will become more obvious in the cases where we might have more implementations that we might want to combine together with hashing. Using mixins also looks more natural and is easier to understand.

What it is good for

As we already said, the bridge design pattern is similar to the adapter. Here, however, we apply it when we design our applications. One obvious benefit of using it is that we don't end up with an exponential number of classes in our application, which could make the use and maintenance of the pattern pretty complicated. The separation of hierarchies allows us to independently extend them without affecting the other one.

What it is not so good for

The bridge design pattern requires us to write some boilerplate. It could complicate the use of the library in terms of which implementation is exactly picked, and it might be a good idea to use the bridge design pattern together with some creational design patterns. All in all, it doesn't have any major drawbacks, but the developer should be wise whether to use it or not depending on the current circumstances.

The composite design pattern

The composite design pattern is used to describe groups of objects that should be treated the same way as a single one.

The purpose of the composite design pattern is to compose objects into tree structures to represent whole-part hierarchies.

The composite design pattern is useful for removing code duplication and avoiding errors in cases where groups of objects are generally treated the same way. A popular example could be a filesystem in which we have directories, which can have other directories or files. Generally, the interface to interact with directories and files is the same, so they are good candidates for a composite design pattern.

Example class diagram

As we mentioned previously, filesystems are a good candidate for the composite design pattern. Essentially, they are just tree structures, so for our example, we will show you how to build a tree using the composite design pattern.

Consider the following class diagram:

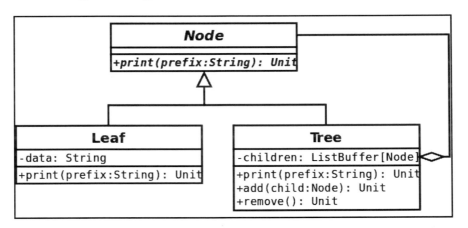

As you can see from the preceding diagram, **Tree** is our composite object. It contains children, which could be either other **Tree** objects with more children nested recursively or just **Leaf** nodes.

Code example

Let's take a look at the code representation for the previous diagram. First of all, we have to define the `Node` interface through a trait:

```
trait Node {
  def print(prefix: String): Unit
}
```

 The `prefix` parameter in the `print` method is used to aid visualization when printing the tree to a console.

After we have the interface, we can now define the implementation:

```
class Leaf(data: String) extends Node {
  override def print(prefix: String): Unit =
    System.out.println(s"${prefix}${data}")
}

class Tree extends Node {
  private val children = ListBuffer.empty[Node]

  override def print(prefix: String): Unit = {
    System.out.println(s"${prefix}(")
    children.foreach(_.print(s"${prefix}${prefix}"))
    System.out.println(s"${prefix})")
  }

  def add(child: Node): Unit = {
    children += child
  }
  def remove(): Unit = {
    if (children.nonEmpty) {
      children.remove(0)
    }
  }
}
```

After this, using our code becomes pretty straightforward. While printing, we don't need to care whether we do it on a leaf or a tree. Our code will automatically take care of this:

```
object CompositeExample {
  def main(args: Array[String]): Unit = {
    val tree = new Tree
    tree.add(new Leaf("leaf 1"))
    val subtree1 = new Tree
    subtree1.add(new Leaf("leaf 2"))
    val subtree2 = new Tree
    subtree2.add(new Leaf("leaf 3"))
    subtree2.add(new Leaf("leaf 4"))
    subtree1.add(subtree2)
    tree.add(subtree1)
    val subtree3 = new Tree
    val subtree4 = new Tree
    subtree4.add(new Leaf("leaf 5"))
    subtree4.add(new Leaf("leaf 6"))
    subtree3.add(subtree4)
    tree.add(subtree3)
    tree.print("-")
  }
}
```

What this code actually does is depth-first traversal of our data structure. The actual example data structure that we have looks as follows:

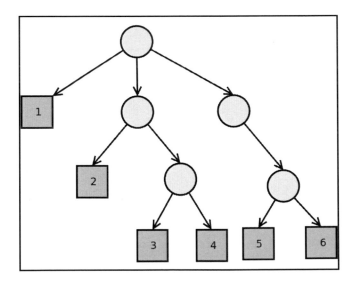

The following screenshot shows the output of our program:

```
volcom@volcom-Dell-System-XPS-L502X:~/workspace/scala-book/structural-design-pat
terns$ java -cp target/structural-1.0.0-SNAPSHOT.jar com.ivan.nikolov.structural
.composite.CompositeExample
-(
--leaf 1
--(
----leaf 2
----(
--------leaf 3
--------leaf 4
----)
--)
--(
----(
--------leaf 5
--------leaf 6
----)
--)
-)
```

As you can see, using composite, we can compose hierarchies of objects that have similar uses.

What it is good for

The composite design pattern is useful for reducing code duplication and simplification when we create hierarchies. The simplification part comes from the fact that clients do not need to know which type of objects they are dealing with. Adding new types of nodes is also easy and won't make us change anything else.

What it is not so good for

The composite design pattern pattern does not have any major drawbacks. It really is applicable in specific cases. One thing developers should be careful about is when they deal with massive hierarchies. The reason is that in such cases, we could have really deeply recursive nested items and this could cause stack overflow issues.

The facade design pattern

Whenever we are building libraries or big systems, we quite often depend on other libraries and functionality. Implementing methods sometimes requires the use of multiple classes at the same time. This requires knowledge. Whenever we build a library for someone, we usually try and make it simpler for the users by assuming they do not have (and do not need) as extensive knowledge as we do. Additionally, developers make sure that components are easy to use throughout their application. This is where the facade design pattern can become useful.

> The purpose of the facade design pattern is to wrap a complex system with a simpler interface in order to hide the usage complexities and ease the client interaction.

We already looked at other design patterns based on wrapping. While the adapter design pattern transforms one interface to another and the decorator adds extra functionality, the facade makes things simpler.

Example class diagram

For the class diagram, let's imagine the following setting—we want our users to be able to download some data from a server and get it de-serialized in the form of objects. The server returns our data in encoded form, so we should decode it first, then parse it, and finally return the right objects. This involves many operations and makes things complicated. That's why we use a facade design pattern:

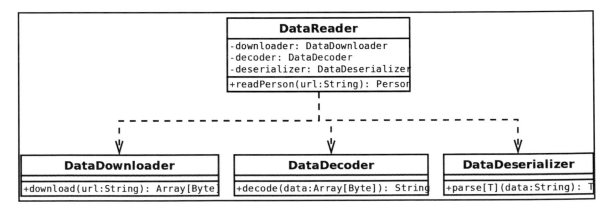

When clients use the preceding application, they will just have to interact with the **DataReader**. Internally, it will take care of downloading, decoding, and deserializing the data.

Code example

The preceding diagram shows the DataDownloader, DataDecoder, and DataDeserializer as composed objects inside DataReader. This is straightforward and clear to achieve—they can be either created with their default constructors, or they can be passed as parameters. For the code representation of our example, however, we have chosen to use traits instead of classes and mix them in with the DataReader class.

Let's first take a look at the DataDownloader, DataDecoder, and DataDeserializer traits:

```scala
trait DataDownloader extends LazyLogging {
  def download(url: String): Array[Byte] = {
    logger.info("Downloading from: {}", url)
    Thread.sleep(5000)
    // {
    // "name": "Ivan",
    // "age": 26
    // }
    // the string below is the Base64 encoded Json above.
    "ew0KICAgICJuYW1lIjogIkl2YW4iLA0KICAgICJhZ2UiOiAyNg0KfQ==".getBytes
  }
}
```

The DataDecoder trait is as follows:

```scala
trait DataDecoder {
  def decode(data: Array[Byte]): String = new
String(Base64.getDecoder.decode(data), "UTF-8")
}
```

The following code snippet is of the DataDeserializer trait:

```scala
trait DataDeserializer {
  implicit val formats = DefaultFormats

  def parse[T](data: String)(implicit m: Manifest[T]): T =
    JsonMethods.parse(StringInput(data)).extract[T]
}
```

The preceding implementations are pretty straightforward and they are separated from each other, since they deal with different tasks. Anyone can use them; however, it requires some knowledge and makes things more complicated. That's why we have a facade class called `DataReader`:

```
class DataReader extends DataDownloader with DataDecoder with
DataDeserializer {
  def readPerson(url: String): Person = {
    val data = download(url)
    val json = decode(data)
    parse[Person](json)
  }
}
```

This example clearly shows that instead of using three different interfaces, we now have a simple method to call. All complexity is hidden inside this method. The following listing shows a sample usage of our class:

```
object FacadeExample {
  def main(args: Array[String]): Unit = {
    val reader = new DataReader
    System.out.println(s"We just read the following person:
      ${reader.readPerson("https://www.ivan-nikolov.com/")}")
  }
}
```

The preceding code makes use of our libraries, which are hidden from the client, really easy. Here is a sample output:

```
volcom@volcom-Dell-System-XPS-L502X:~/workspace/scala-book/structural-design-pat
terns$ java -cp target/structural-1.0.0-SNAPSHOT.jar com.ivan.nikolov.structural
.facade.FacadeExample
[main] INFO  com.ivan.nikolov.structural.facade.DataReader  - Downloading from:
https://www.ivan-nikolov.com/
We just read the following person: Person(Ivan,26)
```

Of course, in the preceding example, we could have used classes inside `DataReader` instead of mixing traits in. This really depends on the requirements and should yield the same results anyway.

What it is good for

The facade design pattern is useful when we want to hide the implementation details of many libraries, make an interface much easier to use, and interact with complex systems.

What it is not so good for

A common mistake some people could make is try and put everything into a facade. This is something that usually doesn't help and the developers remain with a complex system, if not more, as before. Moreover, facade could prove to be restrictive for those users who have enough domain knowledge to use the original functionality. This is especially true if facade is the only way to interact with the underlying system.

The flyweight design pattern

Usually when software is written, developers try to make it fast and efficient. Normally, this means less processing cycles and a smaller memory footprint. There are different ways to achieve these two aspects. Most of the time, a good algorithm will take care of the first one. The amount of used memory can have many causes and solutions, and the flyweight design pattern is there to help and reduce the memory used.

The purpose of the flyweight design pattern is to minimize the memory usage with the help of an object that shares as much data as possible with other similar objects.

There are many cases where many objects share the same information. A common example when talking about flyweight is word processing. Instead of representing each character with all the information about font, size, color, image, and so on, we could just store the positions for similar characters and have a reference to one object that contains the common information. This makes the usage of memory significantly smaller. Otherwise, such applications would become unusable.

Example class diagram

For the class diagram, first let's imagine that we are trying to represent a drawing for a color blindness test similar to the following:

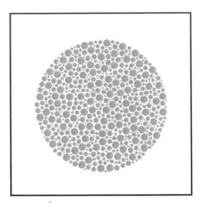

As we can see, it is composed of circles of different sizes and colors. Potentially, this can be an infinitely big picture and it can have any number of circles. To make things simple, let's just set a limitation where we can only have five different circle colors—red, green, blue, yellow, and magenta. Here is what our class diagram will look like in order to represent an image like the preceding one using the flyweight design pattern:

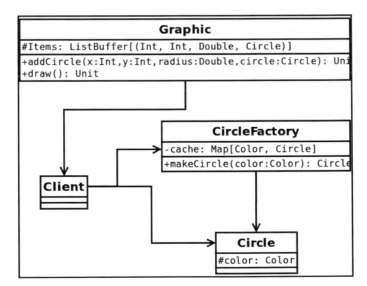

The actual flyweight design pattern is implemented through the **CircleFactory**, **Circle**, and **Client** classes. The client requests the factory and it returns either a new instance of **Circle** or if one with the required parameters exists, it returns it from the cache. For this example, the shared data will be the **Circle** objects with their colors, and then each specific circle will have its own position and a radius. The **Graphic** will contain the actual circles with all of their information. Things will get much clearer with our code example, which the preceding diagram is based on.

Code example

It is time to see how the flyweight design pattern looks like when expressed in Scala code. We will be using the same example as shown previously. It is worth noting that in the code version, some classes have different names than in the diagram. The reasons for this are Scala naming conventions. We will explicitly point out where this happens while going through the code.

An interesting thing about the flyweight design pattern and our example is that it actually uses other design patterns and techniques that we already went through before. We will also point them out while looking at the code.

The first thing we've done is represent the colors. This has nothing to do with the actual flyweight design pattern, but we've decided to use ADTs:

```
sealed abstract class Color
case object Red extends Color
case object Green extends Color
case object Blue extends Color
case object Yellow extends Color
case object Magenta extends Color
```

After we have the colors defined, we can implement our `Circle` class:

```
class Circle(color: Color) {
  System.out.println(s"Creating a circle with $color color.")

  override def toString(): String = s"Circle($color)"
}
```

The circles will be flyweight objects, so the model only has the data that will be shared with the other circle instances. Now that we have the model for the circles, we can create our `CircleFactory`. As the name suggests, it uses the factory design pattern. Here is the code for it:

```
import scala.collection.mutable.Map

object Circle {
  val cache = Map.empty[Color, Circle]

  def apply(color: Color): Circle = cache.getOrElseUpdate(color,
    new Circle(color))

  def circlesCreated(): Int = cache.size
}
```

We have a companion object that is used to implement the factory design pattern in Scala. This is why the name here is different than in the diagram shown previously. This representation allows us to either get an old instance of a circle or create a new one using the following syntax:

```
Circle(Green)
```

Now that we have our circle and factory, we can implement the `Graphic` class:

```
import scala.collection.mutable.ListBuffer

class Graphic {
  val items = ListBuffer.empty[(Int, Int, Double, Circle)]

  def addCircle(x: Int, y: Int, radius: Double, circle: Circle): Unit = {
    items += ((x, y, radius, circle))
  }

  def draw(): Unit = {
    items.foreach {
      case (x, y, radius, circle) =>
        System.out.println(s"Drawing a circle at ($x, $y) with radius
        $radius: $circle")
    }
  }
}
```

The `Graphic` class will actually hold our circles with all other data related to them. The `Client` in the previous diagram does not have a specific representation in our code—it will just be the code that uses the factory to obtain circles. Similarly, the `Graphic` object will retrieve the circle objects by the program and not through explicit access to a client. Here is how all this is implemented in our example:

```scala
object FlyweightExample {
  def main(args: Array[String]): Unit = {
    val graphic = new Graphic
    graphic.addCircle(1, 1, 1.0, Circle(Green))
    graphic.addCircle(1, 2, 1.0, Circle(Red))
    graphic.addCircle(2, 1, 1.0, Circle(Blue))
    graphic.addCircle(2, 2, 1.0, Circle(Green))
    graphic.addCircle(2, 3, 1.0, Circle(Yellow))
    graphic.addCircle(3, 2, 1.0, Circle(Magenta))
    graphic.addCircle(3, 3, 1.0, Circle(Blue))
    graphic.addCircle(4, 3, 1.0, Circle(Blue))
    graphic.addCircle(3, 4, 1.0, Circle(Yellow))
    graphic.addCircle(4, 4, 1.0, Circle(Red))
    graphic.draw()
    System.out.println(s"Total number of circle objects created:
     ${Circle.circlesCreated()}")
  }
}
```

If we run this code, we will get the following output:

```
volcom@volcom-Dell-System-XPS-L502X:~/workspace/scala-book/structural-design-pat
terns$ java -cp target/structural-1.0.0-SNAPSHOT.jar com.ivan.nikolov.structural
.flyweight.FlyweightExample
Creating a circle with Green color.
Creating a circle with Red color.
Creating a circle with Blue color.
Creating a circle with Yellow color.
Creating a circle with Magenta color.
Drawing a circle at (1, 1) with radius 1.0: Circle(Green)
Drawing a circle at (1, 2) with radius 1.0: Circle(Red)
Drawing a circle at (2, 1) with radius 1.0: Circle(Blue)
Drawing a circle at (2, 2) with radius 1.0: Circle(Green)
Drawing a circle at (2, 3) with radius 1.0: Circle(Yellow)
Drawing a circle at (3, 2) with radius 1.0: Circle(Magenta)
Drawing a circle at (3, 3) with radius 1.0: Circle(Blue)
Drawing a circle at (4, 3) with radius 1.0: Circle(Blue)
Drawing a circle at (3, 4) with radius 1.0: Circle(Yellow)
Drawing a circle at (4, 4) with radius 1.0: Circle(Red)
Total number of circle objects created: 5
```

While defining the `Circle` class earlier, we added a print message to the construction. From the preceding figure, we can see that each circle was created with a specific color only once, even though we requested it more times to build our graphic. The last line shows that we have exactly five distinct circle objects, even though our graphic contains 10 different circles.

This is just an example to illustrate how flyweight works. In real life, the flyweight objects will share many more attributes, thus lowering the overall memory footprint of the entire application.

What it is good for

As we already mentioned before, the flyweight design pattern is useful when we are trying to lower the memory used by an application. Using shared objects, our application will require less constructions and destructions of objects, which could further improve performance.

What it is not so good for

Depending on the amount of shared data, sometimes the number of distinct shared objects could dramatically grow and not bring too much benefit. Moreover, it can complicate the factory and its usage. Multithreaded applications need extra care while working with factories. Last but not least, the developers need to be really careful while using shared objects, as any change in them could affect the entire application. Luckily, in Scala, this is less of a concern due to immutability.

The proxy design pattern

In some applications, developers could face the need to provide access control to objects. This could be due to many reasons. Some of them include hiding implementation details, improving interaction with expensive resources, interfacing with remote resources, caching, providing lazy or eager initialization, and so on. The proxy design pattern helps to achieve these.

The purpose of the proxy design pattern is to provide an interface to something else that then gets served behind the scenes to the user.

The proxy design pattern is another example of a wrapper. It is pretty similar to the decorator design pattern, but feels more basic and limited. The reason for this is that the relationship between the proxy and the wrapped object is established during compile time and decorators could be applied at runtime. In the end, its purpose is different.

Example class diagram

For the class diagram, let's imagine that we have an application that visualizes text from files. It might need to visualize the text, or might not depending on user actions. These files could be enormous or could be somewhere in a remote location. Here is how the proxy design pattern could help us achieve this:

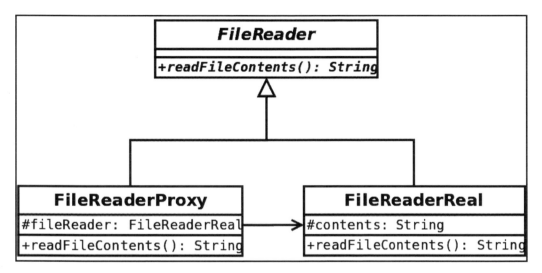

According to the preceding diagram, we could use the **FileReaderProxy** objects and only when someone needs to access the file contents, we will delegate the functionality to the **FileReaderReal**. This design is nice and convenient because we can actually use the **FileReader** object; however, we can keep our application efficient by not needing to load everything at the same time, but just once when needed.

Code example

Now, let's have a closer look at the code that implements the preceding class diagram. The first thing we need to define is the interface (using a Scala trait):

```
trait FileReader {
  def readFileContents(): String
}
```

We then create two classes that implement it—FileReaderReal and FileReaderProxy. First, let's see how the former implements the file read as it has nothing of real significance:

```
class FileReaderReal(filename: String) extends FileReader {
  val contents = {
    val stream = this.getClass.getResourceAsStream(filename)
    val reader = new BufferedReader(
      new InputStreamReader(
        stream
      )
    )
    try {
      reader.lines().iterator().asScala.mkString
      (System.getProperty("line.separator"))
    } finally {
      reader.close()
      stream.close()
    }
  }
  System.out.println(s"Finished reading the actual file: $filename")

  override def readFileContents(): String = contents
}
```

During the construction of the object, it will get the file, read it, and store it in the contents variable. Then, whenever readFileContents is called, the class will return whatever it has buffered. Now, let's take a look at the FileReaderProxy implementation:

```
class FileReaderProxy(filename: String) extends FileReader {
  private var fileReader: FileReaderReal = null

  override def readFileContents(): String = {
    if (fileReader == null) {
      fileReader = new FileReaderReal(filename)
    }
    fileReader.readFileContents()
  }
}
```

The implementation contains an instance of `FileReaderReal`, which is created the first time `readFileContents` is called. The actual file read is then delegated to the `FileReaderReal` class.

 A more elegant implementation of the `FileReaderProxy` would use a `lazy val` instead of a mutable variable. In such a case, the `if` statement won't be needed anymore.

Now, let's see how our proxy can be used in an application:

```
object ProxyExample {
  def main(args: Array[String]): Unit = {
    val fileMap = Map(
      "file1.txt" -> new FileReaderProxy("file1.txt"),
      "file2.txt" -> new FileReaderProxy("file2.txt"),
      "file3.txt" -> new FileReaderProxy("file3.txt"),
      "file4.txt" -> new FileReaderReal("file1.txt")
    )
    System.out.println("Created the map. You should have seen
      file1.txt read because it wasn't used in a proxy.")
    System.out.println(s"Reading file1.txt from the proxy:
      ${fileMap("file1.txt").readFileContents()}")
    System.out.println(s"Reading file3.txt from the proxy:
      ${fileMap("file3.txt").readFileContents()}")
  }
}
```

It's worth noting that each file is actually a resource in the application and contains a line of text in the form of `I am file x`. After running the preceding example, we will get the following output:

```
volcom@volcom-Dell-System-XPS-L502X:~/workspace/scala-book/structural-design-pat
terns$ java -cp target/structural-1.0.0-SNAPSHOT.jar com.ivan.nikolov.structural
.proxy.ProxyExample
Finished reading the actual file: file1.txt
Created the map. You should have seen file1.txt read because it wasn't used in a
 proxy.
Finished reading the actual file: file1.txt
Reading file1.txt from the proxy: I am file 1.
Finished reading the actual file: file3.txt
Reading file3.txt from the proxy: I am file 3.
```

As you can see from the preceding screenshot , the real object is lazily created and so the actual file read is done on demand. This causes our application to skip reading `file2.txt` because we don't even request for it. Someone might come up with a different solution that serves the same purpose, but it will probably be a different design pattern or something similar to proxy.

What it is good for

The proxy design pattern is good when we want to delegate some expensive operations to other classes, do operations lazily, and thus make our applications more efficient.

What it is not so good for

The proxy design pattern is pretty simple and really, there are no drawbacks that could be mentioned. As with every other design pattern, they should be used carefully and only when actually needed.

Summary

In this chapter, we learned about structural design patterns and specifically about the following—adapter, decorator, bridge, composite, facade, flyweight, and proxy. We went through the details of each of them and showed a class diagram as well as a code example for each. Because of the richness of Scala, sometimes there can be a better implementation using some of the nice features of Scala, but sometimes the design pattern just looks the same as it would in a language such as Java.

In many cases, the structural design patterns seem quite similar. This, however, shouldn't confuse you as they still have different purposes. Some examples include:

- **Adapter versus Bridge**: Adapter is used to convert one interface to another when we do not have access to the code. Bridge is used while designing software and it decouples abstraction from implementation for easier extensions in the future.
- **Proxy versus Decorator**: Decorators usually enhance an interface. Proxies provide the same interface, but help with application efficiency.

Now, you should have a good understanding of the structural design patterns and will have enough knowledge to apply them in real-world projects.

In the next chapter, you will learn about *behavioral design patterns*.

8
Behavioral Design Patterns – Part One

Our journey through the Scala design patterns has arrived at the group of **behavioral design patterns**. There are more members in this group than the others we've already been through, so we will split it into two separate parts. In this chapter, we will focus on the following behavioral design patterns:

- Value object
- Null object
- Strategy
- Command
- Chain of responsibility
- Interpreter

This chapter and the next one will give some clarity about what behavioral design patterns are, where they are useful, and how to implement them in Scala. We will be following a path similar to the previous chapters where we presented the patterns, showed a class diagram and a code example, and finally, gave a few hints about what to watch out for and where certain patterns are preferred to be used. Hopefully, you will get a feel for them and be able to confidently identify situations where they are applicable.

Defining behavioral design patterns

Behavioral design patterns, as the name suggests, are to do with behavior. Their purpose is to identify and implement common communication patterns between objects in an application. They define object interaction in such a way that the communication between objects is easy and coupling is still kept at a low level.

Behavioral design patterns describe how objects and classes interact with each other using messages. Contrary to creational and structural design patterns, the behavioral design patterns describe a **flow** or a **process**. This means that a developer should be really familiar with the actual process they are trying to implement. As with every other type of design pattern, behavioral design patterns exist in order to increase the testability, maintainability, and flexibility of the produced code.

The value object design pattern

In programming, there are different ways of comparing data. We can compare object identities or their values. These are useful in different scenarios and here, we will see what value objects are and when they can be used.

Value objects are small and simple immutable objects. Their equality is based not on identity, but on value equality.

Value objects are used to represent numbers, money, dates, and so on. They should be small and immutable; otherwise, changing values could cause bugs and unexpected behavior. They are quite useful in multithreaded applications due to their immutability. They are also commonly used as data transfer objects in enterprise applications.

An example class diagram

In languages such as Java, there is no direct support for value objects. What developers end up doing is to declare the fields as final and implement the `hashCode` and `equals` methods.

Immutability, however, is a concept that is pretty much enforced in Scala. We already saw the **algebraic data types (ADTs)** earlier—they also fall in the value object category. Case classes and tuples are also immutable and they are used to achieve the value object design pattern. The following class diagram shows an example of the value object design pattern in Scala:

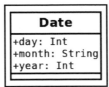

This diagram really doesn't do anything special. It is a representation of a case class called **Date**. This is everything we need to do in order to achieve immutability and be able to implement the value object design pattern.

A code example

In our code example, we will use our `Date` class. Dates are quite commonly used in software products. Of course, there are libraries that provide complete functionality around date manipulations, but this should be good enough for an example. First of all, here is the `Date` class representation:

```
case class Date(
  day: Int,
  month: String,
  year: Int
)
```

This is everything we need in order to get a value object. Scala does everything for us in the background by creating default implementations for the `hashCode`, `equals`, and `toString` methods. Case classes give us extra power, but this is out of this section's scope.

Now, let's use our `Date` class:

```
object DateExample {
  def main(args: Array[String]): Unit = {
    val thirdOfMarch = Date(3, "MARCH", 2016)
    val fourthOfJuly = Date(4, "JULY", 2016)
    val newYear1 = Date(31, "DECEMBER", 2015)
    val newYear2 = Date(31, "DECEMBER", 2015)
    System.out.println(s"The 3rd of March 2016 is the same as
      the 4th of July 2016: ${thirdOfMarch == fourthOfJuly}")
    System.out.println(s"The new year of 2015 is here twice:
      ${newYear1 == newYear2}")
  }
}
```

As you can see, we used our object as values. We should note that here, we have absolutely no validation of the parameters; however, it is something easy to add, but not relevant for the current example. If we run our code now, we will see the following output:

```
volcom@volcom-Dell-System-XPS-L502X:~/workspace/scala-book/behavioral-design-pat
terns$ java -cp target/behavioral-1.0.0-SNAPSHOT.jar com.ivan.nikolov.behavioral
.value_object.DateExample
The 3rd of March 2016 is the same as the 4th of July 2016: false
The new year of 2015 is here twice: true
```

Just to prove that case classes allow us to implement the value object design pattern easily and normal classes don't, let's try and change our `Date` class to a normal one and then use it in the same example. Our class will change to the following:

```
class BadDate(
  day: Int,
  month: String,
  year: Int
)
```

Then, we will take the same example; however this time, we will use the `BadDate`, and since it's not a case class, we will create it with the `new` keyword:

```
object BadDateExample {
  def main(args: Array[String]): Unit = {
    val thirdOfMarch = new BadDate(3, "MARCH", 2016)
    val fourthOfJuly = new BadDate(4, "JULY", 2016)
    val newYear1 = new BadDate(31, "DECEMBER", 2015)
    val newYear2 = new BadDate(31, "DECEMBER", 2015)
    System.out.println(s"The 3rd of March 2016 is the same as the
      4th of July 2016: ${thirdOfMarch == fourthOfJuly}")
    System.out.println(s"The new year of 2015 is here twice:
      ${newYear1 == newYear2}")
  }
}
```

The output of this example will be:

```
volcom@volcom-Dell-System-XPS-L502X:~/workspace/scala-book/behavioral-design-pat
terns$ java -cp target/behavioral-1.0.0-SNAPSHOT.jar com.ivan.nikolov.behavioral
.value_object.BadDateExample
The 3rd of March 2016 is the same as the 4th of July 2016: false
The new year of 2015 is here twice: false
```

As you can see from the preceding output, normal classes do not work in the same way as case classes and some extra work needs to be performed in order to implement the value object design pattern with them. The reason for the preceding result is that classes, by default, are compared with each other by their reference identities and not by the values they carry. In order to change this, `hashCode` and `equals` should be implemented. Scala also allows us to override the `==` operator for the class.

Alternative implementation

The value object design pattern can also be achieved with predefined tuple classes in Scala. In this case, we don't even need to create our class and we can write something like (3, "March", 2016). This would automatically have the same characteristics as value objects. There are implementations of tuples of up to 22 elements, but using them in real applications is not recommended, as readability and quality can degrade dramatically. Moreover, two *n* element tuples can be considered equal, even if semantically they are different types of objects in our application. Last but not least, accessing elements using case classes is much easier and nicer to read than writing something like tuple._3.

What it is good for

As we already mentioned, the value object design pattern is good for multithreading and creating **data transfer objects** (**DTOs**). It is something extremely easy to achieve in Scala, and many people use it on a daily basis without even realizing that it actually is a design pattern. Value objects are another example of the fact that Scala is a really powerful language.

What it is not so good for

Other than using tuples to represent value objects in Scala, there are no other major drawbacks to using this pattern.

The null object design pattern

Most object-oriented languages have a way of specifying the nonexistence of some value. In Scala and Java, for example, this could be the null value that can be assigned to an object. Calling any method on an object that is null would result in a NullPointerException, hence developers should be careful and check whether there is such a possibility. These checks, however, could make the source code hard to follow and extend as developers should always be aware. This is where the null object design pattern is helpful.

 The purpose of the null object design pattern is to define an actual object that represents the null value and has neutral behavior.

Using null objects removes the need to check whether something is set to `null` or not. The code becomes much more readable and easy to understand and makes bug occurrence harder.

An example class diagram

For the class diagram, let's imagine that we have a system that has to poll a queue for messages. Of course, this queue might not always have anything to offer, so it would return nulls. Instead of checking for `null`, we could simply return special null objects that will have empty behavior. Let's show these message classes in a diagram:

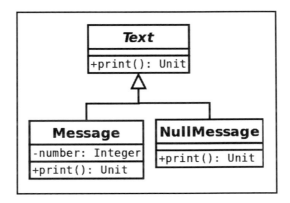

Using the classes from the preceding diagram, whenever there is no number to print, we will return a **NullMessage** object with empty behavior. In some cases, for optimization purposes, people could have the **NullMessage** as a singleton instance.

A code example

Before we actually look at our code, we will note a few observations about the preceding diagram. It represents a classical case using the null object design pattern. However, nowadays, it is not really used this way in either Java or Scala. For example, Java now supports `Optional`, which is used instead (assuming people use new versions of the language). In Scala, things are similar—we can and do use `Option[Message]` instead of null objects. Additionally, we gain all the other nice features of `Option` such as the ability to use them in pattern matching.

So, as mentioned previously, our code is not really going to use the hierarchy of the preceding class diagram. It just doesn't need it and it will be much simpler. Instead, we will be using Option[Message]. First of all, let's see the Message class definition:

```
case class Message(number: Int) {
  def print(): String = s"This is a message with number: $number."
}
```

We mentioned that we will be polling a queue for messages and then displaying them. We have simulated a queue that is being randomly populated using a different thread in our application:

```
import java.util.concurrent.ConcurrentLinkedQueue
import scala.util.Random

class DataGenerator extends Runnable {
  val MAX_VAL = 10
  val MAX_TIME = 10000
  private var isStop = false
  private val queue: ConcurrentLinkedQueue[Int] = new
ConcurrentLinkedQueue[Int]()

  override def run(): Unit = {
    val random = new Random()
    while (!isStop) {
      Thread.sleep(random.nextInt(MAX_TIME))
      queue.add(random.nextInt(MAX_VAL))
    }
  }

  def getMessage(): Option[Message] =
    Option(queue.poll()).map {
    case number => Message(number)
  }

  def requestStop(): Unit = this.synchronized {
    isStop = true
  }
}
```

The preceding code shows what will be run in a different thread. The queue will be populated with random values between 0 (inclusive) and 10 (exclusive) at random intervals. Then, getMessage can be called and whatever is in the queue can be read. Since it is possible for the queue to be empty, we return an Option of Message to the caller. It is probably worth mentioning that in Scala, Option(null) returns None. This is exactly what we took advantage of in the preceding code.

Let's see how everything comes together in our example:

```scala
object MessageExample {
  val TIMES_TO_TRY = 10
  val MAX_TIME = 5000

  def main(args: Array[String]): Unit = {
    val generator = new DataGenerator
    // start the generator in another thread
    new Thread(generator).start()
    val random = new Random()
    (0 to TIMES_TO_TRY).foreach {
      case time =>
        Thread.sleep(random.nextInt(MAX_TIME))
        System.out.println("Getting next message...")
        generator.getMessage().foreach(m =>
          System.out.println(m.print()))
    }
    generator.requestStop()
  }
}
```

The preceding program creates a generator and makes it run on a different thread. Then, it randomly requests items from the generator and prints them if something is actually returned. Due to the use of random generators, the program will print different things every time. Here is an example run:

```
volcom@volcom-Dell-System-XPS-L502X:~/workspace/scala-book/behavioral-design-pat
terns$ java -cp target/behavioral-1.0.0-SNAPSHOT.jar com.ivan.nikolov.behavioral
.null_object.MessageExample
Getting next message...
Getting next message...
Getting next message...
This is a message with number: 4.
Getting next message...
Getting next message...
This is a message with number: 3.
Getting next message...
Getting next message...
This is a message with number: 5.
Getting next message...
Getting next message...
Getting next message...
This is a message with number: 8.
Getting next message...
```

As you can see from our example and the preceding output, we never actually check for nulls and our code just doesn't do anything when the queue returns `null`. This works nicely in large projects and it makes the source code look really elegant and easy to understand.

 In real-life applications, code as in the previous example might not be a good idea. First of all, instead of calling `sleep` on a thread, we can use timers. Secondly, if we want to create producer–consumer applications, we can use libraries such as **Akka** (`https://akka.io/`), which allow us to do reactive programming and have really optimal code.

What it is good for

As you already saw, the null object design pattern is already incorporated in Scala (and newer versions of Java) through the use of `Option` (`Optional` in Java). This makes it really easy to use and shows the power of the language once more. Using null objects makes our code look much more readable and removes the need to take extra care when a value is `null`. It also reduces the risk of bugs.

What it is not so good for

There are no drawbacks of this design pattern that we can think of. One thing probably worth mentioning is this—use it only when it is actually needed, not everywhere.

The strategy design pattern

It is quite a common thing in enterprise applications to have different implementations of specific algorithms and choosing one to use while the application is running. Some examples might include different sorting algorithms that would have a different performance for different sizes or types of data, different parsers for various possible representations of data, and so on.

 The strategy design pattern enables us to define a family of algorithms and select a specific one at runtime.

The strategy design pattern helps with encapsulation as each algorithm can be separately defined and then injected into the classes that use it. The different implementations are also interchangeable.

An example class diagram

For the class diagram, let's imagine that we are writing an application that needs to load some data from a file and then use this data somehow. Of course, the data could be represented in different formats (CSV or JSON, in this case), and depending on the file type, we will be using a different parsing strategy. The class diagram that represents our parser is shown in the following diagram:

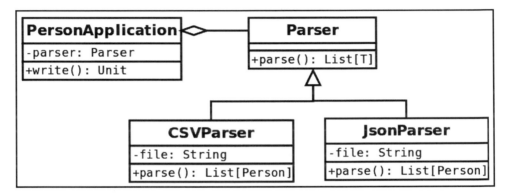

We basically have an interface that the different classes implement, and then depending on which one is needed, **PersonApplication** gets injected with the right one.

The preceding class diagram looks really similar to the one we saw earlier in the book for the bridge design pattern. Even though this is the case, both patterns have different purposes—the builder is concerned with structure, while here it's all about behavior. Also, the strategy design pattern looks somewhat more coupled.

A code example

In the previous section, we showed the class diagram of the example we will show here. As you can see, we used a model class called `Person`. It is just a case class with the following definition:

```
case class Person(name: String, age: Int, address: String)
```

Since there will be different formats available in our application, we have defined a common interface that all parsers will implement:

```
trait Parser[T] {
  def parse(file: String): List[T]
}
```

Now, let's have a look at the implementations. First is the CSVParser:

```
import com.github.tototoshi.csv.CSVReader

class CSVParser extends Parser[Person] {
  override def parse(file: String): List[Person] =
    CSVReader.open(new
InputStreamReader(this.getClass.getResourceAsStream(file))).all().map {
          case List(name, age, address) =>
              Person(name, age.toInt, address)
      }
  }
```

It relies on a library called scala-csv (details in the pom.xml/build.sbt file), which reads each line as a list of strings. Then, they are mapped to the Person objects.

Next is the code for the JsonParser class:

```
import org.json4s._
import org.json4s.jackson.JsonMethods

class JsonParser extends Parser[Person] {
  implicit val formats = DefaultFormats
  override def parse(file: String): List[Person] =
JsonMethods.parse(StreamInput(this.getClass.getResourceAsStream(file))).ext
ract[List[Person]]
}
```

It reads a JSON file and parses it using the json4s library. As you can see, even though both implementations do the same thing, they are quite different. We cannot apply the CSV one when we have a JSON file and vice versa. The files also look really different. Here is the CSV file we are using in our example:

```
Ivan,26,London
Maria,23,Edinburgh
John,36,New York
Anna,24,Moscow
```

This is the JSON file:

```
[
  {
    "name": "Ivan",
    "age": 26,
    "address": "London"
  },
  {
    "name": "Maria",
    "age": 23,
    "address": "Edinburgh"
  },
  {
    "name": "John",
    "age": 36,
    "address": "New York"
  },
  {
    "name": "Anna",
    "age": 24,
    "address": "Moscow"
  }
]
```

Both the preceding datasets contain exactly the same data, but the formats make them look completely different and they require different approaches in parsing.

There is one extra thing we've done in our example. We've used a factory design pattern in order to pick the right implementation at runtime, depending on the file type:

```
object Parser {
  def apply(filename: String): Parser[Person] =
    filename match {
      case f if f.endsWith(".json") => new JsonParser
      case f if f.endsWith(".csv") => new CSVParser
      case f => throw new RuntimeException(s"Unknown format: $f")
    }
}
```

The preceding factory is just an example. It only checks the file extension and of course, could be made much more robust. Using this factory, we can pick the right implementation of the parser for the application class to use, whose code is shown as follows:

```
class PersonApplication[T](parser: Parser[T]) {
  def write(file: String): Unit = {
    System.out.println(s"Got the following data ${parser.parse(file)}")
  }
}
```

The application class looks the same no matter what the implementation is. Different implementations could be plugged in, and as long as there are no errors, everything should run.

Now, let's see how we can use our strategy design pattern in our example:

```
object ParserExample {
  def main(args: Array[String]): Unit = {
    val csvPeople = Parser("people.csv")
    val jsonPeople = Parser("people.json")
    val applicationCsv = new PersonApplication(csvPeople)
    val applicationJson = new PersonApplication(jsonPeople)
    System.out.println("Using the csv: ")
    applicationCsv.write("people.csv")
    System.out.println("Using the json: ")
    applicationJson.write("people.json")
  }
}
```

As you can see, it's pretty simple. The output of the preceding application is shown as follows:

```
volcom@volcom-Dell-System-XPS-L502X:~/workspace/scala-book/behavioral-design-pat
terns$ java -cp target/behavioral-1.0.0-SNAPSHOT.jar com.ivan.nikolov.behavioral
.strategy.ParserExample
Using the csv:
Got the following data List(Person(Ivan,26,London), Person(Maria,23,Edinburgh),
Person(John,36,New York), Person(Anna,24,Moscow))
Using the json:
Got the following data List(Person(Ivan,26,London), Person(Maria,23,Edinburgh),
Person(John,36,New York), Person(Anna,24,Moscow))
```

In both cases, our application coped just fine with the different formats. Adding new implementations for new formats is also straightforward—just implement the `Parser` interface and make sure the factory knows about them.

The strategy design pattern the Scala way

In the preceding section, we showed the strategy design pattern using classes and traits. This is what it would look in a purely object-oriented language. However, Scala is also functional and provides more ways to achieve it by writing far less code. In this subsection, we will show the strategy design pattern by taking advantage of the fact that in Scala, functions are first-class objects.

The first thing that will change is that we will not need to have an interface and classes that implement it. Instead, our `Application` class will look like the following:

```
class Application[T](strategy: (String) => List[T]) {
  def write(file: String): Unit = {
    System.out.println(s"Got the following data ${strategy(file)}")
  }
}
```

The most important thing to note here is that the strategy parameter is a function instead of a normal object. This instantly allows us to pass any function we want there without the need to implement specific classes, as long as it satisfies these requirements—one `String` parameter and returns a `List[T]`. If we have multiple methods in our strategy, we can use a case class or a tuple to group them.

For the current example, we've decided to have the function implementations somewhere so that they are grouped with the factory, which will choose which one to use:

```
import com.github.tototoshi.csv.CSVReader
import org.json4s.{StreamInput, DefaultFormat}
import org.json4s.jackson.JsonMethods

object StrategyFactory {
  implicit val formats = DefaultFormats
  def apply(filename: String): (String) => List[Person] =
    filename match {
      case f if f.endsWith(".json") => parseJson
      case f if f.endsWith(".csv") => parseCsv
      case f => throw new RuntimeException(s"Unknown format: $f")
    }
  def parseJson(file: String): List[Person] =
JsonMethods.parse(StreamInput(this.getClass.getResourceAsStream(file))).ext
```

```
ract[List[Person]]
  def parseCsv(file: String): List[Person] = CSVReader.open(new
    InputStreamReader(this.getClass.getResourceAsStream(file))).all().map
{
      case List(name, age, address) => Person(name, age.toInt, address)
  }
}
```

The preceding code has the same factory as before, but this time it returns methods, which can then be called.

Finally, here is how to use the application:

```
object StrategyExample {
  def main(args: Array[String]): Unit = {
    val applicationCsv = new
Application[Person](StrategyFactory("people.csv"))
    val applicationJson = new
Application[Person](StrategyFactory("people.json"))
    System.out.println("Using the csv: ")
    applicationCsv.write("people.csv")
    System.out.println("Using the json: ")
    applicationJson.write("people.json")
  }
}
```

The output of the preceding example will be absolutely the same as before.

What it is good for

The strategy design pattern helps us when we want to be able to change implementations at runtime. Also, as we can see, the implementations live separately from the code that uses them, so it's quite easy to add new ones without the risk of introducing bugs in other parts of our system.

What it is not so good for

Even though, in the long run, the Scala way of implementing the strategy pattern that uses functions could save a lot on code, sometimes it affects readability and maintainability. The fact that the methods could be stored in an object, class, case class, trait, and so on, indicates the fact that different people could prefer different approaches, and this is not always good while working in a big team. Apart from that, the strategy design pattern doesn't have any major flaws as long as it's used in the right way and in the right places.

The command design pattern

Sometimes in our applications, we might need to pass information to other objects about how to perform some action. Usually, this action will be executed at a later time based on some kind of event. The object that will execute our commands is called **invoker**, and it might not even be aware of the command it actually runs. It just knows about the interface, which means that it knows how to trigger the command. The command design pattern helps us to achieve this.

 The purpose of the command design pattern is to encapsulate the information needed to perform an action at a later stage and pass this information to the object that will be running the actual code.

Usually, the command information will contain the object that owns the method, the method name, and the parameters that should be passed when invoking the method. The command design pattern is useful for many things, some of which include supporting undo actions, implementing parallel processing, or simply optimizing code by deferring, and possibly avoiding code execution.

An example class diagram

When talking about the command design pattern, there are usually a couple of objects, each of which has its specific role:

- **Command**: We can think of this as the interface and its implementations that are being called by the invoker.
- **Receiver**: This is the object that actually knows how commands are executed. Think of this as an object that is being passed to the command and then used in the interface method.
- **Invoker**: It invokes the commands by calling their interface method. As we mentioned earlier, it might not even know what commands are being invoked.
- **Client**: It more or less guides which commands are executed when by using the invoker.

Now that we know the most important objects and their roles in the command design pattern, we can take a look at an example. For the class diagram, let's imagine that we have a robot, which can cook. We connect to it through a controller and send commands to our robot. Things are pretty simplified, but should be good enough to understand how this pattern works. Here is the class diagram:

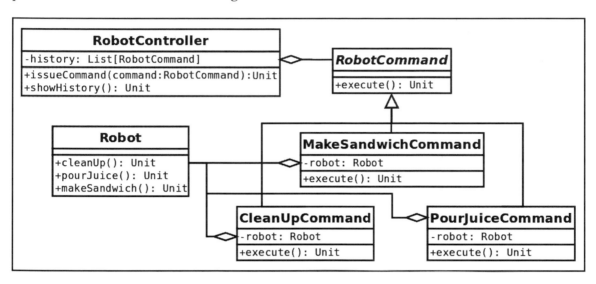

We can quickly identify that here, the **RobotCommand** interface and its implementations are the command. The receiver is the **Robot** class as it knows how to run all the commands issued to it. The **RobotController** class is the invoker. It doesn't know what types of commands it executes, just runs them whenever needed. We haven't shown our client class in the preceding diagram, as it is simply represented by the example application that runs the code, which implements the previously shown class diagram.

You can easily see that if the code representing the preceding diagram is changed, it could easily add multithreaded support and support for undo.

A code example

Now, it's time to see the interesting part representing the previous diagram—the code. As always, we will be going through the individual classes and giving brief explanations where necessary.

The first piece of code that we will look at is the `Robot` class. We already mentioned that it acts as the receiver and knows how to execute some specific functionality:

```
case class Robot() {
  def cleanUp(): Unit = System.out.println("Cleaning up.")
  def pourJuice(): Unit = System.out.println("Pouring juice.")
  def makeSandwich(): Unit = System.out.println("Making a sandwich.")
}
```

We've kept the code simple and the methods just print different things to the command line. Next is the robot command with its different implementations:

```
trait RobotCommand {
  def execute(): Unit
}

case class MakeSandwichCommand(robot: Robot) extends RobotCommand {
  override def execute(): Unit = robot.makeSandwich()
}

case class PourJuiceCommand(robot: Robot) extends RobotCommand {
  override def execute(): Unit = robot.pourJuice()
}

case class CleanUpCommand(robot: Robot) extends RobotCommand {
  override def execute(): Unit = robot.cleanUp()
}
```

There is absolutely nothing special about the preceding code. It is a simple trait, which is implemented by different classes. It relies on the `Robot` receiver, which knows how to execute methods.

The `RobotController` class is our invoker and issues commands given to it according to the `RobotCommand` interface. It doesn't need to know anything about the commands that it issues, as long as the interface is followed. We've decided to add some history of the commands that can be used for rollbacks later. The code for the invoker is shown as follows:

```
class RobotController {
  val history = ListBuffer[RobotCommand]()

  def issueCommand(command: RobotCommand): Unit = {
    command +=: history
    command.execute()
  }

  def showHistory(): Unit = {
```

```
    history.foreach(println)
  }
}
```

Now, let's take a look at the example that uses all of the preceding classes. As we already mentioned earlier, it would actually act as a client. Here is the source code:

```
object RobotExample {
  def main(args: Array[String]): Unit = {
    val robot = Robot()
    val robotController = new RobotController
    robotController.issueCommand(MakeSandwichCommand(robot))
    robotController.issueCommand(PourJuiceCommand(robot))
    System.out.println("I'm eating and having some juice.")
    robotController.issueCommand(CleanUpCommand(robot))
    System.out.println("Here is what I asked my robot to do:")
    robotController.showHistory()
  }
}
```

The output of this application will be the same as in the following screenshot:

```
volcom@volcom-Dell-System-XPS-L502X:~/workspace/scala-book/behavioral-design-pat
terns$ java -cp target/behavioral-1.0.0-SNAPSHOT.jar com.ivan.nikolov.behavioral
.command.RobotExample
Making a sandwich.
Pouring juice.
I'm eating and having some juice.
Cleaning up.
Here is what I asked my robot to do:
CleanUpCommand(Robot())
PourJuiceCommand(Robot())
MakeSandwichCommand(Robot())
```

We can see that our invoker successfully saves the history of the events. This means that as long as our commands and then the receiver (`Robot`) have the undo methods, we can implement these and have extra functionality.

The command design pattern the Scala way

The command design pattern is another example of a design pattern that can be implemented differently in Scala compared to other languages. We will show another implementation of the preceding example. This time, we will use the **by-name parameters** feature of the language. It is replaceable with passing functions as parameters (something we've already seen before for the strategy design pattern), but more verbose. Let's see what it will look like.

Not much of the application actually has to change. We've only refactored and renamed the `RobotController` and `RobotExample` classes. Here is the former class, now called `RobotByNameController`:

```
class RobotByNameController {
  val history = ListBuffer[() => Unit]()

  def issueCommand(command: => Unit): Unit = {
    command _ +=: history
    command
  }

  def showHistory(): Unit = {
    history.foreach(println)
  }
}
```

As you can see, we don't pass an actual command object but just a by-name parameter to the `issueCommand` method. What this method does is defer a call to whatever retrieves the value passed until it is actually needed. In order to make the preceding code work, we had to refactor our example code as well:

```
object RobotByNameExample {
  def main(args: Array[String]): Unit = {
    val robot = Robot()
    val robotController = new RobotByNameController
    robotController.issueCommand(MakeSandwichCommand(robot).execute())
    robotController.issueCommand(PourJuiceCommand(robot).execute())
    System.out.println("I'm eating and having some juice.")
    robotController.issueCommand(CleanUpCommand(robot).execute())
    System.out.println("Here is what I asked my robot to do:")
    robotController.showHistory()
  }
}
```

The by-name parameters method is useful when we don't want to write extra code for the command interface and its implementations. We could just pass any function call (in this case, directly from the receiver) and it will be held off until the data is needed, or not called at all. The output will be the same as before, but with the exception that now we have functions, and the history printout will look slightly different.

What it is good for

The command design pattern is useful for cases where we want to delay, log, or sequence method calls for one reason or another. Another advantage is that it decouples the invoker from the object that actually performs the specific operations. This allows us to have modifications and to add new functionality pretty easily.

What it is not so good for

Even though the by-name parameter method looks nice and could make our writing shorter, it might not be a great idea here. A big disadvantage compared with our previous example is that we could actually plug any `Unit` data there, which could possibly not be relevant to what the receivers are supposed to do. In other cases, though, the by-name parameter technique is quite useful and could dramatically improve our application performance.

The chain of responsibility design pattern

Nowadays, with the growth of data sizes and the hype around big data, stream processing is something that many applications will have to be able to do. Stream processing is characterized by an endless stream of data, which is passed from one object to another while each of them could be doing some processing and then passing it on to the next one. In other cases, data could be moved on in the chain until it arrives at an object which knows how to process a certain command.

The preceding behavior is really suitable for the chain of responsibility design pattern.

 The purpose of the chain of responsibility design pattern is to decouple the sender of a request from its receiver by giving multiple objects the chance to handle the request.

There could be some variations to the chain of responsibility design pattern. The original pattern is that whenever a request reaches an object that can process it, it doesn't go any further. However, in some cases, we might need to push the request further or even multiply it and broadcast to other receivers.

It is worth noting that the chain of responsibility is not data-specific at all, and it can be used in any scenario where the preceding characteristics emerge.

An example class diagram

A common example used to illustrate the chain of responsibility design pattern is about event handling in applications, depending on whether they come from a mouse or a keyboard action. For our class diagram and code example, let's take a look at something else that we use every day—ATMs. How do they return the right amount in different note combinations? The answer is, of course, the chain of responsibility.

We will present two diagrams here—one of the classes that allow us to achieve the chain of responsibility pattern and another that will show how those classes are used together to build our ATM.

First, let's take a look at our classes separately:

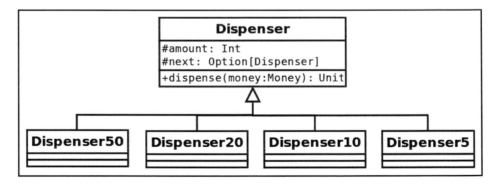

In the preceding diagram, we have a base class (represented as a trait in Scala), which is then extended by the different concrete dispensers. Each dispenser has an optional instance of the same class, and in this way, we can build a chain. The dispense method is the same for all the dispensers, and then each of the dispensers has a different amount and a different next element in the chain.

Things will get much clearer as we present our ATM implementation. It can be seen in the following diagram:

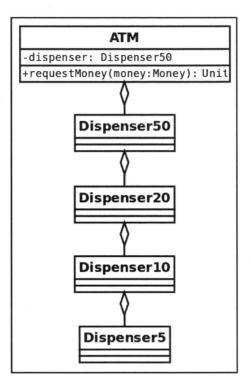

The preceding diagram shows the actual chain that we have in our ATM. Whenever someone requests money, the ATM will go to the dispenser for 50 pound notes, then to a lower dispenser and so on until the request of the user is satisfied. In the following subsection, we will present our code step by step.

A code example

Let's look at the code for the preceding example, one step at a time. First of all, we have defined a Money class that represents the amount the user requests. The definition looks like the following:

```
case class Money(amount: Int)
```

Now, let's have a look at the `Dispenser` trait. It is the one that the concrete dispensers extend, as shown here:

```
trait Dispenser {
  val amount: Int
  val next: Option[Dispenser]

  def dispense(money: Money): Unit = {
    if (money.amount >= amount) {
      val notes = money.amount / amount
      val left = money.amount % amount
      System.out.println(s"Dispensing $notes note/s of $amount.")
      if (left > 0) next.map(_.dispense(Money(left)))
    } else {
      next.foreach(_.dispense(money))
    }
  }
}
```

As we mentioned in the preceding section, the dispense method is the same for everyone who extends our `Dispenser`, but the amount and the next element of the chain are to be defined by whoever extends it. The `dispense` method tries to return as many notes as possible of the given nomination; after this, it passes the responsibility to the next dispenser if there is still money to be given.

The following code block shows our implementations of the different dispensers—for notes of 50, 20, 10, and 5 pounds:

```
class Dispenser50(val next: Option[Dispenser]) extends Dispenser {
  override val amount = 50
}

class Dispenser20(val next: Option[Dispenser]) extends Dispenser {
  override val amount: Int = 20
}

class Dispenser10(val next: Option[Dispenser]) extends Dispenser {
  override val amount: Int = 10
}

class Dispenser5(val next: Option[Dispenser]) extends Dispenser {
  override val amount: Int = 5
}
```

What we have shown so far is the essence of the chain of responsibility design pattern. Using the defined classes, we will now build a chain that can be used easily.

Here is the code for our ATM class:

```
class ATM {
  val dispenser: Dispenser = {
    val d1 = new Dispenser5(None)
    val d2 = new Dispenser10(Some(d1))
    val d3 = new Dispenser20(Some(d2))
    new Dispenser50(Some(d3))
  }

  def requestMoney(money: Money): Unit = {
    if (money.amount % 5 != 0) {
      System.err.println("The smallest nominal is 5 and we cannot
       satisfy your request.")
    } else {
      dispenser.dispense(money)
    }
  }
}
```

In the preceding code, we built the dispenser chain that will be used by our ATM class. The order here is really important for the correct functioning of the system. We have also done some sanity checks. The use of our ATM class is then pretty straightforward with the following application:

```
object ATMExample {
  def main(args: Array[String]): Unit = {
    val atm = new ATM
    printHelp()
    Source.stdin.getLines().foreach {
      case line =>
        processLine(line, atm)
    }
  }

  def printHelp(): Unit = {
    System.out.println("Usage: ")
    System.out.println("1. Write an amount to withdraw...")
    System.out.println("2. Write EXIT to quit the application.")
  }

  def processLine(line: String, atm: ATM): Unit = {
    line match {
      case "EXIT" =>
        System.out.println("Bye!")
        System.exit(0)
      case l =>
```

```scala
        try {
          atm.requestMoney(Money(1.toInt))
          System.out.println("Thanks!")
        } catch {
          case _: Throwable =>
            System.err.println(s"Invalid input: $1.")
            printHelp()
        }
      }
    }
  }
```

This is an interactive application that waits for the user input and then uses the ATM. Let's see how an example run of this will look in the following screenshot:

```
volcom@volcom-Dell-System-XPS-L502X:~/workspace/scala-book/behavioral-design-pat
terns$ java -cp target/behavioral-1.0.0-SNAPSHOT.jar com.ivan.nikolov.behavioral
.chain_of_responsibility.ATMExample
Usage:
1. Write an amount to withdraw...
2. Write EXIT to quit the application.
19
The smallest nominal is 5 and we cannot satisfy your request.
Thanks!
195
Dispensing 3 note/s of 50.
Dispensing 2 note/s of 20.
Dispensing 1 note/s of 5.
Thanks!
35
Dispensing 1 note/s of 20.
Dispensing 1 note/s of 10.
Dispensing 1 note/s of 5.
Thanks!
EXIT
Bye!
```

As you can see in the code, our ATM doesn't have the extra functionality that other ATMs have—check note availability. This, however, is a functionality that can be extended further.

The chain of responsibility design pattern the Scala way

Looking more carefully at the code and the class diagram, you can see some similarities to the decorator design pattern. This means that here, we can use the same stackable traits, which use the `abstract override` construct. We've already seen an example of this and it will not provide you with any new information. However, there is another functionality of the Scala programming language that we can use in order to achieve the chain of responsibility design pattern—partial functions.

Using partial functions, we don't need to define the specific dispenser classes separately. Our dispenser will change to the following:

```
trait PartialFunctionDispenser {
  def dispense(dispenserAmount: Int): PartialFunction[Money, Money] = {
    case Money(amount) if amount >= dispenserAmount =>
      val notes = amount / dispenserAmount
      val left = amount % dispenserAmount
      System.out.println(s"Dispensing $notes note/s of $dispenserAmount.")
      Money(left)
    case m @ Money(amount) => m
  }
}
```

Of course, there are different ways to do this—we can have an abstract trait and then implement the partial function (something similar to the original example) and not specify the `dispenserAmount` parameter, or we can have one trait with different implementations of this function instead of passing the `dispenserAmount` parameter, and so on. Doing this, however, allows us to later simulate the existence of an infinite number of different notes.

After we have our new dispenser, which returns a `PartialFunction` instead of nothing (`Unit`), we can define our ATM class:

```
class PartialFunctionATM extends PartialFunctionDispenser {
  val dispenser =
    dispense(50)
      .andThen(dispense(20))
      .andThen(dispense(10))
      .andThen(dispense(5))

  def requestMoney(money: Money): Unit = {
    if (money.amount % 5 != 0) {
```

```
        System.err.println("The smallest nominal is 5 and we cannot
          satisfy your request.")
      } else {
        dispenser(money)
      }
    }
  }
```

The interesting part here is the `dispenser` field and the way we use it. In the preceding code, we chained multiple partial functions using the `andThen` method and finally, we used the result of them as a method.

 Depending on what chains the developer wants to create, they can use the `orElse` or `andThen` methods of the partial functions. The former is useful for single handlers and the latter for chaining.

Running the original example, but with substituted ATM implementations, will yield absolutely identical results.

As you saw in this subsection, using partial functions can make our application more flexible and will require us to write less code. However, it might be more demanding in terms of understanding advanced Scala language concepts.

Just for completeness, it is worth mentioning that we can also implement the chain of responsibility design pattern using the Akka library. We will be looking into this library in the later chapters of this book, and you will hopefully be able to see how this design pattern can be moved to reactive programming with Scala.

What it is good for

The chain of responsibility design pattern should be used when we want to decouple a sender of a request from the receivers and have these receivers separated into their own entities. It is good for creating pipelines and handling events.

What it is not so good for

As a negative and a possible pitfall of the chain of responsibility design pattern, we will talk about the implementation involving partial functions. This is because it might not always be able to achieve what the developers want, and this could further complicate code and affect readability.

The interpreter design pattern

In modern programming, we sometimes have to deal with problems from well-understood and well-defined domains. In some cases, it makes sense to represent the domain with a language, which could then make it easy to solve problems using an interpreter.

 The interpreter design pattern is useful for specifying how to evaluate sentences in a language by representing it using classes and building syntax trees to evaluate the language expressions.

The interpreter design pattern makes use of the composite design pattern as well. Some common uses of interpreters are for language parsing, protocols, and so on.

An example class diagram

Creating a language and grammar is a complicated task and before getting into it, developers should be confident that it is actually worth the effort. It requires a really good understanding of the domain that is being modeled and usually takes some time. In this section, we will present the class diagram concerning the interpreter part of a program that parses and evaluates an expression in *reverse Polish notation*. This is an important concept in computer science and it shows how computers actually work in performing different operations. The screenshot is shown as follows:

```
volcom@volcom-Dell-System-XPS-L502X:~/workspace/scala-book/behavioral-design-pat
terns$ java -cp target/behavioral-1.0.0-SNAPSHOT.jar com.ivan.nikolov.behavioral
.interpreter.RPNExample
The result of '1 2 + 3 * 9 10 + -' is: -10
The result of '1 2 3 4 5 * * - +' is: -57
'12 -' is invalid.
```

The main concept of our language is the `Expression`. Everything is an expression, which is being interpreted.

We can distinguish two main types of expressions in our diagram:

- **Terminal expression**: This is the `Number` class. It is a terminal in the sense that when building the syntax tree of an expression, it has no other children (leaf node).
- **Nonterminal expression**: These are the `Add`, `Subtract`, and `Multiply` classes. They have children expressions and this is how the entire syntax tree is built.

The preceding screenshot shows only those expressions into which the interpreter will be converting our language. In the following subsection, we will additionally show all the other classes that can make such an application work.

A code example

Here, we will show the code of our interpreter application step by step. We currently have some limitations such as only supporting integers, not having a good error reporting mechanism, and only having three operations, but it is easy to add new ones. You could try and build on top of what we already have.

First of all, let's see the base Expression trait:

```
trait Expression {
  def interpret(): Int
}
```

It is really simple and contains one method that other expressions will have to implement. The terminal expression, which is our Number class, looks like the following:

```
class Number(n: Int) extends Expression {
  override def interpret(): Int = n
}
```

It doesn't do anything special—just returns the number it carries when interpret is called. The nonterminal expressions have a bit more code, but they are all really simple:

```
class Add(right: Expression, left: Expression) extends Expression {
  override def interpret(): Int = left.interpret() + right.interpret()
}

class Subtract(right: Expression, left: Expression) extends Expression {
  override def interpret(): Int = left.interpret() - right.interpret()
}

class Multiply(right: Expression, left: Expression) extends Expression {
  override def interpret(): Int = left.interpret() * right.interpret()
}
```

So far, this is everything that we showed in our diagram, and it is the essential part of the interpreter design pattern. Some people might notice that everywhere in the constructors, we have the right-hand expression first and then the left-hand one. This was done on purpose as it would make the code much cleaner later, when we actually implement our parser.

From now on, we will show how to parse and use the design pattern in real applications. First of all, we need to create a factory that is based on a token that decides which expression it should return:

```
object Expression {
  def apply(operator: String, left: => Expression, right: => Expression):
Option[Expression] =
    operator match {
      case "+" => Some(new Add(right, left))
      case "-" => Some(new Subtract(right, left))
      case "*" => Some(new Multiply(right, left))
      case i if i.matches("\\d+") => Some(new Number(i.toInt))
      case _ => None
    }
}
```

In the preceding code, we applied some of the techniques and design patterns that we already went through—factory and by-name parameters. The latter are really important, as based on which case our code hit determines whether they will be evaluated or not.

We have a parser class that looks like the following:

```
class RPNParser {
  def parse(expression: String): Expression = {
    val tokenizer = new StringTokenizer(expression)
    tokenizer.asScala.foldLeft(mutable.Stack[Expression]()) {
      case (result, token) =>
        val item = Expression(token.toString, result.pop(), result.pop())
        item.foreach(result.push)
        result
    }.pop()
  }
}
```

Here, we relied on a `StringTokenizer` and a stack. We used the factory method we defined before, and this is where the interesting part is—pop will be called on the stack only if we fall in an operator case. It will be called in the order in which we use the parameters inside the factory.

Popping elements from the stack

As you can see from the preceding code, in the factory, we used by-name parameters and everywhere we first access the right parameter and then the left parameter. This, and the fact that our expression classes have the right parameter specified first, makes our code cleaner and makes sure that everything works as expected. The reason this is done is because of the fact that we rely on a stack and it reverses the operator order.

After we process an expression, if everything goes well, we should have only one element in the stack, which will have the complete tree. Then, we will have an interpreter class that just gets an expression and calls the `interpret` method on it:

```
class RPNInterpreter {
  def interpret(expression: Expression): Int = expression.interpret()
}
```

Finally, let's see an application that uses our language and the interpreter design pattern:

```
object RPNExample {
  def main(args: Array[String]): Unit = {
    val expr1 = "1 2 + 3 * 9 10 + -" // (1 + 2) * 3 - (9 + 10) = -10
    val expr2 = "1 2 3 4 5 * * - +" // 1 + 2 - 3 * 4 * 5 = -57
    val expr3 = "12 -" // invalid
    val parser = new RPNParser
    val interpreter = new RPNInterpreter
    System.out.println(s"The result of '${expr1}' is:
     ${interpreter.interpret(parser.parse(expr1))}")
    System.out.println(s"The result of '${expr2}' is:
     ${interpreter.interpret(parser.parse(expr2))}")
    try {
      System.out.println(s"The result is:
       ${interpreter.interpret(parser.parse(expr3))}")
    } catch {
      case _: Throwable => System.out.println(s"'$expr3' is invalid.")
    }
  }
}
```

The output of this application will be the following:

```
volcom@volcom-Dell-System-XPS-L502X:~/workspace/scala-book/behavioral-design-pat
terns$ java -cp target/behavioral-1.0.0-SNAPSHOT.jar com.ivan.nikolov.behavioral
.interpreter.RPNExample
The result of '1 2 + 3 * 9 10 + -' is: -10
The result of '1 2 3 4 5 * * - +' is: -57
'12 -' is invalid.
```

As you can see, our code correctly evaluates the expressions. There are, of course, some improvements that can be made and they are mainly related to error handling and parsing, but this is out of the scope of this subsection. In this subsection, we saw how to use the interpreter design pattern.

What it is good for

The interpreter design pattern is good for applications that deal with well-defined and well-understood domains. They could greatly simplify the application code. You should not confuse the interpreter design pattern with parsing, even though we needed parsing in order to build our expressions.

What it is not so good for

Creating languages and grammar is not an easy job. Developers should thoroughly evaluate the problems they are trying to solve before deciding to use this design pattern.

Summary

In this chapter, we went through the first group of behavioral design patterns. We looked at the value object, null object, strategy, command, the chain of responsibility, and interpreter. As in the previous chapters, we saw that some of these patterns have better alternatives that use the more powerful and flexible features of Scala. In many cases, there are multiple different ways to implement the same design pattern. We've tried to show some good ones and we've also tried to avoid repetition in the cases where more design patterns can use the same features of the Scala programming language. By now, you should have enough knowledge in order to actually use an alternative implementation by yourself when told which approach to use, based on what we've already shown.

We've given some pointers that should help in figuring out what to look for when writing software and identifying potential places to apply behavioral design patterns.

In the following chapter, we will look at the next group of behavioral design patterns, which also puts an end to the *Gang of Four* design patterns we've been focusing on.

9
Behavioral Design Patterns – Part Two

The group of behavioral design patterns is a relatively big one. In the previous chapter, we looked at the first part of behavioral design patterns and understood what their purpose is. As we already know, these patterns are used to deal with behavior and modeling object communication in computer programs.

In this chapter, we will continue going through the different behavioral design patterns as seen from the point of view of Scala. We will look at the following topics:

- Iterator
- Mediator
- Memento
- Observer
- State
- Template method
- Visitor

The design patterns that we will cover in this chapter might not be as relevant to functional programming as some of the others we've seen earlier. They might look like Scala implementations of Java design patterns and this will actually be the case. However, this does not make them unnecessary and they are still important due to the hybrid nature of Scala.

As in the previous chapters, we will follow the same structure, give a pattern definition, show a class diagram and a code example, and talk about the pros and cons of the specific design pattern.

The iterator design pattern

We use iterators in software projects all the time. When we traverse a list or go through the items of a set or a map, we use an **iterator**.

> The iterator design pattern provides a way to access the elements of an aggregate object (collection) in a sequential manner without exposing the underlying representation of the items.

When using the iterator design pattern, the developer doesn't need to know whether there is a linked list, array, tree, or a hash map underneath.

Example class diagram

Using the iterator design pattern, we can create our own objects that act as collections and we can use them in loops. In Java, there is an interface called `Iterator`, which we can implement for this purpose. In Scala, we can mix in the `Iterator` trait and implement its `hasNext` and `next` methods.

For the class diagram and the example, let's have a **ClassRoom** class that will support a foreach loop running through all students. The following diagram shows our class diagram:

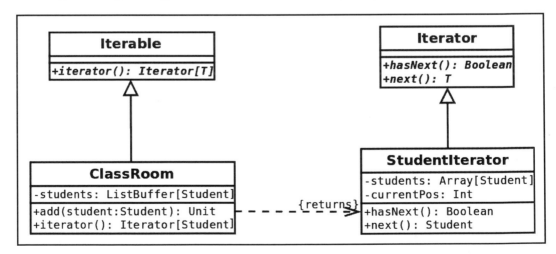

We've decided on our **ClassRoom** class to implement **Iterable**, which should return an **Iterator** and then return a new instance of our iterator when the method is called. The iterator design pattern is represented by the right-hand side of the diagram. The rest of the diagram is something we've done to make working with our class easier.

Code example

Let's see the code that implements the preceding diagram. First of all, the Student class is simply a case class that looks as follows:

```
case class Student(name: String, age: Int)
```

We have implemented the standard Scala Iterator trait in the StudentIterator class. Here is the implementation:

```
class StudentIterator(students: Array[Student]) extends Iterator[Student] {
  var currentPos = 0

  override def hasNext: Boolean = currentPos < students.size

  override def next(): Student = {
    val result = students(currentPos)
    currentPos = currentPos + 1
    result
  }
}
```

One thing to know about iterators is that they work in only one direction and you cannot go back. That's why we simply use a currentPos variable to remember how far we are in an iteration. We have used a mutable variable here, which is against the Scala principles; however, this is just an example and it is not too critical. In practice, you would probably use the iterator design pattern in conjunction with data structures, rather than in this form. The reason we've chosen the underlying structure of the iterator to be an Array is that indexing access of arrays is constant and it will improve the performance of large collections and keep our implementation simple.

The preceding code is really enough to show the iterator design pattern. The rest of the code is here to help us show how it can be used. Let's have a look at the ClassRoom class:

```
import scala.collection.mutable.ListBuffer

class ClassRoom extends Iterable[Student] {
  val students: ListBuffer[Student] = ListBuffer[Student]()
```

```
  def add(student: Student): Unit = {
    student +=: students
  }

  override def iterator: Iterator[Student] = new
StudentIterator(students.toArray)
}
```

We mix in the `Iterable` trait in the preceding code and implement its `iterator` method. We return our `StudentIterator`.

 We've created a custom iterator just as an example. However, in reality, you would just implement `Iterable` in the `ClassRoom` class and return the iterator of the underlying collection (students, in this case).

Let's see an example that uses our `ClassRoom` class:

```
object ClassRoomExample {
  def main(args: Array[String]): Unit = {
    val classRoom = new ClassRoom
    classRoom.add(Student("Ivan", 26))
    classRoom.add(Student("Maria", 26))
    classRoom.add(Student("John", 25))
    classRoom.foreach(println)
  }
}
```

The fact that we have mixed in the `Iterable` trait allows us to use `foreach`, `map`, `flatMap`, and many others on an object of the `ClassRoom` type. The following screenshot shows the output of our example:

```
volcom@volcom-Dell-System-XPS-L502X:~/workspace/scala-book/behavioral-design-pat
terns$ java -cp target/behavioral-1.0.0-SNAPSHOT.jar com.ivan.nikolov.behavioral
.iterator.ClassRoomExample
Student(John,25)
Student(Maria,26)
Student(Ivan,26)
```

As you can see in this example, the user of our `ClassRoom` class has no idea about the underlying data structure that holds our `Student` objects. We could replace it at any time (we can even get the data of the students from a database) and the entire code will keep working as long as we still have the `Iterable` trait in our class.

What it is good for

The iterator design pattern is used all the time in software engineering. It is probably one of the most often used design patterns and everyone knows about it. It is used with almost all collections one can think of, it is pretty simple, and allows us to hide the details of how a composite object is internally organized.

What it is not so good for

One obvious drawback of our implementation, which shows a possible problem with the iteration design pattern, is its use in parallel code. What would happen if another thread adds or removes objects to or from the original collection? Our iterator will not reflect that and it could lead to problems due to lack of synchronization. Making iterators capable of handling multithreaded environments is not a simple task.

The mediator design pattern

Real-world software projects usually contain a large number of different classes. This helps to distribute complexity and logic so that each class does one specific thing, which is simple, rather than many complex tasks. This, however, requires classes to communicate with each other in some way in order to realize some specific functionality, but then keeping the loose coupling principle in place could become a challenge.

The purpose of the mediator design pattern is to define an object that encapsulates how a set of other objects interact with each other in order to promote loose coupling and allow us to vary class interactions independently.

The mediator design pattern defines a specific object called **mediator** that enables other ones to communicate with each other instead of doing this directly. This reduces dependencies between them, which makes a program easy to change and maintain in the future as well as have it properly tested.

Example class diagram

Let's imagine that we are building a system for a school where each student can take multiple classes and each class is taken by multiple students. We might want to have a functionality that notifies all the students of a specific class that it is canceled, or we might want to easily add or remove users from classes. We can impulsively start writing our code and have a list of classes as a part of the `student` class and a list of students in the `group` class. This way, however, our objects will become interconnected and not really reusable. This is a good use case for the mediator pattern.

Let's take a look at our class diagram:

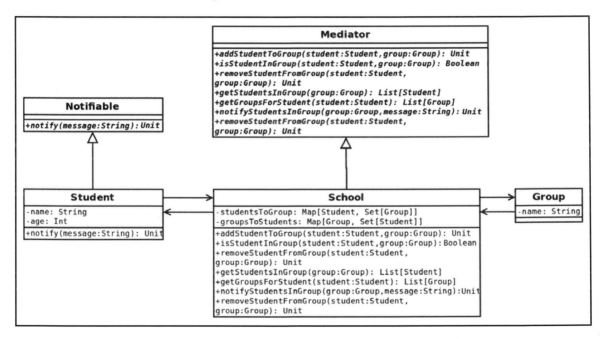

As you can see from the preceding diagram, the school is the mediator and it contains information about users to groups and groups to users. It manages the interaction between these entities and allows us to make our **Student** and **Group** classes reusable and independent from each other.

We've given an example with students and classes; however, this could be easily applied to any many-to-many relationships—permission groups in software, taxi systems, air traffic control systems, and many more.

Code example

Now that we have presented our class diagram, let's take a look at the source code for the example. First of all, let's see the model classes we have:

```scala
trait Notifiable {
  def notify(message: String)
}

case class Student(name: String, age: Int) extends Notifiable {
  override def notify(message: String): Unit = {
    System.out.println(s"Student $name was notified with message:
    '$message'.")
  }
}

case class Group(name: String)
```

The `Notifiable` trait in the preceding code is not needed in the current example; however, for example, if we add teachers, then it would be useful in the cases where we want to send notifications to everyone in the same group. The classes in the previous code can have their own independent functionality.

Our `Mediator` trait has the following definition:

```scala
trait Mediator {
  def addStudentToGroup(student: Student, group: Group)

  def isStudentInGroup(student: Student, group: Group): Boolean

  def removeStudentFromGroup(student: Student, group: Group)

  def getStudentsInGroup(group: Group): List[Student]

  def getGroupsForStudent(student: Student): List[Group]

  def notifyStudentsInGroup(group: Group, message: String)
}
```

As you can see, the preceding code defines methods that allow interactions between students and groups. The implementation of these methods is as follows:

```scala
import scala.collection.mutable.Map
import scala.collection.mutable.Set

class School extends Mediator {
  val studentsToGroups: Map[Student, Set[Group]] = Map()
```

```scala
  val groupsToStudents: Map[Group, Set[Student]] = Map()

  override def addStudentToGroup(student: Student, group: Group): Unit = {
    studentsToGroups.getOrElseUpdate(student, Set()) += group
    groupsToStudents.getOrElseUpdate(group, Set()) += student
  }

  override def isStudentInGroup(student: Student, group: Group): Boolean =
    groupsToStudents.getOrElse(group, Set()).contains(student) &&
      studentsToGroups.getOrElse(student, Set()).contains(group)

  override def getStudentsInGroup(group: Group): List[Student] =
    groupsToStudents.getOrElse(group, Set()).toList

  override def getGroupsForStudent(student: Student): List[Group] =
studentsToGroups.getOrElse(student, Set()).toList

  override def notifyStudentsInGroup(group: Group, message: String): Unit =
{
    groupsToStudents.getOrElse(group, Set()).foreach(_.notify(message))
  }

  override def removeStudentFromGroup(student: Student, group: Group): Unit
= {
    studentsToGroups.getOrElse(student, Set()) -= group
    groupsToStudents.getOrElse(group, Set()) -= student
  }
}
```

The `School` is the actual mediator that our application will be using. As you can see, it does exactly what the mediator design pattern is supposed to do—keeps the objects from directly referring to each other and internally defines their interactions. An application that uses our `School` class is shown in the following code:

```scala
object SchoolExample {
  def main(args: Array[String]): Unit = {
    val school = new School
    // create students
    val student1 = Student("Ivan", 26)
    val student2 = Student("Maria", 26)
    val student3 = Student("John", 25)
    // create groups
    val group1 = Group("Scala design patterns")
    val group2 = Group("Databases")
    val group3 = Group("Cloud computing")
    school.addStudentToGroup(student1, group1)
    school.addStudentToGroup(student1, group2)
```

```
    school.addStudentToGroup(student1, group3)
    school.addStudentToGroup(student2, group1)
    school.addStudentToGroup(student2, group3)
    school.addStudentToGroup(student3, group1)
    school.addStudentToGroup(student3, group2)
    // notify
    school.notifyStudentsInGroup(group1, "Design patterns in Scala
    are amazing!")
    // see groups
    System.out.println(s"$student3 is in groups:
     ${school.getGroupsForStudent(student3)}")
    // remove from group
    school.removeStudentFromGroup(student3, group2)
    System.out.println(s"$student3 is in groups:
     ${school.getGroupsForStudent(student3)}")
    // see students in group
    System.out.println(s"Students in $group1 are
     ${school.getStudentsInGroup(group1)}")
  }
}
```

The preceding example application is really simple—it creates objects of the Student and Group types and uses the mediator object to wire them up and make it possible for them to interact. The output of the example is as follows:

```
volcom@volcom-Dell-System-XPS-L502X:~/workspace/scala-book/behavioral-design-pat
terns$ java -cp target/behavioral-1.0.0-SNAPSHOT.jar com.ivan.nikolov.behavioral
.mediator.SchoolExample
Student Ivan was notified with message: 'Design patterns in Scala are amazing!'.
Student John was notified with message: 'Design patterns in Scala are amazing!'.
Student Maria was notified with message: 'Design patterns in Scala are amazing!'
.
Student(John,25) is in groups: List(Group(Databases), Group(Scala design pattern
s))
Student(John,25) is in groups: List(Group(Scala design patterns))
Students in Group(Scala design patterns) are List(Student(Ivan,26), Student(John
,25), Student(Maria,26))
```

As the output shows, our code does exactly what is expected, and it managed to keep the concepts loosely coupled in the application.

What it is good for

The mediator design pattern is good for keeping coupling between classes loose in an application. It helps to achieve simplicity and maintainability, while still allowing us to model complex interactions between objects in our applications.

What it is not so good for

A possible pitfall when using the mediator design pattern is to put a lot of different interaction functionalities in one class. Mediators tend to become more complex with time, and it will become hard to change or understand what our application can do at all. Moreover, if we actually have many more classes that have to interact with each other, it will imminently affect the mediator as well.

The memento design pattern

Depending on the software we are writing, we might have a requirement to be able to restore the state of an object back to its previous state.

 The purpose of the memento design pattern is to provide the ability to execute an undo action in order to restore an object to a previous state.

The original memento design pattern is implemented with the help of three main objects:

- `Originator`: The object whose state we want to be able to restore
- `Caretaker`: The object that triggers the changes to the `originator` object and uses the `memento` objects for rollback, if needed
- `Memento`: The object that carries the actual state of the originator and can be used to restore to one of the previous states

It is important to know that the `memento` object can be handled only by the originator. The caretaker and all other classes can just store it and nothing else.

Example class diagram

A classic example of the memento design pattern that comes to mind is text editors. We can always undo whatever we have changed. We will present something similar in our class diagram and example.

The following is the class diagram:

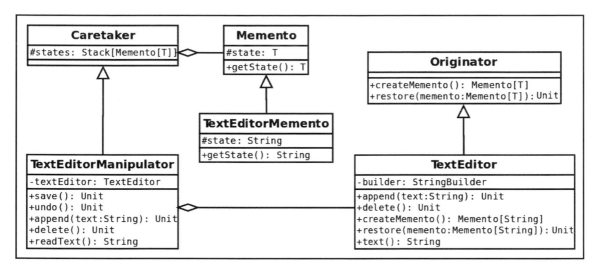

As you can see in the preceding diagram, our caretaker is the **TextEditorManipulator**. It automatically saves the state in the states stack on every manipulation. The **TextEditor** implements the **Originator** and creates a memento object and restores from one. Finally, the **TextEditorMemento** is the concrete memento object that our text editor will be using to save the state. Our state is just the current string representation of the text in the editor.

Code example

In this subsection, we will go through the text editor code one step at a time and see how the memento design pattern could be implemented in Scala.

First of all, let's see the Caretaker, Memento, and Originator traits:

```
trait Memento[T] {
  protected val state: T

  def getState(): T = state
}
```

```
trait Caretaker[T] {
  val states: mutable.Stack[Memento[T]] = mutable.Stack[Memento[T]]()
}

trait Originator[T] {
  def createMemento: Memento[T]

  def restore(memento: Memento[T])
}
```

We have used generics, and this allows us to reuse those traits multiple times when we want to implement the memento design pattern. Now, let's take a look at the specific implementations of the traits that are necessary in our application:

```
class TextEditor extends Originator[String] {
  private var builder: StringBuilder = new StringBuilder

  def append(text: String): Unit = {
    builder.append(text)
  }

  def delete(): Unit = {
    if (builder.nonEmpty) {
      builder.deleteCharAt(builder.length - 1)
    }
  }

  override def createMemento: Memento[String] = new
TextEditorMemento(builder.toString)

  override def restore(memento: Memento[String]): Unit = {
    this.builder = new StringBuilder(memento.getState())
  }

  def text(): String = builder.toString

  private class TextEditorMemento(val state: String) extends
Memento[String]
}
```

The preceding code shows the actual `Originator` implementation as well as the `Memento` one. It is common to create the memento class as being private to the object, which will be creating and restoring from the class, and that's why we have done the same. The reason for this is that the originator should be the only one who knows how to create and restore from a `memento` object and how to read its state.

Finally, let's take a look at the `Caretaker` implementation:

```
class TextEditorManipulator extends Caretaker[String] {
  private val textEditor = new TextEditor

  def save(): Unit = {
    states.push(textEditor.createMemento)
  }

  def undo(): Unit = {
    if (states.nonEmpty) {
      textEditor.restore(states.pop())
    }
  }

  def append(text: String): Unit = {
    save()
    textEditor.append(text)
  }

  def delete(): Unit = {
    save()
    textEditor.delete()
  }

  def readText(): String = textEditor.text()
}
```

In our implementation, the caretaker exposes methods to manipulate the `originator` object. Before every manipulation, we save the state to the stack in order to be able to rollback if needed at a future point.

Now that we've seen all the code for our example, let's see an application that uses it:

```
object TextEditorExample {
  def main(args: Array[String]): Unit = {
    val textEditorManipulator = new TextEditorManipulator
    textEditorManipulator.append("This is a chapter about memento.")
    System.out.println(s"The text is:
    '${textEditorManipulator.readText()}'")
```

```
        // delete 2 characters
        System.out.println("Deleting 2 characters...")
        textEditorManipulator.delete()
        textEditorManipulator.delete()
        // see the text
        System.out.println(s"The text is:
          '${textEditorManipulator.readText()}'")
        // undo
        System.out.println("Undoing...")
        textEditorManipulator.undo()
        System.out.println(s"The text is:
          '${textEditorManipulator.readText()}'")
        // undo again
        System.out.println("Undoing...")
        textEditorManipulator.undo()
        System.out.println(s"The text is:
          '${textEditorManipulator.readText()}'")
    }
}
```

In the preceding code, we just manually added some text to our text editor, deleted some characters, and then did an undo of the deletions. The following screenshot shows the output of this example:

```
volcom@volcom-Dell-System-XPS-L502X:~/workspace/scala-book/behavioral-design-pat
terns$ java -cp target/behavioral-1.0.0-SNAPSHOT.jar com.ivan.nikolov.behavioral
.memento.TextEditorExample
The text is: 'This is a chapter about memento.'
Deleting 2 characters...
The text is: 'This is a chapter about mement'
Undoing...
The text is: 'This is a chapter about memento'
Undoing...
The text is: 'This is a chapter about memento.'
```

One possible issue with our application design that might need improvement is the states stack—we have absolutely no limit and if a lot of changes are made, it could grow too much. In real text editors, we cannot go back infinitely, and this stack is limited to a certain number of operations. Another performance issue could be the fact that we call toString on the internal StringBuilder on each operation. Passing the actual StringBuilder, however, could have undesired effects on the application, as changes will affect all of the builder's references.

What it is good for

The memento design pattern is useful for applications that want to support a revertable state. In our example, we used a stack of states; however, this is not necessary—some applications might need only the last operation to be saved.

What it is not so good for

Developers should be careful when they use the memento design pattern. They should try to have the state saved in value objects if possible because if a mutable type is passed, it would be changed by reference and this will lead to unwanted results. Developers should also be careful about how far back in time they allow changes to be undoable because the more operations are saved in the stack, the more memory will be required. Finally, Scala is immutable and the memento design pattern does not always coincide with the language philosophy.

The observer design pattern

There are sometimes cases where some objects are interested in the state change of another object and want to perform some specific action when this happens. A common example could be whenever you click a button in an app; some other objects subscribe to the click event and perform some actions. The observer design pattern helps us to achieve this.

 The purpose of the observer design pattern is to have an object (called **subject**) that automatically notifies all of its observers of any state change by calling one of their methods.

The observer design pattern is employed in most GUI toolkits. It is also part of the MVC architectural pattern where the view is an observer. Java even comes with the `Observable` class and the `Observer` interface.

Example class diagram

For the class diagram, let's focus on the following example—we have a website with posts, and people can subscribe to get notifications whenever a new comment is added. The following diagram shows how something like this could be represented using the observer design pattern:

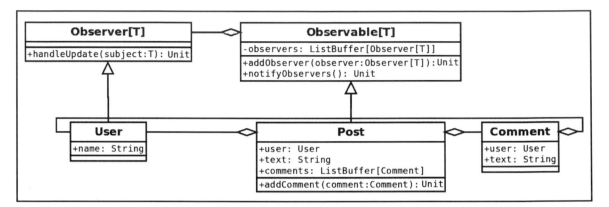

The **Post** class is our observable, and it has observers of the **User** type that are notified whenever the post changes (in our case, when a comment is added).

Note that the preceding scenario is just an example. In reality, subscriptions can be done in a database and people will receive an email notification. However, if we are talking about some kind of notification while you are on the site, then this example is valid.

 The observer pattern in the example could and probably should be replaced with reactive programming in Scala using Akka and actors. This way, we could achieve much better scalability and implement a proper asynchronous publish-subscribe system.

In the following subsection, we will take a look at the code that represents the preceding diagram.

Code example

Now, let's go through all the code that represents the preceding diagram. First, let's see the `Observer` interface. We have decided to have it as a trait that can be mixed in any class:

```
trait Observer[T] {
  def handleUpdate(subject: T)
}
```

This is extremely simple. Next, we will take a look at the `Observable` class. It is a trait that can also be mixed in and can make classes observable:

```
trait Observable[T] {
  this: T =>
  private val observers = ListBuffer[Observer[T]]()

  def addObserver(observer: Observer[T]): Unit = {
    observers.+=:(observer)
  }

  def notifyObservers(): Unit = {
    observers.foreach(_.handleUpdate(this))
  }
}
```

In the preceding code, we have used a self-type in order to make sure that we limit how the `Observable` trait is mixed in. This makes sure that the parameterized type will be the same as that of the object we are mixing it into.

Our implementation of the `Observer` interface will be our `User` class. It has the following code:

```
case class User(name: String) extends Observer[Post] {
  override def handleUpdate(subject: Post): Unit = {
    System.out.println(s"Hey, I'm ${name}. The post got some new comments:
${subject.comments}")
  }
}
```

It is as simple as implementing one method and doing something with the changed `Post` subject.

The `Comment` class is just a simple model class that has nothing special about it:

```
case class Comment(user: User, text: String)
```

The `Post` class will be `Observable`. On every comment that is added, this class will notify all the registered observers. The code is as follows:

```
case class Post(user: User, text: String) extends Observable[Post] {
  val comments = ListBuffer[Comment]()

  def addComment(comment: Comment): Unit = {
    comments.+=:(comment)
    notifyObservers()
  }
}
```

All the preceding code snippets implement our observer design pattern. It is interesting to see how this works in an example. The following block of code has an example of how our classes can be used together:

```
object PostExample extends LazyLogging {
  def main(args: Array[String]): Unit = {
    val userIvan = User("Ivan")
    val userMaria = User("Maria")
    val userJohn = User("John")
    logger.info("Create a post")
    val post = Post(userIvan, "This is a post about the observer
      design pattern")
    logger.info("Add a comment")
    post.addComment(Comment(userIvan, "I hope you like the post!"))
    logger.info("John and Maria subscribe to the comments.")
    post.addObserver(userJohn)
    post.addObserver(userMaria)
    logger.info("Add a comment")
    post.addComment(Comment(userIvan, "Why are you so quiet? Do you
      like it?"))
    logger.info("Add a comment")
    post.addComment(Comment(userMaria, "It is amazing! Thanks!"))
  }
}
```

The output of our application is shown as follows:

```
volcom@volcom-Dell-System-XPS-L502X:~/workspace/scala-book/behavioral-design-pat
terns$ java -cp target/behavioral-1.0.0-SNAPSHOT.jar com.ivan.nikolov.behavioral
.observer.PostExample
[main] INFO  com.ivan.nikolov.behavioral.observer.PostExample$  - Create a post
[main] INFO  com.ivan.nikolov.behavioral.observer.PostExample$  - Add a comment
[main] INFO  com.ivan.nikolov.behavioral.observer.PostExample$  - John and Maria
 subscribe to the comments.
[main] INFO  com.ivan.nikolov.behavioral.observer.PostExample$  - Add a comment
Hey, I'm Maria. The post got some new comments: ListBuffer(Comment(User(Ivan),Wh
y are you so quiet? Do you like it?), Comment(User(Ivan),I hope you like the pos
t!))
Hey, I'm John. The post got some new comments: ListBuffer(Comment(User(Ivan),Why
 are you so quiet? Do you like it?), Comment(User(Ivan),I hope you like the post
!))
[main] INFO  com.ivan.nikolov.behavioral.observer.PostExample$  - Add a comment
Hey, I'm Maria. The post got some new comments: ListBuffer(Comment(User(Maria),I
t is amazing! Thanks!), Comment(User(Ivan),Why are you so quiet? Do you like it?
), Comment(User(Ivan),I hope you like the post!))
Hey, I'm John. The post got some new comments: ListBuffer(Comment(User(Maria),It
 is amazing! Thanks!), Comment(User(Ivan),Why are you so quiet? Do you like it?)
, Comment(User(Ivan),I hope you like the post!))
```

As you can see in the preceding screenshot, the observer design pattern is quite easy to implement. As we mentioned earlier, a better approach would be to use reactive programming in order to make things asynchronous and more scalable. It will be more functional as well. We will see an example of how this can be done with Akka in the future chapters of this book.

What it is good for

The observer design pattern is easy to implement and allows us to add new observers or remove old observers at runtime. It helps to decouple logic and communication, which makes for some good quality classes that have only one responsibility.

What it is not so good for

In functional programming with Scala, one would possibly prefer using Akka and creating a publish-subscribe design instead. Moreover, in the observer design pattern, object references are held in the observer's collection of the subject, which could cause memory leaks or unnecessary allocations during the lifetime of the application or the subject object. Finally, as with any other design pattern, the observer design pattern should be used only where necessary. Otherwise, we might end up complicating our application for no good reason.

The state design pattern

The state design pattern is really similar to the strategy design pattern that we looked at in the previous chapter.

> The purpose of the state design pattern is to allow us to choose a different behavior of an object based on the object's internal state.

Basically, the difference between the state design pattern and the strategy design pattern comes from the following two points:

- The strategy design pattern is about *how* an action is performed. It is usually an algorithm that produces the same results as other algorithms.
- The state design pattern is about *what* action is performed. Depending on the state, an object could be doing different things.

Implementing the state design pattern also closely resembles the implementation of the strategy design pattern.

Example class diagram

Imagine a media player. Most media players have a play button—when we activate it, it usually changes its appearance and becomes a pause button. Clicking the pause button now also does something different—it pauses the playback and reverts to a play button. This is a good candidate for the state design pattern, where depending on which state the player is in, a different action happens.

The following class diagram shows the classes that are needed to implement this functionality for the play and pause buttons:

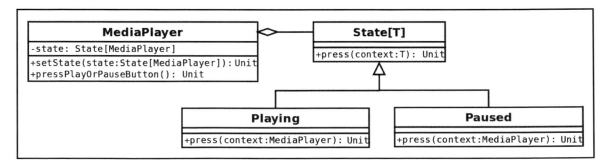

Our **Playing** and **Paused** implementations set the state to the opposite one and make our player functional. Using the state design pattern also makes our code much more elegant—we could, of course, use if statements and depending on the value, perform different actions. However, it could easily get out of control when there are many states.

Code example

Let's have a look at the code for the class diagram that we showed previously. First of all, let's see the `State` trait:

```
trait State[T] {
  def press(context: T)
}
```

It is really simple and allows the extending classes to implement the `press` method. We have two implementations according to our class diagram:

```
class Playing extends State[MediaPlayer] {
  override def press(context: MediaPlayer): Unit = {
    System.out.println("Pressing pause.")
    context.setState(new Paused)
  }
}

class Paused extends State[MediaPlayer] {
  override def press(context: MediaPlayer): Unit = {
    System.out.println("Pressing play.")
    context.setState(new Playing)
  }
}
```

We have made them simple and they only print a relevant message and then change the current state to the opposite state.

Our model defines a `MediaPlayer` class, which looks as follows:

```
case class MediaPlayer() {
  private var state: State[MediaPlayer] = new Paused

  def pressPlayOrPauseButton(): Unit = {
    state.press(this)
  }
}
```

```
    def setState(state: State[MediaPlayer]): Unit = {
      this.state = state
    }
}
```

This really is everything we need. Now, we can use our media player in the following application:

```
object MediaPlayerExample {
  def main(args: Array[String]): Unit = {
    val player = MediaPlayer()
    player.pressPlayOrPauseButton()
    player.pressPlayOrPauseButton()
    player.pressPlayOrPauseButton()
    player.pressPlayOrPauseButton()
  }
}
```

If we run the preceding code, we will see the following output:

```
volcom@volcom-Dell-System-XPS-L502X:~/workspace/scala-book/behavioral-design-pat
terns$ java -cp target/behavioral-1.0.0-SNAPSHOT.jar com.ivan.nikolov.behavioral
.state.MediaPlayerExample
Pressing play.
Pressing pause.
Pressing play.
Pressing pause.
```

As you can see in the example output, the state changes on every button press and it performs a different action, which we've illustrated using a different print message.

A possible improvement to our application would involve making the state objects singletons. As you can see, they are always the same, so there really is no need to create new ones every single time.

What it is good for

The state design pattern is really useful for making code readable and getting rid of conditional statements.

What it is not so good for

The state design pattern has no major drawbacks. One thing that developers should be careful about is the side effects caused by the change of the state of objects.

The template method design pattern

Sometimes when we implement some algorithm or a family of algorithms, we define a common skeleton. Then later, the different implementations deal with the specifics of each method in the skeleton. The template method design pattern allows us to achieve what we mentioned previously.

 The purpose of the template method design pattern is to defer algorithm steps to subclasses using template methods.

The template method design pattern seems really natural to object-oriented programming. Whenever polymorphism is used, this actually represents the design pattern itself. Usually, the template method is implemented using abstract methods.

Example class diagram

The template method design pattern is suitable for implementing frameworks. A typical thing here is that algorithms usually perform the same set of steps, and then these steps are implemented differently by different clients. You can come up with various possible use cases.

For our example, let's imagine that we want to write an application that will read some data from a data source, parse it, and find whether there is an object that satisfies some condition and returns it. If we think about it, we have the following main operations:

- Read the data
- Parse the data
- Search for items satisfying the condition
- Clean up any resources if needed

The following diagram shows the class diagram of our code:

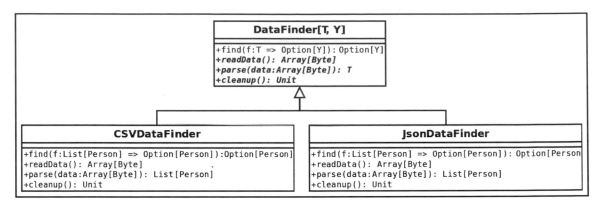

We have used an example that we've shown before—reading data about people from files. Here, however, we use it in order to find data of the person that satisfies a filtering function. Using the template method design pattern, we can have the list of the people read from files with different formats from a server, database, or anything that comes to mind, really. Using polymorphism, our application makes sure that the right methods are called and everything works correctly.

Code example

Let's go through the code that represents the preceding diagram and take a look at what it does. First of all, our model `Person` class:

```
case class Person(name: String, age: Int, address: String)
```

There is nothing special about it. Now, let's move on to the interesting part—the `DataFinder` class:

```
abstract class DataFinder[T, Y] {
  def find(f: T => Option[Y]): Option[Y] =
    try {
      val data = readData()
      val parsed = parse(data)
      f(parsed)
    } finally {
      cleanup()
    }

  def readData(): Array[Byte]
```

```
    def parse(data: Array[Byte]): T

    def cleanup()
}
```

We have used generics in order to make this class usable for various types. As you can see in the preceding code, three of the methods of the DataFinder class have no implementations, but they are still referred to in the find method. The latter is the actual template method, and the abstract methods will be implemented in the different classes that extend the DataFinder.

For our example, we have provided two different implementations, one for JSON and one for the CSV files. The JSON finder looks as follows:

```
import org.json4s.{StringInput, DefaultFormats}
import org.json4s.jackson.JsonMethods

class JsonDataFinder extends DataFinder[List[Person], Person] {
  implicit val formats = DefaultFormats

  override def readData(): Array[Byte] = {
    val stream = this.getClass.getResourceAsStream("people.json")
    Stream.continually(stream.read).takeWhile(_ !=
-1).map(_.toByte).toArray
  }

  override def cleanup(): Unit = {
    System.out.println("Reading json: nothing to do.")
  }

  override def parse(data: Array[Byte]): List[Person] =
    JsonMethods.parse(StringInput(new String(data,
"UTF-8"))).extract[List[Person]]
}
```

The CSV finder has the following code:

```
import com.github.tototoshi.csv.CSVReader

class CSVDataFinder extends DataFinder[List[Person], Person] {
  override def readData(): Array[Byte] = {
    val stream = this.getClass.getResourceAsStream("people.csv")
    Stream.continually(stream.read).takeWhile(_ !=
-1).map(_.toByte).toArray
  }

  override def cleanup(): Unit = {
```

```
            System.out.println("Reading csv: nothing to do.")
        }

    override def parse(data: Array[Byte]): List[Person] =
        CSVReader.open(new InputStreamReader(new
ByteArrayInputStream(data))).all().map {
            case List(name, age, address) => Person(name, age.toInt, address)
        }
    }
```

Whenever we use it, depending on what specific instance we have, the `find` method will call the right implementations through polymorphism. It is possible to add new formats and data sources by extending the `DataFinder` class.

Using our data finders is now straightforward:

```
object DataFinderExample {
    def main(args: Array[String]): Unit = {
        val jsonDataFinder: DataFinder[List[Person], Person] = new
JsonDataFinder
        val csvDataFinder: DataFinder[List[Person], Person] = new CSVDataFinder
        System.out.println(s"Find a person with name Ivan in the json:
            ${jsonDataFinder.find(_.find(_.name == "Ivan"))}")
        System.out.println(s"Find a person with name James in the json:
            ${jsonDataFinder.find(_.find(_.name == "James"))}")
        System.out.println(s"Find a person with name Maria in the csv:
            ${csvDataFinder.find(_.find(_.name == "Maria"))}")
        System.out.println(s"Find a person with name Alice in the csv:
            ${csvDataFinder.find(_.find(_.name == "Alice"))}")
    }
}
```

We have provided some example data files. The CSV has the following contents:

```
Ivan,26,London
Maria,23,Edinburgh
John,36,New York
Anna,24,Moscow
```

The following data is for the JSON file:

```
[
    {
        "name": "Ivan",
        "age": 26,
        "address": "London"
    },
    {
```

```
      "name": "Maria",
      "age": 23,
      "address": "Edinburgh"
    },
    {
      "name": "John",
      "age": 36,
      "address": "New York"
    },
    {
      "name": "Anna",
      "age": 24,
      "address": "Moscow"
    }
  ]
```

Running the preceding example against these datasets will produce the following output:

```
volcom@volcom-Dell-System-XPS-L502X:~/workspace/scala-book/behavioral-design-pat
terns$ java -cp target/behavioral-1.0.0-SNAPSHOT.jar com.ivan.nikolov.behavioral
.template.DataFinderExample
Reading json: nothing to do.
Find a person with name Ivan in the json: Some(Person(Ivan,26,London))
Reading json: nothing to do.
Find a person with name James in the json: None
Reading csv: nothing to do.
Find a person with name Maria in the csv: Some(Person(Maria,23,Edinburgh))
Reading csv: nothing to do.
Find a person with name Alice in the csv: None
```

The code in our example uses an abstract class. This makes it slightly limiting in the sense that we can only extend one class. However, it would be straightforward to change the abstract class to a trait and then mix it into classes.

What it is good for

As you can see, whenever we have a use case where the structure of an algorithm is the same and we provide different implementations, we can use the template method design pattern. This is a really good fit for creating frameworks.

What it is not so good for

Whenever the frameworks we implement using the template method design pattern become large, it is harder to simply extend a huge class and implement a few of its methods. In cases like these, passing an interface to the constructor and using it in the skeleton might be a better idea (strategy design pattern).

The visitor design pattern

There are some applications out there where during design time, not all possible use cases are known. There might be new application features coming out from time to time, and in order to implement them, some refactoring has to be done.

 The visitor design pattern helps us add new operations to existing object structures without modifying them.

This helps us to design our structures separately and then use the visitor design pattern to add functionality on top.

Another case where the visitor design pattern could be useful is if we are building a big object structure with many different types of nodes that support different operations. Instead of creating a base node that has all the operations and only a few of them are implemented by the concrete nodes or use type casting, we could create visitors that will add the functionality we need where we need it.

Example class diagram

Initially, when a developer sees the visitor design pattern, it seems that it can be easily replaced using polymorphism and can rely on the dynamic types of the classes. However, what if we have a huge type hierarchy? In such a case, every single change will have to change an interface as well, which will lead to changing a whole bunch of classes, and so on.

For our class diagram and example, let's imagine that we are writing a text editor and we have documents. We want to be able to save each document in at least two data formats, but new ones could come. The following diagram shows the class diagram for our application that uses the visitor design pattern:

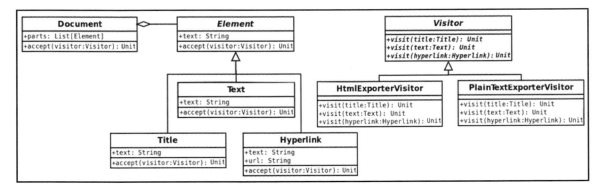

As you can see in the preceding diagram, we have two seemingly disconnected hierarchies. The one to the left represents our document—each document is simply a list of different elements. All of them subclass the **Element** abstract class, which has an `accept` method that accepts a **Visitor**. To the right, we have the visitor hierarchy—each of our visitors will mix in the `Visitor` trait, which contains the `visit` methods with overrides for each of our document elements.

The way the visitor pattern will work is that it will create an instance of `Visitor` depending on what needs to be done, and then it will be passed to the `Document accept` method. This way, we can add extra functionality really easily (different formats, in our case), and the extra functionality will not involve any changes to the model.

Code example

Let's take a step-by-step look at the code that implements the visitor design pattern for the previous example. First of all, we have our model of the document and all the elements that can build it:

```
abstract class Element(val text: String) {
  def accept(visitor: Visitor)
}

class Title(text: String) extends Element(text) {
  override def accept(visitor: Visitor): Unit = {
    visitor.visit(this)
```

```
    }
  }

  class Text(text: String) extends Element(text) {
    override def accept(visitor: Visitor): Unit = {
      visitor.visit(this)
    }
  }

  class Hyperlink(text: String, val url: String) extends Element(text) {
    override def accept(visitor: Visitor): Unit = {
      visitor.visit(this)
    }
  }

  class Document(parts: List[Element]) {
    def accept(visitor: Visitor): Unit = {
      parts.foreach(p => p.accept(visitor))
    }
  }
```

There is nothing special about the preceding code, just a simple subclassing for the different document elements and a composition for the Document class and the elements it contains. The important method here is accept. It takes a visitor, and since the trait type is given, we can pass different visitor implementations. In all the cases, it calls the visit method of the visitor with the current instance passed as a parameter.

Now, let's have a look on the other side—the Visitor trait and its implementations. The Visitor trait looks as simple as this:

```
trait Visitor {
  def visit(title: Title)
  def visit(text: Text)
  def visit(hyperlink: Hyperlink)
}
```

In this case, it has overloads of the visit method with different concrete element types. In the preceding code, the visitors and elements allow us to use **double dispatch** in order to determine which calls will be made.

Now, let's have a look at the concrete `Visitor` implementations. The first one is the
`HtmlExporterVisitor`:

```
class HtmlExporterVisitor extends Visitor {
  val line = System.getProperty("line.separator")
  val builder = new StringBuilder

  def getHtml(): String = builder.toString

  override def visit(title: Title): Unit = {
    builder.append(s"<h1>${title.text}</h1>").append(line)
  }

  override def visit(text: Text): Unit = {
    builder.append(s"<p>${text.text}</p>").append(line)
  }

  override def visit(hyperlink: Hyperlink): Unit = {
    builder.append(s"""<a
href=\"${hyperlink.url}\">${hyperlink.text}</a>""").append(line)
  }
}
```

It simply provides different implementations depending on what type of `Element` it gets.
There are no conditional statements, just overloads.

If we want to save the document we have in plain text, we can use the
`PlainTextExporterVisitor`:

```
class PlainTextExporterVisitor extends Visitor {
  val line = System.getProperty("line.separator")
  val builder = new StringBuilder

  def getText(): String = builder.toString

  override def visit(title: Title): Unit = {
    builder.append(title.text).append(line)
  }

  override def visit(text: Text): Unit = {
    builder.append(text.text).append(line)
  }

  override def visit(hyperlink: Hyperlink): Unit = {
    builder.append(s"${hyperlink.text} (${hyperlink.url})").append(line)
  }
}
```

After having the visitors and the document structure, wiring everything up is pretty straightforward:

```
object VisitorExample {
  def main(args: Array[String]): Unit = {
    val document = new Document(
      List(
        new Title("The Visitor Pattern Example"),
        new Text("The visitor pattern helps us add extra functionality
          without changing the classes."),
        new Hyperlink("Go check it online!", "https://www.google.com/"),
        new Text("Thanks!")
      )
    )
    val htmlExporter = new HtmlExporterVisitor
    val plainTextExporter = new PlainTextExporterVisitor
    System.out.println(s"Export to html:")
    document.accept(htmlExporter)
    System.out.println(htmlExporter.getHtml())
    System.out.println(s"Export to plain:")
    document.accept(plainTextExporter)
    System.out.println(plainTextExporter.getText())
  }
}
```

The preceding example shows how to use both the visitors we implemented. The output of our program is shown in the following screenshot:

```
volcom@volcom-Dell-System-XPS-L502X:~/workspace/scala-book/behavioral-design-pat
terns$ java -cp target/behavioral-1.0.0-SNAPSHOT.jar com.ivan.nikolov.behavioral
.visitor.VisitorExample
Export to html:
<h1>The Visitor Pattern Example</h1>
<p>The visitor pattern helps us add extra functionality without changing the cla
sses.</p>
<a href="https://www.google.com/">Go check it online!</a>
<p>Thanks!</p>

Export to plain:
The Visitor Pattern Example
The visitor pattern helps us add extra functionality without changing the classe
s.
Go check it online! (https://www.google.com/)
Thanks!
```

As you can see, using the visitor is simple. Adding new visitors and new formats in our case is even easier. We just need to create a class that implements all the visitor methods and use it.

The visitor design pattern the Scala way

As with many other design patterns we saw earlier, the visitor design pattern could be represented in a way that is less verbose and closer to Scala. The way things can be done in order to implement a visitor in Scala is the same as the strategy design pattern—pass functions to the `accept` method. Moreover, we can also use pattern matching instead of having multiple different `visit` methods in the `Visitor` trait.

In this subsection, we will show both the improvement steps. Let's start with the latter.

First of all, we need to make the model classes case classes in order to be able to use them in pattern matching:

```
abstract class Element(text: String) {
  def accept(visitor: Visitor)
}

case class Title(text: String) extends Element(text) {
  override def accept(visitor: Visitor): Unit = {
    visitor.visit(this)
  }
}

case class Text(text: String) extends Element(text) {
  override def accept(visitor: Visitor): Unit = {
    visitor.visit(this)
  }
}

case class Hyperlink(text: String, val url: String) extends Element(text) {
  override def accept(visitor: Visitor): Unit = {
    visitor.visit(this)
  }
}

class Document(parts: List[Element]) {
  def accept(visitor: Visitor): Unit = {
    parts.foreach(p => p.accept(visitor))
  }
}
```

Then, we change our `Visitor` trait to the following:

```
trait Visitor {
  def visit(element: Element)
}
```

Since we will be using pattern matching, we will only need one method to implement it. Finally, we can have our visitor implementations as follows:

```scala
class HtmlExporterVisitor extends Visitor {
  val line = System.getProperty("line.separator")
  val builder = new StringBuilder

  def getHtml(): String = builder.toString

  override def visit(element: Element): Unit = {
    element match {
      case Title(text) =>
        builder.append(s"<h1>${text}</h1>").append(line)
      case Text(text) =>
        builder.append(s"<p>${text}</p>").append(line)
      case Hyperlink(text, url) =>
        builder.append(s"""<a href=\"${url}\">${text}</a>""").append(line)
    }
  }
}

class PlainTextExporterVisitor extends Visitor {
  val line = System.getProperty("line.separator")
  val builder = new StringBuilder

  def getText(): String = builder.toString

  override def visit(element: Element): Unit = {
    element match {
      case Title(text) =>
        builder.append(text).append(line)
      case Text(text) =>
        builder.append(text).append(line)
      case Hyperlink(text, url) =>
        builder.append(s"${text} (${url})").append(line)
    }
  }
}
```

Pattern matching is similar to the `instanceOf` checks in Java; however, it is a powerful feature of Scala and it is quite commonly used. Our example, then, doesn't need to change at all and the output will be the same as before.

Next, we will show how we can pass functions instead of visitor objects. The fact that we will be passing functions means that now, we can change our model to the following:

```
abstract class Element(text: String) {
  def accept(visitor: Element => Unit): Unit = {
    visitor(this)
  }
}

case class Title(text: String) extends Element(text)

case class Text(text: String) extends Element(text)

case class Hyperlink(text: String, val url: String) extends Element(text)

class Document(parts: List[Element]) {
  def accept(visitor: Element => Unit): Unit = {
    parts.foreach(p => p.accept(visitor))
  }
}
```

We moved the `accept` method implementation to the base `Element` class (which can also be represented as a trait) and inside this, we simply called the function passed as parameter. Since we will be passing functions, we can get rid of the `Visitor` trait and its implementations. Everything we have now is the example, which looks as follows:

```
object VisitorExample {
  val line = System.getProperty("line.separator")

  def htmlExporterVisitor(builder: StringBuilder): Element => Unit = {
      case Title(text) =>
        builder.append(s"<h1>${text}</h1>").append(line)
      case Text(text) =>
        builder.append(s"<p>${text}</p>").append(line)
      case Hyperlink(text, url) => builder.append(s"""<a
href=\"${url}\">${text}</a>""").append(line)
    }

  def plainTextExporterVisitor(builder: StringBuilder): Element => Unit = {
      case Title(text) => builder.append(text).append(line)
      case Text(text) => builder.append(text).append(line)
      case Hyperlink(text, url) => builder.append(s"${text}
(${url})").append(line)
    }

  def main(args: Array[String]): Unit = {
    val document = new Document(
```

```
        List(
          Title("The Visitor Pattern Example"),
          Text("The visitor pattern helps us add extra functionality
           without changing the classes."),
          Hyperlink("Go check it online!", "https://www.google.com/"),
          Text("Thanks!")
        )
      )
      val html = new StringBuilder
      System.out.println(s"Export to html:")
      document.accept(htmlExporterVisitor(html))
      System.out.println(html.toString())
      val plain = new StringBuilder
      System.out.println(s"Export to plain:")
      document.accept(plainTextExporterVisitor(plain))
      System.out.println(plain.toString())
    }
  }
```

We have moved the visitor functionality inside the functions that are part of the `VisitorExample` object. In the initial examples, we had a `StringBuilder` as part of the visitor classes. We have used curried functions in order to be able to pass one here. Passing these functions to the `Document` structure is then straightforward. Again, the result here will be identical to the previous versions of the example. However, we can see how much code and boilerplate classes we have saved.

What it is good for

The visitor design pattern is really good for applications that have large object hierarchies, where adding a new functionality will involve a lot of refactoring. Whenever we need to be able to do multiple different things with an object hierarchy and when changing the object classes could be problematic, the visitor design pattern is a useful alternative.

What it is not so good for

As you saw in the initial version of our example, the visitor design pattern could be bulky and include quite a lot of boilerplate code. Moreover, if some component is not designed to support the pattern, we cannot really use it if we are not allowed to change the original code.

Summary

In this chapter, we went through the second group of behavioral design patterns. You are now familiar with iterators, mediators, memento, observer, state, template method, and the visitor design pattern. You might feel that these are purely object-oriented design patterns that don't have much to do with functional programming, and you would be correct. However, they are still relevant to Scala due to its hybrid nature and it is important to be aware of them and to know when to use them.

Some of the design patterns in this chapter are quite commonly used and can be seen in many projects, while others are a bit more rare and specific to some use cases. These patterns, combined with all the other ones you learned about in the previous chapters, can be used together in order to build elegant and powerful solutions to real-world problems.

In the next chapter, we will dive deep into functional programming theory. We will cover some advanced concepts that will show us how powerful Scala and functional programming languages in general are.

10
Functional Design Patterns – the Deep Theory

The Scala programming language is a hybrid between a functional and object-oriented language. Most of the object-oriented design patterns are still applicable. However, in order to facilitate the full power of Scala, you also need to be aware of the purely functional aspects of it. When using the language and reading tutorials or best practices, developers will most likely notice terms such as **monoids**, **monads**, and **functors** appearing more often as the problems become harder or the solutions are desired to be more elegant. In this chapter, we will focus on the following functional design patterns:

- Monoids
- Functors
- Monads

There are a lot of resources on the preceding topics all over the internet. The problem is that many of them are extremely theoretical and hard to understand by someone who is not really familiar with mathematics, and more specifically, category theory. As it happens, in practice, many developers lack the deep mathematical background needed to grasp the topics, and it is not unusual to completely avoid these concepts in the code.

In my experience, most of the Scala developers I know have tried to read tutorials on the topics covered in this chapter, and they've found these topics difficult to understand and have given up. Expert mathematicians seem to find these concepts much easier. However, despite repeated attempts at understanding, most people admit that they are not completely comfortable with the deep functional programming theory. In this chapter, we will try and present this theory in a way that is easy to understand, and we will give an idea of how and when to apply the theory.

Abstraction and vocabulary

A big part of programming is abstraction. We find common functionality, laws, and behavior and encapsulate them into classes, interfaces, functions, and so on, which are abstract and allow code reuse. Then, we refer to them and reuse them to minimize code duplication and the possibility of errors. Some of these abstractions are more common than others and are observed in different projects and used by more people. These abstractions lead to the creation of a common vocabulary, which additionally helps in communication and understanding. Everybody knows certain data structures such as trees and hash maps, and so there is no need to get into detail about them because their behavior and requirements are well-known. Similarly, when someone gains enough experience in design patterns, they can see them and easily apply the patterns to the problems they are trying to tackle.

In this chapter, we will try to look at monoids, monads, and functors from a point of view that will teach us how to recognize them and when to use them.

Monoids

All monoids, monads, and functors are derived from mathematics. One thing about this subject is that similarly to programming, it tries to find abstractions. If we try to map mathematics to programming, we can think about the different datatypes we have—`Int`, `Double`, `Long`, or custom datatypes. Each type can be characterized by the operations it supports and the laws of these operations, and this is called the *algebra* of the type.

Now, if we think about it, we can identify the operations that are shared by multiple types, for example, addition, multiplication, subtraction, and so on. Different types can share the same operations and they can conform to exactly the same laws. This is something we can take advantage of because this allows us to write generic programs that apply to different types that follow some specific rules.

What are monoids?

After the preceding brief introduction to monoids, let's get straight to business and look at a formal definition of a *monoid*:

A monoid is a purely algebraic structure, which means that it is defined only by its algebra. All monoids must conform to the so-called **monoid laws**.

The preceding definition is definitely not enough to have a good understanding of monoids, so let's break it into pieces in this section and try to come up with a better one.

First, let's clarify the term **algebraic structure**:

Algebraic: It is defined only by its algebra, for example, the operations it supports and the laws it conforms to.

Now that we know that monoids are defined only by the operations they support, let's have a look at the monoid laws:

- A monoid contains a T type.
- A monoid contains one associative binary operation. This means that for any x, y, and z of the T type, the following is true:
  op(op(x, y), z) == op(x, op(y, z)).
- A structure must have an *identity element*—zero. This element is characterized by the fact that the previous operation will always return the other element—op(x, zero) == x and op(zero, x) == x.

Other than the preceding laws, different monoids might not have absolutely anything to do with each other—they can have any type. Now let's look at a better definition of a monoid that would actually mean more to you as a developer:

A monoid is a type with an associative binary operation over it, which also has an identity element.

The monoid rules are extremely simple but they give us great power to write polymorphic functions based just on the fact that monoids always conform to the same rules. With the use of monoids, we can easily facilitate parallel computation and build complex calculations from small pieces.

Monoids in real life

We use monoids all the time without realizing it—string concatenation, sums of integers, products, Boolean operations, lists, and so on—they are all examples of monoids. Let's look at integer addition:

- **Our type**: Int.
- **Our associative operation**: add. It is indeed associative because ((1 + 2) + 3) == (1 + (2 + 3)).
- **Our identity element**: 0. It does nothing when added to another integer.

We can easily come up with similar examples for string concatenation, where the identity element will be an empty string, or for list concatenation, where the identity element will be an empty list, and many others. Similar examples can be found absolutely everywhere.

Everything we mentioned previously takes us to the following Scala representation of a monoid:

```
trait Monoid[T] {
  def op(l: T, r: T): T
  def zero: T
}
```

Starting from this base trait, we can define just about any monoid we want. The following are a few implementations of a integer addition monoid, integer multiplication monoid, and a string concatenation monoid:

```
package object monoids {
  val intAddition: Monoid[Int] = new Monoid[Int] {
    val zero: Int = 0

    override def op(l: Int, r: Int): Int = l + r
  }
  val intMultiplication: Monoid[Int] = new Monoid[Int] {
    val zero: Int = 1

    override def op(l: Int, r: Int): Int = l * r
  }
```

```
val stringConcatenation: Monoid[String] = new Monoid[String] {
  val zero: String = ""

  override def op(l: String, r: String): String = l + r
  }
}
```

Using the same framework as shown previously, we can define monoids for as many different types as we can think of, as long as they always satisfy the rules. However, you should note that not every operation follows the monoid rules. For example, integer division— $(6/3)/2 \mathrel{!=} 6/(3/2)$.

We saw how to write monoids. But how do we use them? What are they helpful for and can we just write generic functions based only on the rules we know? Of course we can, and we will see this in the following subsection.

Using monoids

In the preceding section, we already mentioned that monoids can be used for parallel computation and to build complex computations using small and simple chunks. Monoids can also be naturally used with lists and collections, in general.

In this subsection, we will look at different use cases with examples for monoids.

Monoids and foldable collections

To show how useful monoids are with collections that support the `foldLeft` and `foldRight` functions, let's take a look at the standard Scala list and the declarations of these two functions:

```
def foldLeft[B](z: B)(f: (B, A) => B): B

def foldRight[B](z: B)(f: (A, B) => B): B
```

Usually, the z parameter in these two functions is called the zero value, so if A and B are of the same type, we will end up with the following:

```
def foldLeft[A](z: A)(f: (A, A) => A): A

def foldRight[A](z: A)(f: (A, A) => A): A
```

Looking at the functions now, we can see that these are exactly monoid rules. This means that we can write an example as shown in the following code, which uses the monoids we created previously:

```
object MonoidFolding {
  def main(args: Array[String]): Unit = {
    val strings = List("This is\n", "a list of\n", "strings!")
    val numbers = List(1, 2, 3, 4, 5, 6)
    System.out.println(s"Left
folded:\n${strings.foldLeft(stringConcatenation.zero)(stringConcatenation.o
p)}")
    System.out.println(s"Right
folded:\n${strings.foldRight(stringConcatenation.zero)(stringConcatenation.
op)}")
    System.out.println(s"6! is:
${numbers.foldLeft(intMultiplication.zero)(intMultiplication.op)}")
  }
}
```

Another thing to note in the preceding code is that it doesn't actually matter for the final result whether we use `foldLeft` or `foldRight` because our monoids have an associative operation. It does, however, matter in terms of performance.

The output of the preceding example is as shown here:

```
volcom@volcom-Dell-System-XPS-L502X:~/workspace/scala-book/deep-theory$ java -cp
  target/deep-theory-1.0.0-SNAPSHOT.jar com.ivan.nikolov.monoids.Monoid
com.ivan.nikolov.monoids.Monoid
com.ivan.nikolov.monoids.MonoidFolding
volcom@volcom-Dell-System-XPS-L502X:~/workspace/scala-book/deep-theory$ java -cp
  target/deep-theory-1.0.0-SNAPSHOT.jar com.ivan.nikolov.monoids.MonoidFolding
Left folded:
 This is
a list of
strings!
Right folded:
 This is
a list of
strings!
6! is: 720
```

Looking at the preceding example, you can see that we can write a generic function that will fold a list using a monoid and do different things depending on the monoid operation. Here is the code for it:

```
object MonoidOperations {
  def fold[T](list: List[T], m: Monoid[T]): T = list.foldLeft(m.zero)(m.op)
}
```

We can now rewrite our example and use our generic function as follows:

```
object MonoidFoldingGeneric {
  def main(args: Array[String]): Unit = {
    val strings = List("This is\n", "a list of\n", "strings!")
    val numbers = List(1, 2, 3, 4, 5, 6)
    System.out.println(s"Left folded:\n${MonoidOperations.fold(strings,
      stringConcatenation)}")
    System.out.println(s"Right folded:\n${MonoidOperations.fold(strings,
      stringConcatenation)}")
    System.out.println(s"6! is: ${MonoidOperations.fold(numbers,
      intMultiplication)}")
  }
}
```

The output, of course, will be exactly the same. However, things are much neater now, and this is how monoids can become useful when used together with lists.

In the preceding examples, we made the A and B types to be the same in the foldLeft and foldRight functions. However, we might build a different data structure with a different type, or our algorithm might rely on a different type that has a different monoid to the type of the list we have. In order to support such a scenario, we have to add the possibility of mapping the type of the original list to a different type:

```
object MonoidOperations {
  def fold[T](list: List[T], m: Monoid[T]): T = foldMap(list, m)(identity)

  def foldMap[T, Y](list: List[T], m: Monoid[Y])(f: T => Y): Y =
    list.foldLeft(m.zero) {
      case (t, y) => m.op(t, f(y))
    }
}
```

The preceding code shows how our fold functions will change. This would give us the possibility of implementing even more complex operations on top of our lists using different types of monoids.

Monoids and parallel computations

The fact that a monoid operation is associative means that if we have to chain multiple operations, we could probably do it in parallel. For example, if we have the numbers 1, 2, 3, and 4 and wanted to find 4!, we can use what we used previously, which would end up being evaluated to the following:

```
op(op(op(1, 2), 3), 4)
```

The associativity, however, would allow us to do the following:

```
op(op(1, 2), op(3, 4))
```

Here, the nested operations could be done independently and in parallel. This is also called **balanced fold**. An implementation of a balanced fold would look like the following:

```
def balancedFold[T, Y](list: IndexedSeq[T], m: Monoid[Y])(f: T => Y): Y =
  if (list.length == 0) {
    m.zero
  } else if (list.length == 1) {
    f(list(0))
  } else {
    val (left, right) = list.splitAt(list.length / 2)
    m.op(balancedFold(left, m)(f), balancedFold(right, m)(f))
  }
```

It is worth mentioning that we've used an `IndexedSeq` here, as it will guarantee that getting elements by index will be efficient. Also, this code is not parallel, but we've switched the order of the operations as we mentioned previously. In the case of integers, it might not make much of a difference but for other types such as strings, it will improve the performance. The reason is that strings are immutable and every concatenation will create a new string by allocating new space. So, if we are simply going from the left-hand side to the right-hand side, we will be allocating more and more space and throwing away the intermediate results all the time.

The next code listing shows how to use our `balancedFold` function:

```
object MonoidBalancedFold {
  def main(args: Array[String]): Unit = {
    val numbers = Array(1, 2, 3, 4)
    System.out.println(s"4! is: ${MonoidOperations.balancedFold(numbers,
intMultiplication)(identity)}")
  }
}
```

The result would be as follows:

```
volcom@volcom-Dell-System-XPS-L502X:~/workspace/scala-book/deep-theory$ java -cp
 target/deep-theory-1.0.0-SNAPSHOT.jar com.ivan.nikolov.monoids.MonoidBalancedFo
ld
4! is: 24
```

There are a few ways to make this code parallel. The hard way would involve quite a lot of extra code writing in order to manage threads, and it is really advanced. It probably deserves a chapter (if not an entire book) of its own, and we will just mention it for the more curious readers—*purely functional parallelism*. There are some materials on GitHub (https:/ /github.com/fpinscala/fpinscala/wiki/Chapter-7:-Purely-functional-parallelism) that cover this concept nicely with examples.

We can also use the par method that most Scala collections have. Due to the laws that monoids conform to, we are guaranteed to always get the correct results, no matter how the underlying collections are parallelized. The following listing shows example implementations of our fold methods:

```scala
def foldPar[T](list: List[T], m: Monoid[T]): T =
  foldMapPar(list, m)(identity)

def foldMapPar[T, Y](list: List[T], m: Monoid[Y])(f: T => Y): Y =
  list.par.foldLeft(m.zero) {
    case (t, y) => m.op(t, f(y))
  }
```

The only difference between these methods and what we had before is the call to par before we use foldLeft. Using the methods is exactly the same as we did previously:

```scala
object MonoidFoldingGenericPar {
  def main(args: Array[String]): Unit = {
    val strings = List("This is\n", "a list of\n", "strings!")
    val numbers = List(1, 2, 3, 4, 5, 6)
    System.out.println(s"Left folded:\n${MonoidOperations.foldPar(strings,
      stringConcatenation)}")
    System.out.println(s"Right folded:\n${MonoidOperations.foldPar(strings,
      stringConcatenation)}")
    System.out.println(s"6! is: ${MonoidOperations.foldPar(numbers,
      intMultiplication)}")
  }
}
```

As you would expect, the result here would be exactly the same as it was for the sequential example.

Monoids and composition

So far, we have seen some examples where monoids are used to improve efficiency and write generic functions. They, however, are even more powerful. The reason is that they follow another useful rule:

> Monoids support *composition*; if A and B are monoids, then their product (A, B) is also a monoid.

What does this mean exactly and how can we take advantage of this? Let's look at the following function:

```
def compose[T, Y](a: Monoid[T], b: Monoid[Y]): Monoid[(T, Y)] =
  new Monoid[(T, Y)] {
    val zero: (T, Y) = (a.zero, b.zero)

    override def op(l: (T, Y), r: (T, Y)): (T, Y) =
      (a.op(l._1, r._1), b.op(l._2, r._2))
  }
```

In the preceding code, we showed a function that applies the composition exactly as we mentioned in our definition. This would now allow us to simultaneously apply multiple operations using a monoid, and we can compose even more and apply even more operations. Let's see an example that will calculate the sum and the factorial of the numbers given to it:

```
object ComposedMonoid {
  def main(args: Array[String]): Unit = {
    val numbers = Array(1, 2, 3, 4, 5, 6)
    val sumAndProduct = compose(intAddition, intMultiplication)
    System.out.println(s"The sum and product is:
${MonoidOperations.balancedFold(numbers, sumAndProduct)(i => (i, i))}")
  }
}
```

In the preceding example, we took advantage of the map function as well because our new monoid expects a tuple of integers rather than just the single integers we have in our array. Running the example will yield the following result:

```
volcom@volcom-Dell-System-XPS-L502X:~/workspace/scala-book/deep-theory$ java -cp
 target/deep-theory-1.0.0-SNAPSHOT.jar com.ivan.nikolov.monoids.ComposedMonoid
The sum and product is: (21,720)
```

The preceding `compose` function is really powerful, and we can do a lot of things with it. We can also efficiently calculate the mean of all items in a list—we just need to use the `intAddition` monoid twice and map the numbers to `(number, 1)` in order to have the count together with the sum.

So far, we have seen how to compose monoids with operations. However, monoids are quite useful for building data structures as well. Data structures can also form monoids as long as their values also form monoids.

Let's go through an example. In machine learning, we might need to extract the features from some text. Then, each feature will be weighted using a coefficient and a number equal to the number of times we've seen it. Let's try and get to a monoid that can be used to fold a collection and give us what we need—the count of each feature.

First of all, it is clear that we will be counting how many times we see each feature. Building a map of features to be counted sounds like a good idea! We will be incrementing the count for a feature every time we see it. So, if we imagine that each element in our feature list becomes a map of one element, we will have to fold these maps and use our integer sum monoid to sum the values for the same keys.

Let's build a function that can return a monoid, which can be used to fold items into a map and will apply any monoid to the values of the same key of the map:

```
def mapMerge[K, V](a: Monoid[V]): Monoid[Map[K, V]] =
  new Monoid[Map[K, V]] {
    override def zero: Map[K, V] = Map()

    override def op(l: Map[K, V], r: Map[K, V]): Map[K, V] =
      (l.keySet ++ r.keySet).foldLeft(zero) {
        case (res, key) => res.updated(key, a.op(l.getOrElse(key,
          a.zero), r.getOrElse(key, a.zero)))
      }
  }
```

We can now use this monoid to do different aggregations—sums, multiplications, concatenations, and so on. For our features counting, we will have to use sums and here is how we've done it:

```
object FeatureCounting {
  def main(args: Array[String]): Unit = {
    val features = Array("hello", "features", "for", "ml", "hello",
      "for", "features")
    val counterMonoid: Monoid[Map[String, Int]] = mapMerge(intAddition)
    System.out.println(s"The features are:
${MonoidOperations.balancedFold(features, counterMonoid)(i => Map(i ->
```

```
1))}")
   }
}
```

The output of the preceding program will be as follows:

```
volcom@volcom-Dell-System-XPS-L502X:~/workspace/scala-book/deep-theory$ java -cp
 target/deep-theory-1.0.0-SNAPSHOT.jar com.ivan.nikolov.monoids.FeatureCounting
The features are: Map(hello -> 2, features -> 2, for -> 2, ml -> 1)
```

The `mapMerge` function that we defined previously can now take any monoid, and we can even easily create maps of maps and so on, without extra code writing.

When to use monoids

In the preceding examples, we showed how to use monoids in order to achieve certain things. However, if we look at the previous example, we could simplify it in the following way:

```scala
object FeatureCountingOneOff {
  def main(args: Array[String]): Unit = {
    val features = Array("hello", "features", "for", "ml", "hello",
      "for", "features")
    System.out.println(s"The features are: ${
      features.foldLeft(Map[String, Int]()) {
        case (res, feature) => res.updated(feature,
          res.getOrElse(feature, 0) + 1)
      }
    }")
  }
}
```

In fact, each example could be rewritten to a representation similar to the preceding code.

While someone might be tempted to do things this way, it might not always be scalable. As we already mentioned, the purpose of monoids is to actually allow us to write generic and reusable code. With the help of monoids, we can focus on simple operations and then just compose them together rather than build concrete implementations for everything we want. It might not be worth it for one-off functions, but using monoids would definitely have a positive effect when we are reusing functionality. Moreover, as you already saw, composition here is extremely easy, and with time it will save us from writing a huge amount of code (read less code duplication and possibilities to introduce bugs).

Functors

A **functor** is one of those terms that comes from category theory in mathematics and causes a lot of pain to developers who come into functional programming and have less of a mathematical background. It is a requirement for monads, and here we will try to explain it in a way that will be easy to understand.

What is a functor? In the preceding section, we looked at monoids as a way to abstract some computation and then used them in different ways for optimization or to create more complex computations. Even though some people might not agree with the correctness of this approach, let's look at functors from the same point of view—something that will abstract some specific computations.

 In Scala, a functor is a class that has a `map` method and conforms to a few laws. Let's call them **functor laws**.

The `map` method for a functor of the `F[T]` type takes a function from `T` to `Y` as a parameter and returns a `F[Y]` as a result. This will become much clearer in the next subsection, where we will show some actual code.

Functors also obey some functor laws:

- **Identity**: Whenever the `identity` function is mapped over some data, it doesn't change it, in other words, `map(x)(i => i) == x`.
- **Composition**: Multiple maps must compose together. It should make no difference if we do this operation: `map(map(x)(i => y(i)))(i => z(i))` or `map(x)(i => z(y(i)))`.
- The `map` function preserves the structure of the data, for example, it does not add or remove elements, change their order, and so on. It just changes the representation.

The preceding laws give developers some grounds to assume certain things when performing different computations. For example, we can now safely postpone different mappings of data in time or just do them all together, and be sure that the final result will be the same.

From what we mentioned previously, we can actually come up with the conclusion that functors set a specific set of laws on their operations (`map`, in this case) that must be in place and allow us to automatically reason about their results and effects.

Now that we have a definition for functors and we showed the laws they should follow, in the next subsection we can create a base trait that all functors will be able to extend.

Functors in real life

Before we show an example functor trait based on the laws we showed in the preceding section, you can conclude that standard Scala types such as `List`, `Option`, and others that define a `map` method are functors.

 The `map` method in the built-in Scala types such as `List` has a different signature from the example we show here. In our examples, the first parameter is the functor and the second one is the transformation function we apply to it. In the standard Scala types, the first parameter doesn't need to be passed, as it is the actual object we're calling it on (`this`).

If we want to create our own types that follow the functor laws, we can create a base trait and make sure to implement it:

```
trait Functor[F[_]] {
  def map[T, Y](l: F[T])(f: T => Y): F[Y]
}
```

Now, let's create a list functor that will simply call the `map` function of the Scala `List`:

```
package object functors {
  val listFunctor = new Functor[List] {
    override def map[T, Y](l: List[T])(f: (T) => Y): List[Y] = l.map(f)
  }
}
```

In the preceding code, the fact that an object is a functor simply allows us to assume that certain laws are in place.

Using our functors

A simple example of using our `listFunctor` that we defined in the preceding section can be seen as follows:

```
object FunctorsExample {
  def main(args: Array[String]): Unit = {
    val numbers = List(1, 2, 3, 4, 5, 6)
    val mapping = Map(
      1 -> "one",
```

```
        2 -> "two",
        3 -> "three",
        4 -> "four",
        5 -> "five",
        6 -> "six"
      )
    System.out.println(s"The numbers doubled are:
      ${listFunctor.map(numbers)(_ * 2)}")
    System.out.println(s"The numbers with strings are:
      ${listFunctor.map(numbers)(i => (i, mapping(i)))}")
  }
}
```

The output of the preceding example is shown in the following screenshot:

```
volcom@volcom-Dell-System-XPS-L502X:~/workspace/scala-book/deep-theory$ java -cp
 target/deep-theory-1.0.0-SNAPSHOT.jar com.ivan.nikolov.functors.FunctorsExample

The numbers doubled are: List(2, 4, 6, 8, 10, 12)
The numbers with strings are: List((1,one), (2,two), (3,three), (4,four), (5,fiv
e), (6,six))
```

As you can see, functors don't really do much by themselves. They are not exciting at all. However, they set some specific rules that help us understand the results from specific operations. This means that we can define methods based on the abstract map inside the Functor trait, which rely on the rules we've stated previously.

Functors are an important concept that are required for monads, which we will look at in the following subsection.

Monads

In the preceding section, we defined functors. With their map methods, the standard Scala collections seem to be good examples of functors. We should, however, emphasize again that a functor doesn't mean a collection—it can be a container and any custom-defined class. Based on an abstract map method and the rules it follows, we can define other functions that will help us reduce code duplication. However, there are not many exciting things we can do based on a mapping only. In our programs, we will have different operations, some of which not only transform a collection or an object, but also modify it in some way.

Monads are another one of those scary terms that come from category theory, which we will try to explain in a way that you will be able to easily understand, identify, and use in your daily routine as a developer.

What is a monad?

We already talked about laws earlier in this chapter. The monoid is defined based on some laws it follows, and these laws allow us to implement generic functionality with certainty, just because we expect certain conditions to hold. If a law is broken, then there is no way for us to know for sure what to expect in terms of how something will behave. In such cases, things would most probably end up returning wrong results.

Similar to the other concepts we already saw in this chapter, monads are defined in terms of the laws they follow. In order for a structure to be considered a monad, it must satisfy all the rules. Let's start with a short definition, which we will expand on later:

 Monads are functors that have the `unit` and `flatMap` methods and follow the **monad rules**.

So, what does the preceding definition mean? First of all, it means that monads follow all the rules we previously defined about functors. Additionally, they take things further and add support for two more methods.

The flatMap method

Before we formally define the rules, let's have a brief discussion about `flatMap`. We assume that you are familiar with Scala collections and are aware of the existence of the `flatten` method. So, just the name of `flatMap` tells us that it maps and then flattens, as shown here:

```
def flatMap[T](f: Y => Monad[T]) : Monad[T] = flatten(map(f))
```

We don't have the monad definition we referred to in the preceding code yet, but that's fine. We will get there. For now, let's just look at it as another generic parameter. You should also know that `flatten` has the following declaration:

```
def flatten[T](x: F[F[T]]): M[T]
```

For example, if F is actually a `List`, `flatten` will convert a list of lists into a simple list of whatever the type of the internal one is. If F is an `Option`, then the ones with the `None` value in the nested option will disappear and the rest will remain. These two examples show us that the `flatten` result actually depends on the specifics of the type being flattened, but in any case, it is clear how it transforms our data.

The unit method

The other method we mentioned previously is `unit`. It actually doesn't matter how this method is called and it could be different for different languages based on their standards. What is important is its functionality. The signature of `unit` can be written in the following way:

```
def unit[T](value: T): Monad[T]
```

What does the preceding line mean? It is pretty simple—it takes a value of the T type and turns it into a monad of the T type. This is nothing more than a single argument constructor or just a factory method. In Scala, this can be expressed using a companion object with an `apply` method as well. As long as it does the right thing, the implementation doesn't really matter. In Scala, we have many of the collection types as examples—`List`, `Array`, `Seq`—they all have an `apply` method that supports the following:

```
List(x)
Array(x)
Seq(x)
```

The connection between map, flatMap, and unit

In the preceding section, we showed how `flatMap` can be defined using `map` and `flatten`. We can, however, take a different approach and define `map` using `flatMap`. Here is what the definition would look like in our pseudo code:

```
def map[T](f: Y => T): Monad[T] = flatMap { x => unit(f(x)) }
```

The preceding definition is important because it draws the relationship between all the `map`, `flatMap`, and `unit` methods.

Depending on what kind of monads we implement, it could sometimes be easier to implement `map` first (usually, if we build collection-like monads) and then `flatMap` based on it and `flatten`, while other times it could be easier to first implement `flatMap` instead. As long as the monad laws are satisfied, it shouldn't matter which approach we take.

The names of the methods

In the preceding section, we mentioned that it doesn't actually matter how the `unit` method is called. While it is true for `unit` and it could be propagated to any of the other methods, it is recommended that `map` and `flatMap` actually remain this way. It doesn't mean that it is not possible to make things work, but following common conventions would make things much simpler. Moreover, `map` and `flatMap` give us something extra—the possibility of using our classes in *for comprehensions*. Consider the following example, which is only here to illustrate how having methods with such names helps:

```
case class ListWrapper(list: List[Int]) {
  // just wrap
  def map[B](f: Int => B): List[B] = list.map(f)

  // just wrap
  def flatMap[B](f: Int => GenTraversableOnce[B]): List[B] =
    list.flatMap(f)
}
```

In the preceding example, we just wrap a list in an object and define the `map` and `flatMap` methods. If we didn't have the preceding object, we could have written something like this:

```
object ForComprehensionWithLists {
  def main(args: Array[String]): Unit = {
    val l1 = List(1, 2, 3, 4)
    val l2 = List(5, 6, 7, 8)
    val result = for {
      x <- l1
      y <- l2
    } yield x * y
    // same as
    // val result = l1.flatMap(i => l2.map(_ * i))
    System.out.println(s"The result is: ${result}")
  }
}
```

With our wrapper object, we could do the same as follows:

```
object ForComprehensionWithObjects {
  def main(args: Array[String]): Unit = {
    val wrapper1 = ListWrapper(List(1, 2, 3, 4))
    val wrapper2 = ListWrapper(List(5, 6, 7, 8))
    val result = for {
      x <- wrapper1
      y <- wrapper2
    } yield x * y
    System.out.println(s"The result is: ${result}")
  }
}
```

Both applications do the same and will have exactly the same output:

```
volcom@volcom-Dell-System-XPS-L502X:~/workspace/scala-book/deep-theory$ java -cp
 target/deep-theory-1.0.0-SNAPSHOT.jar com.ivan.nikolov.monads.ForComprehensionW
ithObjects
The result is: List(5, 6, 7, 8, 10, 12, 14, 16, 15, 18, 21, 24, 20, 24, 28, 32)
```

What the second application uses, however, is the fact that our wrapper class contains methods specifically with the names such as `map` and `flatMap`. If we rename any of them, we would get a compilation error—we could still manage to write the same code but it will not be able to use syntactic sugar in Scala. Another point here is that the *for comprehension* would work correctly in the case where both the methods actually follow the rules for `map` and `flatMap`.

The monad laws

After going a bit through the methods a monad is supposed to support, now we can formally define the monad laws. You already saw that monads are functors and they follow the functor laws. Being explicit is always better, so here we will mix the laws together:

- **Identity law**: Doing `map` over the identity function doesn't change the data—`map(x)(i => i) == x`. Flat mapping over the `unit` function also keeps the data the same—`x.flatMap(i => unit(i)) == x`. The latter basically says that `flatMap` undoes `unit`. Using the connection between `map`, `flatMap`, and `unit` we defined earlier, we can derive one of these two rules from the other and vice versa. The `unit` method can be thought of as the zero element in monoids.

- **The unit law**: From the definition of `unit`, we can also say this:
  `unit(x).flatMap { y => f(y) } == f(x)`. From this, we will get
  `unit(x).map { y => f(x) } == unit(f(x))`. This gives us some interesting
  connections between all the methods.
- **Composition**: Multiple maps must be composed together. It should make no
  difference if we do `x.map(i => y(i)).map(i => z(i))` or `x.map(i =>
  z(y(i)))`. Moreover, multiple `flatMap` calls must also compose, making the
  following true:
  `x.flatMap(i => y(i)).flatMap(i => z(i)) == x.flatMap(i =>
  y(i).flatMap(j => z(j)))`.

Monads, similarly to monoids, also have a zero element. Some real-world examples of
monadic zeros are `Nil` in the Scala List and the `None` option. However, here we can also
have multiple zero elements, which are represented by an algebraic datatype with a
constructor parameter to which we can pass different values. In order to be complete, we
might not have zeros at all if there is no such concept for the monads we are modeling. In
any case, the zero monad represents some kind of emptiness and follows some extra laws:

- **Zero identity**: This one is pretty straightforward. It says that no matter what
  function we apply to a zero monad, it is still going to be zero—`zero.flatMap(i
  => f(i)) == zero` and `zero.map(i => f(i)) == zero`. `Zero` shouldn't be
  confused with `unit`, as they are different and the latter doesn't represent
  emptiness.
- **Reverse zero**: This is straightforward as well. Basically, if we replace everything
  with zero, our final result will also be zero—`x.flatMap(i => zero) == zero`.
- **Commutativity** : Monads can have a concept of addition, whether it is
  concatenation or something else. In any case, this kind of operation when done
  with the zero monad will be commutative, for example, `x plus zero == zero
  plus x == x`.

Monads and side effects

When presenting the composition law, we kind of assumed that an operation has no side effects. We said the following:
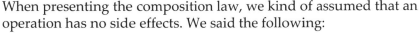
x.map(i => y(i)).map(i => z(i)) == x.map(i => z(y(i))).
However, let's now think about what would happen if y or z cause some side effects. On the left-hand side, we first run all ys and then all zs. On the right-hand side, however, we interleave them, doing y and z all the time. Now, if an operation causes a side effect, it would mean that the two might end up producing different results. That's why developers should prefer using the left-hand side version, especially when there might be side effects such as IO.

We have discussed the monad laws. For those who have more experience with Scala, monads might seem pretty close to the collection classes, and the rules we defined previously might seem logical. However, we are pointing out once more that it is not necessary for a monad to be a collection, and it is important that these rules are followed in order to be able to call an algebraic data structure a monad.

Monads in real life

After going through a lot of theory about monads, it would now be useful to go through some code that demonstrates how to implement and use the theoretical concepts, which real-world situations they are good for, and so on.

Let's now do something similar to what we did before, and show what a monad trait will look like in Scala. Before doing this, however, let's slightly change our functor definition:

```
trait Functor[T] {
  def map[Y](f: T => Y): Functor[Y]
}
```

In the preceding code, instead of passing the element that will be mapped, we assume that the type that mixes Functor will have a way to pass it to the map implementation. We also changed the return type so that we can chain multiple functors using map. After we've done this, we can show our Monad trait:

```
trait Monad[T] extends Functor[T] {
  def unit[Y](value: Y): Monad[Y]

  def flatMap[Y](f: T => Monad[Y]): Monad[Y]
```

```
    override def map[Y](f: T => Y): Monad[Y] =
        flatMap(i => unit(f(i)))
}
```

The preceding code follows a convention similar to what we used for monoids. The methods the monad has are exactly the same as we have already mentioned earlier in the theoretical part of this chapter. The signatures might be slightly different, but mapping them to the theoretical code, which was made to be understood easily, shouldn't cause any issues.

As you can see, the monads extend functors. Now, whenever we want to write monads, we just need to extend the preceding trait and implement the methods.

Using monads

Simply having a monad trait puts us in a framework that we can follow. We already went through the theory of monads and the laws that they follow. However, in order to understand how monads work and what they are useful for, looking at an actual example is invaluable.

However, how are we supposed to even use monads if we don't know what their purpose is? Let's call them computation builders, as this is exactly what they are used for. This gives the ordinary developer much more understanding about when and where to use monad's computation builder chain operations in some way, which are then performed.

The Option monad

We have already mentioned a few times that the standard Scala Option is a monad. In this subsection, we will provide our own monadical implementation of this standard class and show one of the many possible uses of monads.

In order to show how useful the option is, we will see what happens if we don't have it. Let's imagine that we have the following classes:

```
case class Doer() {
  def getAlgorithm(isFail: Boolean) =
    if (isFail) {
      null
    } else {
      Algorithm()
    }
}
```

```scala
case class Algorithm() {
  def getImplementation(isFail: Boolean, left: Int, right: Int):
Implementation =
    if (isFail) {
      null
    } else {
      Implementation(left, right)
    }
}

case class Implementation(left: Int, right: Int) {
  def compute: Int = left + right
}
```

In order to test, we have added a `Boolean` flag that will or will not fail to get the required objects. In reality, this could be some complicated function that, depending on parameters or something else, could return `null` in some specific cases. The following piece of code shows how the preceding classes should be used in order to be completely protected from failure:

```scala
object NoMonadExample {
  def main(args: Array[String]): Unit = {
    System.out.println(s"The result is: ${compute(Doer(), 10, 16)}")
  }

  def compute(doer: Doer, left: Int, right: Int): Int =
    if (doer != null) {
      val algorithm = doer.getAlgorithm(false)
      if (algorithm != null) {
        val implementation = algorithm.getImplementation(false,
          left, right)
        if (implementation != null) {
          implementation.compute
        } else {
          -1
        }
      } else {
        -1
      }
    } else {
      -1
    }
}
```

The `compute` method in the `NoMonadExample` object looks really bad and hard to read. We shouldn't write code like that.

Looking at what's happening in the preceding code, we can see that we are actually trying to build a chain of operations, which can individually fail. Monads can help us and abstract this protective logic. Now, let's show a much better solution.

First of all, let's define our own `Option` monad:

```
sealed trait Option[A] extends Monad[A]

case class Some[A](a: A) extends Option[A] {
  override def unit[Y](value: Y): Monad[Y] = Some(value)

  override def flatMap[Y](f: (A) => Monad[Y]): Monad[Y] = f(a)
}

case class None[A]() extends Option[A] {
  override def unit[Y](value: Y): Monad[Y] = None()

  override def flatMap[Y](f: (A) => Monad[Y]): Monad[Y] = None()
}
```

We have two concrete cases in the preceding code—one where we can get a value and other where the result will be empty. Now, let's rewrite our computation classes so that they use the new monad we just created:

```
case class Doer_v2() {
  def getAlgorithm(isFail: Boolean): Option[Algorithm_v2] =
    if (isFail) {
      None()
    } else {
      Some(Algorithm_v2())
    }
}

case class Algorithm_v2() {
  def getImplementation(isFail: Boolean, left: Int, right: Int):
Option[Implementation] =
    if (isFail) {
      None()
    } else {
      Some(Implementation(left, right))
    }
}
```

Finally, we can use them in the following way:

```
object MonadExample {
  def main(args: Array[String]): Unit = {
    System.out.println(s"The result is: ${compute(Some(Doer_v2()), 10,
16)}")
  }

  def compute(doer: Option[Doer_v2], left: Int, right: Int) =
    for {
      d <- doer
      a <- d.getAlgorithm(false)
      i <- a.getImplementation(false, left, right)
    } yield i.compute

  // OR THIS WAY:
  //  doer.flatMap {
  //    d =>
  //      d.getAlgorithm(false).flatMap {
  //        a =>
  //          a.getImplementation(false, left, right).map {
  //            i => i.compute
  //          }
  //      }
  //  }
}
```

In the preceding code, we've shown a *for comprehension* usage of our monad, but the part that is commented out is also valid. The first one is preferred because it makes things look really simple, and some completely different computations end up looking the same, which is good for understanding and changing code.

Of course, everything we showed in our example can be implemented using the standard Scala Option. It is almost certain that you have already seen and used this class before, which means that you have actually used monads before, maybe without realizing this was the case.

A more advanced monad example

The previous example was pretty simple, and it showed a great use of monads. We made our code much more straightforward, and we abstracted some logic inside the monads. Also, our code became much more readable than it was before.

In this subsection, let's see another use of monads, which is much more advanced this time. All the software we write becomes much more challenging and interesting whenever we add I/O to it. This can be reading and writing data to and from files, communicating with a user, making web requests, and so on. Monads can be used in order to write I/O applications in a purely functional way. There is a really important feature here: I/O has to deal with side effects, operations are usually performed in a sequence, and the result depends on a state. This state can be anything—if we ask the user what cars they like, the response would vary depending on the user, and if we ask them what they ate for breakfast, or what the weather is like, the responses to these question will also depend on the user. Even if we try and read the same file twice, there might be differences—we might fail, the file could be changed, and so on. Everything we have described so far is a state. Monads help us hide this state from the user and just expose the important parts as well as abstract the way we deal with errors, and so on.

There are a few important aspects about the state we will be using:

- The state changes between different I/O operations
- The state is only one and we can't just create a new one whenever we want
- At any moment in time, there can be only one state

All of the previous statements are quite logical, but they will actually guide the way we implement our state and our monads.

We will write an example, which will read the lines from a file and then go through them and write them in a new file with all the letters capitalized. This can be written in a really easy and straightforward way with Scala, but as soon as some of the operations become more complex or we try to handle errors properly, it can become pretty difficult.

Throughout the example, we will try to show what steps we have taken in order to make sure the previous statements about our state are correct.

The following example we will show doesn't really need to use state. It just performs a file read and write in a monadic manner. The reader should have enough knowledge by now to take the state out of the code, if needed.

We've decided to show a very simple usage of state, where we just increment a number. This can give the reader an idea of how a state can be used and wired up in applications that might actually need it. Additionally, the use of state can actually modify the behavior of our program and trigger different actions depending on it—for example, a vending machine and a user trying to request something that is out of stock.

Let's start with the state. For the current example, we don't really need a special state, but we have used one anyway. It is just to show how to handle cases when one is actually needed:

```
sealed trait State {
  def next: State
}
```

The preceding trait has a `next` method, which will return the next state when we move between different operations. Just by calling it when we pass a state, we make sure that different operations cause a change in state.

We need to make sure that our application has only one state and that nobody can create a state whenever they want. The fact that the trait is sealed helps us to make sure nobody can extend our state outside the file, where we have defined it. Being sealed is not enough, though. We need to make sure all the implementations of the state are hidden:

```
abstract class FileIO {

  // this makes sure nobody can create a state
  private class FileIOState(id: Int) extends State {
    override def next: State = new FileIOState(id + 1)
  }

  def run(args: Array[String]): Unit = {
    val action = runIO(args(0), args(1))
    action(new FileIOState(0))
  }

  def runIO(readPath: String, writePath: String): IOAction[_]
}
```

The preceding code defines the state as a private class, and this means that nobody else will be able to create one. Let's ignore the other methods for now, as we will come back to them later.

The third rule we defined for our state earlier is much trickier to achieve. We have taken multiple steps in order to make sure the state behaves correctly. First of all, as can be seen from the previous listing, there is no clue of a state that the user can get to, except the private class that nobody can instantiate. Instead of loading the user with the burden of executing a task and passing a state, we only expose an IOAction to them, which is defined as follows:

```
sealed abstract class IOAction[T] extends ((State) => (State, T)) {
  // START: we don't have to extend. We could also do this...
  def unit[Y](value: Y): IOAction[Y] = IOAction(value)

  def flatMap[Y](f: (T) => IOAction[Y]): IOAction[Y] = {
    val self = this
    new IOAction[Y] {
      override def apply(state: State): (State, Y) = {
        val (state2, res) = self(state)
        val action2 = f(res)
        action2(state2)
      }

    }
  }

  def map[Y](f: T => Y): IOAction[Y] =
    flatMap(i => unit(f(i)))

  // END: we don't have to extend. We could also do this...
}
```

First, let's focus only on the IOAction signature. It extends a function from an old state to a tuple of the new state and the result of the operation. So, it turns out that we are still exposing the state to our users in a way—it is just in the form of a class. However, we already saw that it is pretty straightforward to hide a state by creating a private class that nobody can instantiate. Our users will be working with the IOAction class, so we need to make sure they don't have to deal with states themselves. We have already defined the IOAction to be sealed. Additionally, we can create a factory object, which will help us create new instances:

```
object IOAction {
  def apply[T](result: => T): IOAction[T] =
    new SimpleAction[T](result)
```

```
private class SimpleAction[T](result: => T) extends IOAction[T] {
  override def apply(state: State): (State, T) =
    (state.next, result)
}

}
```

The preceding code is quite important in terms of how things will get wired up later. First of all, we have a private implementation of IOAction. It only takes a by-name parameter, which means that it will only be evaluated when the apply method is called—this is really important. Moreover, in the preceding code, we have an apply method for the IOAction object, which allows the users to instantiate actions. Again, here the value is passed by name.

The preceding code, basically, enables us to define actions and only execute them whenever we have a state available.

If we now have a think, you can see that we've managed to satisfy all three requirements for our state. Indeed, by hiding the state behind a class, whose instance creations are controlled by us, we have managed to protect the state so that we don't have more than one at the same time.

Now that we have everything in place, we can make sure our IOAction is a monad. It will need to satisfy the monad laws and define the required methods. We've already shown them, but let's have a closer look at the methods again:

```
// START: we don't have to extend. We could also do this...
def unit[Y](value: Y): IOAction[Y] = IOAction(value)

def flatMap[Y](f: (T) => IOAction[Y]): IOAction[Y] = {
  val self = this
  new IOAction[Y] {
    override def apply(state: State): (State, Y) = {
      val (state2, res) = self(state)
      val action2 = f(res)
      action2(state2)
    }

  }
}

def map[Y](f: T => Y): IOAction[Y] =
  flatMap(i => unit(f(i)))

// END: we don't have to extend. We could also do this...
```

We haven't specifically extended our `Monad` trait, but instead we have just defined the methods here. We already know that `map` can be defined using `flatMap` and `unit`. For the latter, we have used the factory method for the `SimpleAction`. Our implementation of the former is quite interesting—it performs the current operation first and then sequentially after that, based on the resulting state, the second operation. This allows us to chain multiple I/O operations together.

Let's look at our `IOAction` class again. Does it satisfy the monad rules? The answer is no, but there is a really easy fix. The problem is that our `unit` method, if we look into it, would change the state because it uses a `SimpleAction`. But it shouldn't. What we have to do is create another `IOAction` implementation that doesn't change the state, and we use it for `unit`:

```
private class EmptyAction[T](value: T) extends IOAction[T] {
  override def apply(state: State): (State, T) =
    (state, value)
}
```

Then, our `IOAction` object will get an extra function:

```
def unit[T](value: T): IOAction[T] = new EmptyAction[T](value)
```

We will also have to change the unit method in the `IOAction` abstract class:

```
def unit[Y](value: Y): IOAction[Y] = IOAction.unit(value)
```

So far, we have defined our monad, made sure the state is handled properly, and that the actions can be created by a user in a controlled manner. What we need to do now is just add some useful methods and try them out:

```
package object io {
  def readFile(path: String) =
    IOAction(Source.fromFile(path).getLines())

  def writeFile(path: String, lines: Iterator[String]) =
    IOAction({
      val file = new File(path)
      printToFile(file) { p => lines.foreach(p.println) }
    })

  private def printToFile(file: File)(writeOp: PrintWriter => Unit): Unit =
  {
    val writer = new PrintWriter(file)
    try {
      writeOp(writer)
```

```
    } finally {
      writer.close()
    }
  }
}
```

The preceding is the code of a package object that reads and writes files and returns instances of `IOAction` (in the current case, `SimpleAction` is created using the `IOAction` `apply` method). Now that we have these methods and our monad, we can use the framework we have defined and wire everything up:

```
abstract class FileIO {

  // this makes sure nobody can create a state
  private class FileIOState(id: Int) extends State {
    override def next: State = new FileIOState(id + 1)
  }

  def run(args: Array[String]): Unit = {
    val action = runIO(args(0), args(1))
    action(new FileIOState(0))
  }

  def runIO(readPath: String, writePath: String): IOAction[_]
}
```

The preceding code defines a framework that the users of our library will follow; they will have to extend `FileIO`, implement `runIO`, and call the `run` method whenever they are ready to use our application. By now, you should be familiar enough with monads and see that the only thing the highlighted code will do is *build a computation*. It can be thought of as a graph of operations that have to be performed. It will not execute anything until the next line, where it actually gets the state passed to it:

```
object FileIOExample extends FileIO {
  def main(args: Array[String]): Unit = {
    run(args)
  }

  override def runIO(readPath: String, writePath: String): IOAction[_] =
    for {
      lines <- readFile(readPath)
      _ <- writeFile(writePath, lines.map(_.toUpperCase))
    } yield ()
}
```

The preceding code shows an example usage of the `FileIO` library that we created. We can now run it with the following input file:

```
this is a file, which
will be completely capitalized
in a monadic way.

Enjoy!
```

The command that we need to use is shown as follows:

```
volcom@volcom-Dell-System-XPS-L502X:~/workspace/scala-book/deep-theory$ java -cp
 target/deep-theory-1.0.0-SNAPSHOT.jar com.ivan.nikolov.monads.io.FileIOExample
input.txt output.txt
```

As expected, the output file will contain the same text with all uppercase letters. You can, of course, try with different inputs and see how the code performs.

Monad intuition

In this section, we went through some theory and real-world examples with monads. Hopefully, we have managed to give an easy to understand explanation of what is what, and how and why it works. Monads are not as scary as they initially seem to be and some time spent with them would give an even better understanding of how and why things work in a certain way.

 The last example could seem pretty complicated, but some extra time spent with it using an IDE will make it clear and easy for you to realize how exactly everything gets wired up. Then, you will be able to easily spot and use monads on your own.

Of course, a developer can probably get away without monads, but using them can help with hiding details about exception handling, specific operations, and so on. Monads are actually good because of the extra work that happens inside them, and they can be used to implement some of the design patterns we saw earlier in this book. We can implement better states, rollbacks, and many, many more. It is also worth mentioning that it is likely that many times we use monads without even realizing.

Summary

This chapter was dedicated to some of the functional programming theories that seem to put many people off pure functional programming. Because the majority of explanations require a strong mathematical background, we see people avoiding the concepts covered in this chapter.

We talked about monoids, monads, and functors, and we showed some examples of how to use them and the difference between having and not having them. It turns out that we use these concepts more often than we think, but we just don't realize it.

We saw that monoids, functors, and monads can be used for a variety of purposes—performance optimization, abstraction, and removal of code duplication. Properly understanding these concepts and feeling comfortable with them might take some time initially, but after some practice, developers tend to get a much better understanding and use them much more often than before. Hopefully, this chapter has made monoids, monads, and functors look much simpler than you may have thought and you will make them a part of the production code more often.

In the next chapter, we will cover some functional programming design patterns that are specific to Scala, due to its expressiveness. Some of them will be new and previously unseen, while others we have already met, but we will look at from a different perspective.

11
Applying What We Have Learned

We have already come a long way in Scala and in learning about the various design patterns in the language. Now, you should be at a stage where you are confident about when to use specific design patterns and when to avoid them. You saw some of the specifics and nice features of Scala that lead to its expressiveness. We went through the *Gang of Four* design patterns as well as some important functional programming concepts, such as monads. Throughout this book, we have tried to keep mathematical theories to a really basic level, and we have tried to avoid some scary Greek letters in formulas that are hard to understand for non-mathematicians, who may also want to use a functional programming language to its full potential.

The aim of this and the next chapter is to look at Scala from a more practical point of view. Knowing about a language and some design patterns is not always enough for a developer to see the whole picture and the potential of language possibilities. In this chapter, we will show how some of the concepts we presented before can be combined to write even more powerful and cleaner programs. We will look at the following topics:

- The lens design pattern
- The cake design pattern
- The pimp my library design pattern
- The stackable traits design pattern
- The type class design pattern
- Lazy evaluation
- Partial functions
- Implicit injection
- Duck typing
- Memoization

Some of the sections in this chapter will show concepts that we haven't seen before. Others will combine some of the features of Scala and the design patterns we have learned so far in order to achieve something else. In all the cases, though, these concepts will deal with either a specific language feature or a limitation we have already seen, or help in achieving something commonly seen in actual software engineering projects.

The lens design pattern

We have already mentioned that, in Scala, objects are immutable. You can, of course, make sure that a specific class has its fields declared as `vars`, but this is discouraged and considered bad practice. After all, immutability is good and we should try to aim for it.

The lens design pattern was created specifically for that purpose and allows us to overcome the immutability limitation and at the same time preserve the code's readability. In the following subsections, we will start with some code that doesn't use the lens design pattern and we will go step by step to show how to use it and how it improves our applications.

Lens example

In order to show the lens design pattern in practice, we will create a class hierarchy that is usually seen in enterprise applications. Let's imagine that we are building a system for a library that can be used by the employees of different companies. We might end up with the following classes:

```
case class Country(name: String, code: String)
case class City(name: String, country: Country)
case class Address(number: Int, street: String, city: City)
case class Company(name: String, address: Address)
case class User(name: String, company: Company, address: Address)
```

The representation of these classes as a class diagram will look like the following figure:

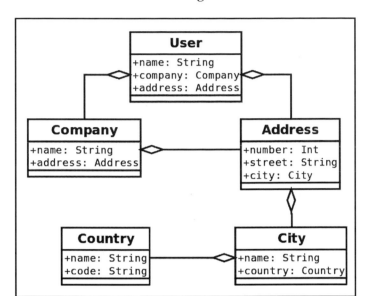

The diagram is pretty clear and it doesn't need too much explanation. We basically have a User class that has other information about the user. Other classes contain others and so on. There is absolutely no challenge in using our classes if we don't want to modify anything. However, as soon as we go on to modify something, it becomes complicated.

Without the lens design pattern

In this subsection, we will see how to use our classes if we want to modify some of their properties.

Immutable and verbose

Without getting into too much detail, let's see what an example application would look like:

```scala
object UserVerboseExample {
  def main(args: Array[String]): Unit = {
    val uk = Country("United Kingdom", "uk")
    val london = City("London", uk)
    val buckinghamPalace = Address(1, "Buckingham Palace Road", london)
    val castleBuilders = Company("Castle Builders", buckinghamPalace)
    val switzerland = Country("Switzerland", "CH")
    val geneva = City("geneva", switzerland)
```

```
      val genevaAddress = Address(1, "Geneva Lake", geneva)
      val ivan = User("Ivan", castleBuilders, genevaAddress)
      System.out.println(ivan)
      System.out.println("Capitalize UK code...")
      val ivanFixed = ivan.copy(
        company = ivan.company.copy(
          address = ivan.company.address.copy(
            city = ivan.company.address.city.copy(
              country = ivan.company.address.city.country.copy(
                code = ivan.company.address.city.country.code.toUpperCase
              )
            )
          )
        )
      )
      System.out.println(ivanFixed)
    }
  }
```

The preceding application creates one user for our library and then decides to change the company country code, as we initially created it in lowercase characters. The output of the application looks like this:

```
volcom@volcom-Dell-System-XPS-L502X:~/workspace/scala-book/functional-design-pat
terns$ java -cp target/functional-design-patterns-1.0.0-SNAPSHOT.jar com.ivan.ni
kolov.lens.UserVerboseExample
User(Ivan,Company(Castle Builders,Address(1,Buckingham Palace Road,City(London,C
ountry(United Kingdom,uk)))),Address(1,Geneva Lake,City(geneva,Country(Switzerla
nd,CH))))
Capitalize UK code...
User(Ivan,Company(Castle Builders,Address(1,Buckingham Palace Road,City(London,C
ountry(United Kingdom,UK)))),Address(1,Geneva Lake,City(geneva,Country(Switzerla
nd,CH))))
```

Our application works correctly but as you can see in the highlighted code, it is extremely verbose and long and making a mistake is really easy. We don't want to write code like this, as it will be hard to maintain and change in the future.

Using mutable properties

The first thought that might come into your head is to change the classes and make the properties variable. Here is how our case classes would change:

```
case class Country(var name: String, var code: String)
case class City(var name: String, var country: Country)
```

```
case class Address(var number: Int, var street: String, var city: City)
case class Company(var name: String, var address: Address)
case class User(var name: String, var company: Company, var address:
Address)
```

After this, using these classes will be as easy as this:

```
object UserBadExample {
  def main(args: Array[String]): Unit = {
    val uk = Country("United Kingdom", "uk")
    val london = City("London", uk)
    val buckinghamPalace = Address(1, "Buckingham Palace Road", london)
    val castleBuilders = Company("Castle Builders", buckinghamPalace)
    val switzerland = Country("Switzerland", "CH")
    val geneva = City("geneva", switzerland)
    val genevaAddress = Address(1, "Geneva Lake", geneva)
    val ivan = User("Ivan", castleBuilders, genevaAddress)
    System.out.println(ivan)
    System.out.println("Capitalize UK code...")
    ivan.company.address.city.country.code =
ivan.company.address.city.country.code.toUpperCase
    System.out.println(ivan)
  }
}
```

 In the preceding code example, we could have also changed the country code using this—uk.code = uk.code.toUpperCase. This would work, because we use a reference of the country in our User object.

The preceding example will produce absolutely the same output. However, here we broke the rule that everything in Scala is immutable. This might not look like a big deal in the current example but, in reality, it goes against the Scala principles. This is considered bad code and we should try to avoid it.

With the lens design pattern

In the previous subsection, we saw how complicated something such as changing one property of a nested class can be. We are going after nice, clean, and correct code, and we also don't want to go against the principles of Scala.

Luckily for us, cases such as the one we just mentioned previously are exactly the reason for the creation of the lens design pattern. In this chapter, we will see the Scalaz library for the first time in this book. It defines many functional programming abstractions for us, and we can easily use them straight away without worrying whether they follow some specific set of rules or not.

So, what are lenses anyway? We won't get too deep into the theoretical aspects here, as this is out of the scope of this book. It is enough for us to know what they are used for, and if you want to know more, there is plenty of material on lenses, store, and comonads online, which can make these concepts clearer. A simple way to represent a lens is the following:

```
case class Lens[X, Y](get: X => Y, set: (X, Y) => X)
```

This basically lets us get and set different properties of an object of the X type. This means that, in our case, we will have to define different lenses for the different properties we want to set:

```
import scalaz.Lens

object User {
  val userCompany = Lens.lensu[User, Company](
    (u, company) => u.copy(company = company), _.company
  )
  val userAddress = Lens.lensu[User, Address](
    (u, address) => u.copy(address = address), _.address
  )
  val companyAddress = Lens.lensu[Company, Address](
    (c, address) => c.copy(address = address), _.address
  )
  val addressCity = Lens.lensu[Address, City](
    (a, city) => a.copy(city = city), _.city
  )

  val cityCountry = Lens.lensu[City, Country](
    (c, country) => c.copy(country = country), _.country
  )
  val countryCode = Lens.lensu[Country, String](
    (c, code) => c.copy(code = code), _.code
  )
  val userCompanyCountryCode = userCompany >=> companyAddress >=>
addressCity >=> cityCountry >=> countryCode
}
```

The preceding code is a companion object to our `User` class. There are a lot of things going on here, so we will explain this. You can see the calls to `Lens.lensu[A, B]`. They create actual lenses so that for an object of the `A` type, the calls get and set a value of the `B` type. There is nothing special about them really, and they simply look like boilerplate code. The interesting part here is the highlighted code—it uses the `>=>` operator, which is an alias for `andThen`. This allows us to compose lenses and this is exactly what we will do. We will define a composition that allows us to go from a `User` object through the chain and set the country code of the country of the `Company`. We could have used `compose` as well, which has an alias of `<=<` because `andThen` internally calls `compose` and it would look like the following:

```
val userCompanyCountryCodeCompose = countryCode <=< cityCountry <=<
addressCity <=< companyAddress <=< userCompany
```

The latter, however, is not as intuitive as the former.

Using our lens is now very easy. We need to make sure to import our companion object and then we can simply use the following code where we change the country code to uppercase:

```
val ivanFixed = userCompanyCountryCode.mod(_.toUpperCase, ivan)
```

You saw how the lens design pattern allows us to cleanly set properties of our case class without breaking the immutability rule. We simply need to define the right lenses and then use them.

Minimizing the boilerplate

The preceding example showed quite a lot of boilerplate code. It is not complicated, but it requires us to write quite a lot of extra stuff, and then any refactoring will likely affect these manually defined lenses. There has been an effort in creating libraries that automatically generate lenses for all user-defined classes that can then be used easily. One example of a library that seems to be maintained well is Monocle: `https://github.com/julien-truffaut/Monocle`. It is well-documented and can be used so that we don't have to write any boilerplate code. It has its limitations though, and users should make sure they are okay with what the library provides. It also provides other optics concepts that could be useful.

The cake design pattern

Actual software projects will usually combine multiple components that will have to be used together. Most of the time, these components will depend on others, which in turn depend on other components, and so on. This makes creating objects in an application hard because we also need to create the objects they depend on and so on. This is where dependency injection comes in handy.

Dependency injection

So, what exactly is dependency injection? It turns out to be something really simple—every single class that has an object as a parameter in their constructor is actually an example of a dependency injection. The reason is that the dependency is injected into the class rather than instantiated inside it. Developers should actually try to use this kind of approach instead of creating objects inside a constructor. There are many reasons for this, but one of the most important ones is the fact that components can become tightly coupled and practically untestable.

Dependency injection, however, could degrade the code quality if implemented using constructor parameters. This would make constructors take a large number of parameters and, as a consequence, it will become really difficult to use the constructors. Of course, using the factory design pattern could help, but there are other approaches that are much more common in enterprise applications. In the following subsections, we will briefly mention the alternatives and show how, using only the features of Scala, we can easily implement dependency injection.

Dependency injection libraries and Scala

Many developers with a background in Java might be already familiar with some of the famous dependency injection libraries. Some popular examples are Spring (`https://spring.io/`) and Guice (`https://github.com/google/guice`). In Spring, dependencies are usually managed in an XML file, where they are described, and the file tells the framework how to create instances and where to inject the objects into classes. Some of the terms used are beans.

On the other hand, Guice uses annotations that are then evaluated and replaced with the right objects. These are quite popular frameworks and they can also be used in Scala pretty easily. Those of you familiar with Play Framework will know that it uses exactly Guice to wire things up.

Using external libraries, however, adds dependencies to projects, increases the jar size, and so on. Nowadays, this is not really an issue. Scala, however, is quite an expressive language, as we have already seen, and we can implement dependency injection natively without any extra libraries. We will see how this can be done in the following subsections.

Dependency injection in Scala

In order to implement dependency injection in Scala, we can use a special design pattern. It is called the cake design pattern. Without getting into too much detail, let's create an application. The application that we are creating will need to have a bunch of classes that depend on each other so that we can demonstrate how injection works.

Writing our code

We will create an application that can read from a database data about people, classes, and who has signed up to which classes. We will have a user service which will implement some simple business logic with the data, and a service that will access the data. It will be a small application, but it will clearly show how dependency injection works.

Let's start with the simple stuff. We will need to have a model for the objects that we will be representing:

```
case class Class(id: Int, name: String)
case class Person(id: Int, name: String, age: Int)
```

In the preceding code, we have two classes that will be used in our application. There is nothing special about them, so let's go further.

We said that we want our application to be able to read data from a database. There are different databases—MySQL, PostgreSQL, Oracle, and so on. If we want to use any of these, however, you will need to install some extra software that will require extra knowledge and will be tricky. Luckily, there is an in-memory database engine called H2 (`https://www.h2database.com/html/main.html`) that we can use instead. Using this is as simple as adding a dependency to our `pom.xml` or `build.sbt` file and then using the database. We will see how this all works really soon.

Also, let's make things more interesting and make sure that a different database engine could easily be plugged in. For this to work, we will need some kind of interface that will be implemented by different database services:

```
trait DatabaseService {
  val dbDriver: String
  val connectionString: String
  val username: String
  val password: String
  val ds = {
    JdbcConnectionPool.create(connectionString, username, password)
  }

  def getConnection: Connection = ds.getConnection
}
```

In the preceding code, we used a trait and will extend this trait whenever we want to create an H2 database service, or an Oracle database service, and so on. Everything in the preceding code seems to be quite straightforward and doesn't need additional explanation.

The order of the vals

In the preceding code, listing the order of the variable definitions matters. This means that if we had declared `ds` first and then everything else, we would have faced a `NullPointerException`. This can be easily overcome using a `lazy val` instead.

For our example, we will be implementing a service for the H2 database engine, as follows:

```
trait DatabaseComponent {
  val databaseService: DatabaseService
  class H2DatabaseService(val connectionString: String, val username:
String, val password: String) extends DatabaseService {
    val dbDriver = "org.h2.Driver"
  }
}
```

The actual implementation of the database service is in the nested `H2DatabaseService` class. Nothing special about it. But what about the `DatabaseComponent` trait? It is simple—we want to have a database component that we will mix in our classes and it will provide functionality to connect to the databases. The `databaseService` variable is left to be abstract and will have to be implemented when the component is mixed in.

Having a database component by itself is not useful at all. We will need to use it in some way. Let's create another component, which creates our database and its tables and fills them up with data. Obviously, it will depend on the database component mentioned previously:

```
trait MigrationComponent {
  this: DatabaseComponent =>

  val migrationService: MigrationService

  class MigrationService() {
    def runMigrations(): Unit = {
      val connection = databaseService.getConnection
      try {
        // create the database
        createPeopleTable(connection)
        createClassesTable(connection)
        createPeopleToClassesTable(connection)
        // populate
        insertPeople(
          connection,
          List(Person(1, "Ivan", 26), Person(2, "Maria", 25),
            Person(3, "John", 27))
        )
        insertClasses(
          connection,
          List(Class(1, "Scala Design Patterns"), Class(2,
            "JavaProgramming"), Class(3, "Mountain Biking"))
        )
        signPeopleToClasses(
          connection,
          List((1, 1), (1, 2), (1, 3), (2, 1), (3, 1), (3, 3))
        )
      } finally {
        connection.close()
      }
    }

    private def createPeopleTable(connection: Connection): Unit = {
      // implementation
    }

    private def createClassesTable(connection: Connection): Unit = {
      // implementation
    }

    private def createPeopleToClassesTable(connection: Connection):
```

```
     Unit = {
       // implementation
     }

     private def insertPeople(connection: Connection, people: List[Person]):
   Unit = {
       // implementation
     }

     // Other methods
   }

 }
```

Now this is a lot of code! There is nothing scary about it, though. Let's go through it and try to understand it. First, we followed the same pattern as before—we created a component trait with an abstract variable, in this case, called `migrationService`. We don't need to have multiple different migrations, so we simply created a class inside the component trait.

The interesting part here is the first line that we highlighted—`this: DatabaseComponent =>`. What does this mean? Luckily, we have already seen this syntax before in the book—it is nothing more than a **self type annotation**. What it does, however, is really interesting—it tells the compiler that whenever we mix in the `MigrationComponent`, we also need to mix in the `DatabaseComponent`. And this is exactly the piece of the puzzle that tells Scala that the migration component will depend on the database component. As a consequence, we are now able to run the code in the second highlighted row. And if we look carefully, it actually accesses `databaseService`, which is a part of `DatabaseComponent`.

In the preceding code, we've skipped most of the other implementations, but they are straightforward and have nothing to do with the cake design pattern. Let's see two of them:

```
private def createPeopleTable(connection: Connection): Unit = {
  val statement = connection.prepareStatement(
    """
      |CREATE TABLE people(
      | id INT PRIMARY KEY,
      | name VARCHAR(255) NOT NULL,
      | age INT NOT NULL
      |)
    """.stripMargin
  )
  try {
    statement.executeUpdate()
  } finally {
    statement.close()
```

```
    }
  }

  private def insertPeople(connection: Connection, people: List[Person]):
  Unit = {
    val statement = connection.prepareStatement(
      "INSERT INTO people(id, name, age) VALUES (?, ?, ?)"
    )
    try {
      people.foreach {
        case person =>
          statement.setInt(1, person.id)
          statement.setString(2, person.name)
          statement.setInt(3, person.age)
          statement.addBatch()
      }
      statement.executeBatch()
    } finally {
      statement.close()
    }
  }
}
```

The preceding code is just database code that creates a table and inserts data into it. The rest of the methods in the class are similar, but they differ in the table definitions and what is inserted into them. The full code can be seen in the examples that are provided with this book. Here, we will just extract the statements that create the database model so that you can have an idea of how the database is structured and what we can do with it:

```
CREATE TABLE people(
  id INT PRIMARY KEY,
  name VARCHAR(255) NOT NULL,
  age INT NOT NULL
)

CREATE TABLE classes(
  id INT PRIMARY KEY,
  name VARCHAR(255) NOT NULL,
)

CREATE TABLE people_classes(
  person_id INT NOT NULL,
  class_id INT NOT NULL,
```

```
    PRIMARY KEY(person_id, class_id),
    FOREIGN KEY(person_id) REFERENCES people(id) ON DELETE CASCADE ON UPDATE
CASCADE,
    FOREIGN KEY(class_id) REFERENCES classes(id) ON DELETE CASCADE ON UPDATE
CASCADE
)
```

Our migration service in the preceding code simply creates tables in a database and inserts some information into them so that we can then use the service. We saw that this migration service depends on the database service, and we also saw how this dependency is implemented.

Just by having these classes, our application will not be that useful. We need to be able to interact with the data and do something interesting with it. We can say that the migration component just makes sure we have the data. In real-world scenarios, we might already have a prepopulated database and we will need to work with what is inside this database. Whatever the case, we will need to have a data access layer to retrieve what we need. We have created the following component:

```
trait DaoComponent {
  this: DatabaseComponent =>
  val dao: Dao

  class Dao() {
    def getPeople: List[Person] = {
      // skipped
    }

    def getClasses: List[Class] = {
      // skipped
    }

    def getPeopleInClass(className: String): List[Person] = {
      val connection = databaseService.getConnection
      try {
        val statement = connection.prepareStatement(
          """
            |SELECT p.id, p.name, p.age
            |FROM people p
            | JOIN people_classes pc ON p.id = pc.person_id
            | JOIN classes c ON c.id = pc.class_id
            |WHERE c.name = ?
          """.stripMargin
        )
        statement.setString(1, className)
        executeSelect(statement) {
```

```
        rs =>
          readResultSet(rs) {
            row =>
              Person(row.getInt(1), row.getString(2), row.getInt(3))
          }
      }
    } finally {
      connection.close()
    }
  }

  private def executeSelect[T](preparedStatement: PreparedStatement)(f:
(ResultSet) => List[T]): List[T] =
    try {
      f(preparedStatement.executeQuery())
    } finally {
      preparedStatement.close()
    }

  private def readResultSet[T](rs: ResultSet)(f: ResultSet => T): List[T]
=
    Iterator.continually((rs.next(), rs)).takeWhile(_._1).map {
      case (_, row) => f(rs)
    }.toList
  }
}
```

This `DaoComponent` is similar to the `DatabaseComponent` in terms of its dependency. It just defines queries to retrieve data. We've skipped the simple `select` statements. It could, of course, define even more methods for insertions, updates, and deletes. It nicely hides the complexity of dealing with data from a database, and now we can actually create something useful in our application.

What is commonly seen in enterprise applications is different services that could access data in a database, perform some business logic on it, return results, and write it back into the database. We have created a simple service that deals with users:

```
trait UserComponent {
  this: DaoComponent =>
  val userService: UserService

  class UserService {
    def getAverageAgeOfUsersInClass(className: String): Double = {
      val (ageSum, peopleCount) =
dao.getPeopleInClass(className).foldLeft((0, 0)) {
        case ((sum, count), person) =>
          (sum + person.age, count + 1)
```

```
      }
    if (peopleCount != 0) {
      ageSum.toDouble / peopleCount.toDouble
    } else {
      0.0
    }
  }
  }
}
```

In our `UserComponent`, we follow the same pattern we already know, but this time our dependency is on `DaoComponent`. We can then have other components that depend on this component and on others as well. We haven't shown any example here in which a component depends on multiple ones at the same time, but this is not hard to do at all. We just use the following:

```
this: Component1 with Component2 with Component3 ... =>
```

We can have dependencies on as many components as we want, and this is where the cake design pattern starts to shine and shows its benefits.

Wiring it all up

In the preceding code, we saw a bunch of components with their implementations that declare dependencies to others. We still haven't seen how everything will be used together. By defining our components as traits, we can just mix them in together and they will be available to us. This is how we have done it:

```
object ApplicationComponentRegistry
  extends UserComponent
    with DaoComponent
    with DatabaseComponent
    with MigrationComponent {
  override val dao: ApplicationComponentRegistry.Dao = new Dao
  override val databaseService: DatabaseService = new
H2DatabaseService("jdbc:h2:mem:test;DB_CLOSE_DELAY=-1", "", "")
  override val migrationService:
ApplicationComponentRegistry.MigrationService = new MigrationService
  override val userService: ApplicationComponentRegistry.UserService = new
UserService
  }
```

In the preceding code, the `ApplicationComponentRegistry` can be a class as well, instead of a Scala object. It mixes the components in and, since each of them had an abstract variable, it forces us to assign actual values to them. The nicest part of this is that, if we know that our application will need a `UserComponent`, the compiler will tell us that we also need a `DaoComponent`, and so on, down the chain. The compiler will basically make sure that we have the entire dependency chain available during compilation, and it won't let us run our application until we have done things properly. This is extremely useful. In other libraries, this is not the case and we often find out that our dependency graph is not built properly at runtime. Also, this way of wiring things up makes sure we have only one instance of each.

If we had used a class instead of an object for the `ApplicationComponentRegistry`, the statement about having only one instance of each component doesn't automatically become true. We need to take extra care, otherwise each instance of the registry might have different instances of the components.

After we have created our component registry, we can easily use everything in our application:

```scala
object Application {

  import ApplicationComponentRegistry._

  def main(args: Array[String]): Unit = {
    migrationService.runMigrations()
    System.out.println(dao.getPeople)
    System.out.println(dao.getClasses)
    System.out.println(dao.getPeopleInClass("Scala Design Patterns"))
    System.out.println(dao.getPeopleInClass("Mountain Biking"))
    System.out.println(s"Average age of everyone in Scala Design Patterns:
${userService.getAverageAgeOfUsersInClass("Scala Design Patterns")}")
  }
}
```

In the preceding code, we simply imported everything from the registry and then we used it. The output of this application is shown in the following screenshot:

```
volcom@volcom-Dell-System-XPS-L502X:~/workspace/scala-book/functional-design-pat
terns$ java -cp target/functional-design-patterns-1.0.0-SNAPSHOT.jar com.ivan.ni
kolov.cake.Application
List(Person(1,Ivan,26), Person(2,Maria,25), Person(3,John,27))
List(Class(1,Scala Design Patterns), Class(2,Java Programming), Class(3,Mountain
 Biking))
List(Person(1,Ivan,26), Person(2,Maria,25), Person(3,John,27))
List(Person(1,Ivan,26), Person(3,John,27))
Average age of everyone in Scala Design Patterns: 26.0
```

This is how easy it is to use the cake design pattern in Scala.

Unit testing our application

Testing is an important part of every application. We need to make sure that the changes we add do not negatively affect the other parts of our system and that every unit behaves correctly. Testing with the cake design pattern is also really simple to achieve.

The cake design pattern allows us to easily create different environments. This is why we can create the following test environment:

```
trait TestEnvironment
  extends UserComponent
    with DaoComponent
    with DatabaseComponent
    with MigrationComponent
    with MockitoSugar {
  override val dao: Dao = mock[Dao]
  override val databaseService: DatabaseService = mock[DatabaseService]
  override val migrationService: MigrationService = mock[MigrationService]
  override val userService: UserService = mock[UserService]
}
```

The preceding code simply contains every component and mocks every service with Mockito. Let's write a test class for our `UserComponent` using our new test environment:

```
class UserComponentTest extends FlatSpec with Matchers with MockitoSugar
with TestEnvironment {
  val className = "A"
  val emptyClassName = "B"
  val people = List(
    Person(1, "a", 10),
```

```
    Person(2, "b", 15),
    Person(3, "c", 20)
  )
  override val userService = new UserService
  when(dao.getPeopleInClass(className)).thenReturn(people)
  when(dao.getPeopleInClass(emptyClassName)).thenReturn(List())
  "getAverageAgeOfUsersInClass" should "properly calculate the average of
all ages." in {
    userService.getAverageAgeOfUsersInClass(className) should equal(15.0)
  }
  it should "properly handle an empty result." in {
    userService.getAverageAgeOfUsersInClass(emptyClassName) should
equal(0.0)
  }
}
```

In the preceding code, we override the `userService` to be an actual implementation and then we use it for the tests. We use Mockito to simulate our database access and then we simply write a test that checks whether things work correctly. We have decided to simulate our database access. However, in some cases, people have test databases or use H2 for tests. Using our test environment, we have the flexibility to do whatever we decide.

Running the tests we wrote previously can be achieved with the `mvn clean test` or `sbt test` command.

Our test environment allows us to enable as many components in our tests as we want. We could simply override multiple such components in our test classes.

Other dependency injection alternatives

One thing about the cake design pattern that we presented previously is the amount of boilerplate code that we need to write in order to wire everything up properly. In large applications, this could become an issue, so there are other alternatives that can be used to deal with this. We will briefly discuss here.

Implicits for dependency injection

Using implicits is something that removes the requirement of having the component traits and self type annotations of the cake design pattern. Implicits, however, can quickly complicate method definitions because every method has to declare implicit parameters to whatever components it depends on.

Reader monad for dependency injection

The `Reader` monad is available in the Scalaz library. The way dependency injection works with it is that we make each method return a function wrapped in the `Reader` monad, for example:

```
def getAverageAgeOfUsersInClass(className: String) =
  Reader((userService: UserService) =>
userService.getAverageAgeOfUsersInClass(className))
```

In the preceding code, we only expose `getAverageAgeOfUsersInClass(className: String)` to the users. Typically, for monads, computation here is built, but nothing is done until the last moment. We can build complex operations, use `map`, `flatMap`, and for comprehensions. We defer injecting the dependencies until the last moment, where we can simply call `apply` on a reader with the actual component or components it needs. The preceding explanation might sound a bit abstract, but things are pretty simple and can be seen in many places online.

In some cases, this method is used together with the cake design pattern.

The pimp my library design pattern

In our daily job as developers, we often use different libraries. They, however, are usually made to be generic and allow many people to use them, so sometimes we need to do something extra that is specific to our use case in order to make things work properly. The fact that we cannot really modify the original library code means that we have to do something different. We have already looked at the decorator and the adapter design patterns. Well, pimp my library achieves something similar, but it does this in the Scala way and some of the extra work is given to the compiler to deal with.

The pimp my library design pattern is really similar to extension methods in C#. We will see some examples in the following subsections.

Using pimp my library

The pimp my library design pattern is really easy to use. Let's see an example in which we want to add some useful methods to the standard `String` class. Of course, we cannot modify its code, so we need to do something else:

```
package object pimp {
```

```
implicit class StringExtensions(val s: String) extends AnyVal {
  def isAllUpperCase: Boolean =
    !(0 until s.length).exists {
      case index =>
        s.charAt(index).isLower
    }
}
}
```

In the preceding code, we have a package object. It gives us the convenience to not do anything extra in order to be able to access its members from the classes in the same package in Scala. It can be a simple object, but then we will have to `import ObjectName._` in order to gain access to the members.

The preceding object is just a detail and is not related to the design pattern. The pimp my library code is the internal class. There are a few important things about this:

- It is implicit
- It extends `AnyVal`

These features allow us to write the following application:

```
object PimpExample {
  def main(args: Array[String]): Unit = {
    System.out.println(s"Is 'test' all upper case:
      ${"test".isAllUpperCase}")
    System.out.println(s"Is 'Tes' all upper case:
      ${"Test".isAllUpperCase}")
    System.out.println(s"Is 'TESt' all upper case:
      ${"TESt".isAllUpperCase}")
    System.out.println(s"Is 'TEST' all upper case:
      ${"TEST".isAllUpperCase}")
  }
}
```

We basically added an extension method to the standard string that checks whether the entire string is in uppercase or not. The only thing we need to do is make sure that the implicit class is available in the scope where we want to use the methods defined by it.

The output of the preceding application is shown as follows:

```
volcom@volcom-Dell-System-XPS-L502X:~/workspace/scala-book/functional-design-pat
terns$ java -cp target/functional-design-patterns-1.0.0-SNAPSHOT.jar com.ivan.ni
kolov.pimp.PimpExample
Is 'test' all upper case: false
Is 'Tes' all upper case: false
Is 'TESt' all upper case: false
Is 'TEST' all upper case: true
```

In our example, we didn't have to write code that wraps strings in our extension class. Our code shows the type as a normal string; however, we can just do extra things with it. Additionally, the decorator design pattern will suffer in the cases where the class we are trying to decorate is final. Here, there is no issue. Again, all the magic happens because we have an implicit class, and the Scala compiler automatically figures out that it can wrap and unwrap a string depending on the methods we call on it.

We can, of course, add more methods to the `StringExtensions` class and they will be available to all the strings where the implicit class is available. We can also add other classes:

```
implicit class PersonSeqExtensions(val seq: Iterable[Person]) extends
AnyVal {
  def saveToDatabase(): Unit = {
    seq.foreach {
      case person =>
        System.out.println(s"Saved: ${person} to the database.")
    }
  }
}
```

The preceding code is capable of saving an entire collection of the `Person` type to a database (even though, in the example, we just print the collection to the standard output). For completeness, our `Person` model class is defined as follows:

```
case class Person(name: String, age: Int)
```

Using the new extension is then similar to the earlier extension:

```
object PimpExample2 {
  def main(args: Array[String]): Unit = {
    val people = List(
      Person("Ivan", 26),
      Person("Maria", 26),
      Person("John", 25)
    )
```

```
        people.saveToDatabase()
    }
}
```

The preceding example will produce the expected result, as follows:

```
volcom@volcom-Dell-System-XPS-L502X:~/workspace/scala-book/functional-design-pat
terns$ java -cp target/functional-design-patterns-1.0.0-SNAPSHOT.jar com.ivan.ni
kolov.pimp.PimpExample2
Saved: Person(Ivan,26) to the database.
Saved: Person(Maria,26) to the database.
Saved: Person(John,25) to the database.
```

We can also apply the pimp my library design pattern to our custom classes if we need to and if it makes sense.

Pimp my library in real life

As you can see from the preceding section, the pimp my library design pattern is extremely easy to use. This is seen quite often, especially when a decorator or adapter design pattern is needed. We can, of course, figure out ways to deal with issues without this library design but, in reality, it helps us to avoid boilerplate code. It also really helps in making our code more readable. Last but not least, it can be used to simplify the use of specific libraries.

The stackable traits design pattern

There are sometimes cases where we want to be able to provide different implementations for a method of a class. We might not even know all the possibilities that could exist at the moment of writing, but we can add them later and combine them or we can allow someone else to do this instead. This is another use case of the decorator design pattern, which for this purpose could be implemented with the stackable traits design pattern. We have already seen this pattern before in this book in Chapter 7, *Structural Design Patterns*, but we used it to read data, which adds a really important catch there. We will see another example here, which will make sure everything is completely clear.

Using stackable traits

The stackable traits design pattern is based on mixin composition—something we became familiar with in the early chapters of this book. We usually have an abstract class or a trait that defines an interface, a base implementation, and traits that extend the abstract class to stack modifications on it.

For our example, let's implement the following diagram:

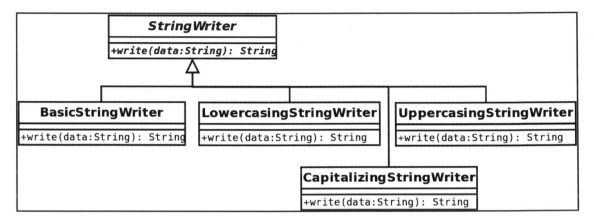

The preceding diagram is of a really simple application. We have a base `StringWriter` class, which has a basic implementation (`BasicStringWriter`) that just returns a message containing the string. On the right-hand side, we have traits that can add stackable modifications to the `StringWriter`.

Let's see the following code:

```
abstract class StringWriter {
  def write(data: String): String
}

class BasicStringWriter extends StringWriter {
  override def write(data: String): String =
    s"Writing the following data: ${data}"
}
```

The preceding code is of the abstract class and the basic implementation. There is nothing special about these. Now, let's look at the stackable traits:

```
trait CapitalizingStringWriter extends StringWriter {
  abstract override def write(data: String): String = {
    super.write(data.split("\\s+").map(_.capitalize).mkString(""))
  }
}

trait UppercasingStringWriter extends StringWriter {
  abstract override def write(data: String): String = {
    super.write(data.toUpperCase)
  }
}

trait LowercasingStringWriter extends StringWriter {
  abstract override def write(data: String): String = {
    super.write(data.toLowerCase)
  }
}
```

The whole magic in the preceding code happens because of the `abstract override` modifier on the methods. It allows us to call `super` on an abstract method of the `super` class. This would otherwise fail, but here it just requires us to mix the traits in with a class or a trait that has `write` implemented. If we don't, we won't be able to compile our code.

Let's see an example use of our traits:

```
object Example {
  def main(args: Array[String]): Unit = {
    val writer1 = new BasicStringWriter
      with UppercasingStringWriter
      with CapitalizingStringWriter
    val writer2 = new BasicStringWriter
      with CapitalizingStringWriter
      with LowercasingStringWriter
    val writer3 = new BasicStringWriter
      with CapitalizingStringWriter
      with UppercasingStringWriter
      with LowercasingStringWriter
    val writer4 = new BasicStringWriter
      with CapitalizingStringWriter
      with LowercasingStringWriter
      with UppercasingStringWriter
    System.out.println(s"Writer 1: '${writer1.write("we like learning
      scala!")}'")
    System.out.println(s"Writer 2: '${writer2.write("we like learning
```

```
        scala!")}'")
    System.out.println(s"Writer 3: '${writer3.write("we like learning
      scala!")}'")
    System.out.println(s"Writer 4: '${writer4.write("we like learning
      scala!")}'")
  }
}
```

In the preceding code, we simply stack modifications together using mixin composition. In the current example, they are just illustrations that don't do anything smart, but, in reality, we can have variations that will provide powerful modifications. The following figure shows the output of our example:

```
volcom@volcom-Dell-System-XPS-L502X:~/workspace/scala-book/functional-design-pat
terns$ java -cp target/functional-design-patterns-1.0.0-SNAPSHOT.jar com.ivan.ni
kolov.stackable.Example
Writer 1: 'Writing the following data: WE LIKE LEARNING SCALA!'
Writer 2: 'Writing the following data: We Like Learning Scala!'
Writer 3: 'Writing the following data: WE LIKE LEARNING SCALA!'
Writer 4: 'Writing the following data: We Like Learning Scala!'
```

The modifications we have in our code would depend on the order in which they are applied. For example, if we put everything in uppercase first, then capitalization will not have any effect. Let's see the code and the relevant output and try to figure out how the modifications are applied. If you look at all the examples and outputs, you will see that the modifications are applied *from right to left* in the order we have mixed the traits in.

If we look back at the example in Chapter 7, *Structural Design Patterns*, however, we will see that the actual modifications are reversed. The reason for this is that each trait does `super.readLines` and then maps. Well, this actually means that we will be pushing calls on the stack until we get to the basic implementation, and then we will be going back to do all the mappings. So in Chapter 7, *Structural Design Patterns*, the modifications are also applied from right to left, but because we just get the output and don't pass anything on, things are applied in left to right order.

The stackable traits order of execution

Stackable traits are always executed from the right mixin to the left. Sometimes, however, if we only get output and it doesn't depend on what is passed to the method, we simply end up with method calls on a stack, which then get evaluated and it will appear as if things are applied from left to right.

Understanding the preceding explanation is really important for using stackable traits. It actually perfectly matches what we saw about linearization in `Chapter 2`, *Traits and Mixin Compositions*.

The type class design pattern

A lot of times when we write software, we encounter similarities between different implementations. An important principle of good code design is to avoid repetition and it is known as **do not repeat yourself (DRY)**. There are multiple ways that help us to avoid repetitions—inheritance, generics, and so on.

One way to make sure we do not repeat ourselves is through type classes.

 The purpose of type classes is to define some behavior in terms of operations that a type must support in order to be considered a member of the type class.

A concrete example would be `Numeric`. We can say that it is a type class and defines the operations—addition, subtraction, multiplication, and so on, for the `Int`, `Double`, and such other classes. We have actually already encountered type classes earlier in this book in `Chapter 4`, *Abstract and Self Types*. Type classes are the ones that allow us to implement ad hoc polymorphism.

Type class example

Let's see an actual example that is also somehow useful to developers in this case. In machine learning, developers tend to use some statistical functions quite often in their work. There are statistical libraries and, if we try them out, we will see that these functions exist for different numeric types—`Int`, `Double`, and so on. Now, we could come up with something simple and implement these functions for all the numeric types we think about. This, however, is not feasible and makes our library impossible to extend. Moreover, statistical functions have the same definitions, no matter the type, so we don't want to repeat our code as many times as there are numeric types.

So let's first define our type class:

```
trait Number[T] {
  def plus(x: T, y: T): T
  def minus(x: T, y: T): T
  def divide(x: T, y: Int): T
  def multiply(x: T, y: T): T
  def sqrt(x: T): T
}
```

The preceding is just a trait that defines some operations that will require numbers to support it.

Numeric in Scala

The Scala programming language has a `Numeric` trait that defines many of the previously mentioned operations.

If we had used the `Numeric` trait in the preceding code, we could have saved ourselves from some code writing, but for the sake of this example, let's use our custom type.

After we have defined a trait for the numbers, we can now write our library as follows:

```
object Stats {
  // same as
  // def mean[T](xs: Vector[T])(implicit ev: Number[T]): T =
  // ev.divide(xs.reduce(ev.plus(_, _)), xs.size)
  def mean[T: Number](xs: Vector[T]): T =
    implicitly[Number[T]].divide(
      xs.reduce(implicitly[Number[T]].plus(_, _)),
      xs.size
    )

  // assumes the vector is sorted
  def median[T: Number](xs: Vector[T]): T =
    xs(xs.size / 2)

  def variance[T: Number](xs: Vector[T]): T = {
    val simpleMean = mean(xs)
    val sqDiff = xs.map {
      case x =>
        val diff = implicitly[Number[T]].minus(x, simpleMean)
        implicitly[Number[T]].multiply(diff, diff)
    }
    mean(sqDiff)
  }
```

```
def stddev[T: Number](xs: Vector[T]): T =
  implicitly[Number[T]].sqrt(variance(xs))
}
```

There is quite a lot of code in the preceding example. Defining the functions is pretty straightforward. Let's, however, explain the role of the `implicitly` keyword. It uses the so-called **context bounds** from Scala, and it is the crucial part that allows us to implement the type class design pattern. In order to use the preceding methods, it requires a type class member of `Number` for the `T` type to be implicitly available. As you can see in the comment above `mean`, we can alternatively have an implicit parameter to the methods.

Now, let's write some example code that will use the previously mentioned methods:

```
import Stats._

object StatsExample {
  def main(args: Array[String]): Unit = {
    val intVector = Vector(1, 3, 5, 6, 10, 12, 17, 18, 19, 30, 36, 40, 42,
66)
    val doubleVector = Vector(1.5, 3.6, 5.0, 6.6, 10.9, 12.1, 17.3, 18.4,
19.2, 30.9, 36.6, 40.2, 42.3, 66.0)
    System.out.println(s"Mean (int): ${mean(intVector)}")
    System.out.println(s"Median (int): ${median(intVector)}")
    System.out.println(s"Std dev (int): ${stddev(intVector)}")
    System.out.println(s"Mean (double): ${mean(doubleVector)}")
    System.out.println(s"Median (double): ${median(doubleVector)}")
    System.out.println(s"Std dev (double): ${stddev(doubleVector)}")
  }
}
```

Compiling the preceding code right now will not be successful and we will see error similar to the following:

```
Error:(9, 44) could not find implicit value for evidence parameter of type
com.ivan.nikolov.type_classes.Number[Int]
    System.out.println(s"Mean (int): ${mean(intVector)}")
                                          ^
```

The reason for this is that we have not yet defined any implicitly available `Number` members for `Int` and `Double`. Let's define them in the companion object for the `Number` trait:

```
import Math.round

object Number {
  implicit object DoubleNumber extends Number[Double] {
    override def plus(x: Double, y: Double): Double = x + y
    override def divide(x: Double, y: Int): Double = x / y
```

```
      override def multiply(x: Double, y: Double): Double = x * y
      override def minus(x: Double, y: Double): Double = x - y
      override def sqrt(x: Double): Double = Math.sqrt(x)
    }
  implicit object IntNumber extends Number[Int] {
    override def plus(x: Int, y: Int): Int = x + y
    override def divide(x: Int, y: Int): Int = round(x.toDouble /
y.toDouble).toInt
    override def multiply(x: Int, y: Int): Int = x * y
    override def minus(x: Int, y: Int): Int - x - y
    override def sqrt(x: Int): Int = round(Math.sqrt(x)).toInt
  }
}
```

Now, our code will compile successfully. But how did this whole thing work when we had just defined these implicits in a companion object in a completely different file? First of all, our nested objects are implicit, and second of all, they are available in the companion object.

Defining your default type class members in the companion object

The companion object of the implicit type class parameter is the last place the compiler looks for implicit values. This means that nothing extra has to be done and users can easily override our implementations.

We can now run our code easily:

```
volcom@volcom-Dell-System-XPS-L502X:~/workspace/scala-book/functional-design-pat
terns$ java -cp target/functional-design-patterns-1.0.0-SNAPSHOT.jar com.ivan.ni
kolov.type_classes.StatsExample
Mean (int): 22
Median (int): 18
Std dev (int): 18
Mean (double): 22.185714285714287
Median (double): 18.4
Std dev (double): 17.96881652605254
```

Of course, we can put our implicit values anywhere we want. If they are not in the companion object, however, we will have to do extra imports in order to make them available.

Type class design pattern alternatives

There are, of course, alternatives to the type class design pattern. We can use the adapter design pattern. It will, however, make it much harder to read our code because things will be wrapped all the time and they will be much more verbose. The type class design pattern takes advantage of the nice features of the Scala type system.

Looking at our preceding code, we can also see that there is a fair bit of boilerplate code. This can become problematic in bigger projects, or when we try to define more complex type classes. A library that was written specifically to deal with these issues can be found at `https://github.com/mpilquist/simulacrum/`.

Lazy evaluation

Writing efficient code is an important part of software engineering. A lot of times, we will see cases where an expression is expensive to evaluate due to different possible reasons—database access, complex calculations, and so on. There are cases where we might even be able to exit the application without even evaluating these expensive expressions. This is where lazy evaluation becomes helpful.

 Lazy evaluation makes sure that an expression is evaluated only once when it is actually needed.

Scala supports lazy evaluation in a couple of flavors—lazy variables and by-name parameters. We have already seen both in this book the former we saw when we looked at creational design patterns in `Chapter 6`, *Creational Design Patterns,* and more specifically, lazy initialization. We saw the latter in a few places, but we encountered it for the first time in `Chapter 8`, *Behavioral Design Patterns - Part 1*, where we showed you how to implement the command design pattern in a way that is closer to how Scala does it.

There is an important difference between lazy variables and by-name parameters. The lazy variables will be calculated only once, whereas the by-name parameters will be calculated every time they are referred to in a method. There is a really simple trick we will show here that will fix this issue.

Evaluating by-name parameters only once

Let's imagine that we have an application that takes data about people from a database. The reading operation is something that is expensive, and it is a good candidate for lazy evaluation. For this example, we will simply simulate reading from the database. First of all, our model will be as simple as the following:

```
case class Person(name: String, age: Int)
```

Now, let's create a companion object that will have a method that simulates getting the data about people from a database:

```
object Person {
  def getFromDatabase(): List[Person] = {
    // simulate we're getting people from database by sleeping
    System.out.println("Retrieving people...")
    Thread.sleep(3000)
    List(
      Person("Ivan", 26),
      Person("Maria", 26),
      Person("John", 25)
    )
  }
}
```

The preceding code simply makes the current thread sleep for three seconds and returns a static result. Calling the `getFromDatabase` method multiple times will make our application slow, so we should consider lazy evaluation. Now, let's add the following method to our companion object:

```
def printPeopleBad(people: => List[Person]): Unit = {
  System.out.println(s"Print first time: ${people}")
  System.out.println(s"Print second time: ${people}")
}
```

As you can see, we simply printed the list of data about people twice and we accessed the by-name parameter twice. This is bad because it will evaluate the function twice and we will have to wait for twice the amount of time. Let's write another version that will fix this issue:

```
def printPeopleGood(people: => List[Person]): Unit = {
  lazy val peopleCopy = people
  System.out.println(s"Print first time: ${peopleCopy}")
  System.out.println(s"Print second time: ${peopleCopy}")
}
```

This time, we will assign the by-name parameter to a `lazy val` and then use it instead. This will only evaluate the by-name parameter once and, again, if we end up not using it, it will not be evaluated at all.

Let's see an example:

```scala
object Example {

  import Person._

  def main(args: Array[String]): Unit = {
    System.out.println("Now printing bad.")
    printPeopleBad(getFromDatabase())
    System.out.println("Now printing good.")
    printPeopleGood(getFromDatabase())
  }
}
```

If we run this application, we will see the following output:

```
volcom@volcom-Dell-System-XPS-L502X:~/workspace/scala-book/functional-design-pat
terns$ java -cp target/functional-design-patterns-1.0.0-SNAPSHOT.jar com.ivan.ni
kolov.laziness.Example
Now printing bad.
Retrieving people...
Print first time: List(Person(Ivan,26), Person(Maria,26), Person(John,25))
Retrieving people...
Print second time: List(Person(Ivan,26), Person(Maria,26), Person(John,25))
Now printing good.
Retrieving people...
Print first time: List(Person(Ivan,26), Person(Maria,26), Person(John,25))
Print second time: List(Person(Ivan,26), Person(Maria,26), Person(John,25))
```

As you can see from the program output, the first version of our method retrieves the by-name parameter value twice, while the second version does it only once. The fact that we use a `lazy val` inside the second method also has the possibility of not evaluating our expensive expression at all if we don't actually use it.

Alternative lazy evaluation

There is another way to implement lazy evaluations in Scala. It is through using anonymous functions and taking advantage of the fact that functions are a part of unifications in Scala and we can also pass them as parameters easily. This is done as follows—a value is represented as `() => value` rather than just the value itself. It is somewhat pointless, though, especially because we already have two mechanisms that can do quite a lot. Using anonymous functions for a lazy evaluation is not recommended.

Passing a function to a method can also be considered as a way of lazily evaluating some data. This, however, can be useful and should not be confused with what we just said about anonymous functions.

Partial functions

In mathematics and, as a consequence, in programming, there are functions that are not defined for all possible inputs. A simple example is the square root function—it will only work for real numbers if they are non-negative. In this section, we will look at partial functions and how we can use them.

Partial functions are not partially applied functions

There seems to be some confusion around what partial functions are and what they are not. It is important for you to understand that these functions are not partially applied functions. Partially applied functions are simply functions that might take multiple parameters and we've specified some of them and then they return functions with fewer parameters that we can specify. There is another term—**curried functions**—that is related to partially applied functions. In terms of functionality, they provide the same functionality. Let's see a quick example:

```
/**
  * Note that these are not partially defined functions!
  */
object PartiallyAppliedFunctions {
  val greaterOrEqual = (a: Int, b: Int) => a >= b
  val lessOrEqual = (a: Int, b: Int) => a <= b

  def greaterOrEqualCurried(b: Int)(a: Int) = a >= b
```

```
def lessOrEqualCurried(b: Int)(a: Int) = a <= b

val greaterOrEqualCurriedVal: (Int) => (Int) => Boolean = b => a => a >=
b
val lessOrEqualCurriedVal: (Int) => (Int) => Boolean = b => a => a <= b
}
```

In the preceding code, we have different definitions of greater and lesser or equal functions. First, we have them as normal functions. The second version is with multiple parameter lists and the last one is an actual curried function. Here is how to use them:

```
object PartiallyAppliedExample {

  import PartiallyAppliedFunctions._

  val MAX = 20
  val MIN = 5

  def main(args: Array[String]): Unit = {
    val numbers = List(1, 5, 6, 11, 18, 19, 20, 21, 25, 30)
    // partially applied
    val ge = greaterOrEqual(_: Int, MIN)
    val le = lessOrEqual(_: Int, MAX)
    // curried
    val geCurried = greaterOrEqualCurried(MIN) _
    val leCurried = lessOrEqualCurried(MAX) _
    // won't work because of the argument order
    // val geCurried = greaterOrEqual.curried(MIN)
    // val leCurried = lessOrEqual.curried(MAX)
    // will work normally
    // val geCurried = greaterOrEqualCurriedVal(MIN)
    // val leCurried = lessOrEqualCurriedVal(MAX)
    System.out.println(s"Filtered list: ${numbers.filter(i => ge(i) &&
le(i))}")
    System.out.println(s"Filtered list: ${numbers.filter(i => geCurried(i)
&& leCurried(i))}")
  }
}
```

The way we use partially applied functions is as follows:

```
greaterOrEqual(_: Int, MIN)
```

This returns a function of Int to Boolean, which we can use to check whether the parameter is greater or equal to the MIN value. This is a partially applied function.

For the curried versions of these functions, as you can see, we have switched the parameters. The reason is that curried functions are simply a chain of single parameter functions and the parameters are applied in the order we see them. The line `greaterOrEqualCurried(MIN) _` partially applies the function and returns a curried function that we can use similarly to above. As you can see in the code comments, we can actually convert any multiple parameter function into a curried function. The reason for `greaterOrEqual` and `lessOrEqual` not working in our example is that the parameters are applied in the order they are seen. Finally, we have a pure curried version in `greaterOrEqualCurriedVal` and `lessOrEqualCurriedVal`. This type of function is returned when we partially apply a function with multiple parameter lists.

If we run the preceding example, we will see the following output:

```
volcom@volcom-Dell-System-XPS-L502X:~/workspace/scala-book/functional-design-pat
ternns$ java -cp target/functional-design-patterns-1.0.0-SNAPSHOT.jar com.ivan.ni
kolov.partial_functions.PartiallyAppliedExample
Filtered list: List(5, 6, 11, 18, 19, 20)
Filtered list: List(5, 6, 11, 18, 19, 20)
```

Choosing whether to use partially applied functions or curried functions depends on many things, including personal preference. In both cases, we can achieve the same objectives with a slightly different syntax. As you can see, we can go from a normal to a curried function using `.curried`. We can also go the other way round using the `Function.uncurried` call and passing the function to it. This call makes sense when the curried function has more than one function in the chain.

Using partially applied functions for dependency injection

Because of the way partially applied functions and curried functions work, we can use them for dependency injection. We can basically apply the dependencies to a function and then get another function, which we can use afterward.

Partially defined functions

We already said that partial functions are only defined for specific subsets of all possible values the functions can get. This is quite useful, as we can basically perform `filter` and `map` at once. This means fewer CPU cycles and more readable code. Let's see an example:

```
object PartiallyDefinedFunctions {
  val squareRoot: PartialFunction[Int, Double] = {
```

```
    case a if a >= 0 => Math.sqrt(a)
  }
}
```

We defined a partial function from `Int` to `Double`. It checks whether a number is non-negative and returns the square root of that number. This partial function can be used as follows:

```
object PartiallyDefinedExample {

  import PartiallyDefinedFunctions._

  def main(args: Array[String]): Unit = {
    val items = List(-1, 10, 11, -36, 36, -49, 49, 81)
    System.out.println(s"Can we calculate a root for -10:
      ${squareRoot.isDefinedAt(-10)}")
    System.out.println(s"Square roots: ${items.collect(squareRoot)}")
  }
}
```

We are using the `collect` method that takes a partial function. We've also shown one of the methods that partial functions have—`isDefinedAt`, whose name tells us exactly what it does. The output of our program will be this:

```
volcom@volcom-Dell-System-XPS-L502X:~/workspace/scala-book/functional-design-pat
terns$ java -cp target/functional-design-patterns-1.0.0-SNAPSHOT.jar com.ivan.ni
kolov.partial_functions.PartiallyDefinedExample
Can we calculate a root for -10: false
Square roots: List(3.1622776601683795, 3.3166247903554, 6.0, 7.0, 9.0)
```

Our partial function filtered out the negative numbers and returned the square roots of the rest.

Partial functions can also be used to chain operations or do something different if one operation is not possible. They have the `orElse`, `andThen`, `runWith`, and such other methods. It is clear from their names what the first two methods do. The third method uses the results of the partially applied function and performs an action that could potentially cause side effects. Let's see an example of `orElse`:

```
val square: PartialFunction[Int, Double] = {
  case a if a < 0 => Math.pow(a, 2)
}
```

First, we define another partial function that squares negative numbers. Then, we can add some extra code to our example:

```
object PartiallyDefinedExample {

  import PartiallyDefinedFunctions._

  def main(args: Array[String]): Unit = {
    val items = List(-1, 10, 11, -36, 36, -49, 49, 81)
    System.out.println(s"Can we calculate a root for -10:
      ${squareRoot.isDefinedAt( 10)}")
    System.out.println(s"Square roots: ${items.collect(squareRoot)}")
    System.out.println(s"Square roots or squares:
      ${items.collect(squareRoot.orElse(square))}")
  }
}
```

This will produce the following output:

```
volcom@volcom-Dell-System-XPS-L502X:~/workspace/scala-book/functional-design-pat
terns$ java -cp target/functional-design-patterns-1.0.0-SNAPSHOT.jar com.ivan.ni
kolov.partial_functions.PartiallyDefinedExample
Can we calculate a root for -10: false
Square roots: List(3.1622776601683795, 3.3166247903554, 6.0, 7.0, 9.0)
Square roots or squares: List(1.0, 3.1622776601683795, 3.3166247903554, 1296.0,
6.0, 2401.0, 7.0, 9.0)
```

We will basically square the negative numbers and square root the positive ones. It might not make much sense in terms of the operations we do in this example, but it shows how we can chain partial functions. If, after combining the different partial functions, we end up covering the whole possible input space, then it might make more sense to use pattern matching and a normal function. If we don't match all the possible values, however, we can get runtime exceptions.

Implicit injection

We already saw implicits in a few places in this book. We used them in the type class design pattern and the pimp my library design pattern, and we also mentioned that they can be used for dependency injection. Implicits are also used for conversions from one type to another silently.

They are nothing more than some objects, values, or methods that the compiler knows about and injects for us into methods or places that need them. What we need to make sure is to make these implicits available to the scope of the methods that will use them.

Implicit conversions

We have already mentioned that implicits can be used for silent conversions. Sometimes, it might be useful to be able to assign a `Double` to an `Int` and not get an error. Other times, we might want to wrap an object of one type into another and take advantage of the methods the new one provides:

```
package object implicits {
    implicit def doubleToInt(a: Double): Int = Math.round(a).toInt
}
```

In the preceding code listing, we have a package object that defines a method, which converts a `Double` to `Int`. This will allow us to write and successfully compile the following code:

```
object ImplicitExamples {
  def main(args: Array[String]): Unit = {
    val number: Int = 7.6
    System.out.println(s"The integer value for 7.6 is ${number}")
  }
}
```

We don't have to do anything extra, as long as the `ImplicitExamples` object is in the same package as our package object. Another alternative would be to define our implicit conversions inside an object and import the object in the scope we will need it in.

We can even wrap types in new objects. There are some examples in the `LowPriorityImplicits` class that is part of Scala, which can convert strings to sequences and so on. Now, let's add an implicit conversion that will convert a list of `Int` to a `String`:

```
implicit def intsToString(ints: List[Int]): String =
ints.map(_.toChar).mkString
```

Now, we can use our implicit conversion in order to print a list of ASCII character codes as a `String`:

```scala
object ImplicitExamples {
  def main(args: Array[String]): Unit = {
    val number: Int = 7.6
    System.out.println(s"The integer value for 7.6 is ${number}")
    // prints HELLO!
    printAsciiString(List(72, 69, 76, 76, 79, 33))
  }

  def printAsciiString(s: String): Unit = {
    System.out.println(s)
  }
}
```

Running this example will produce the following output:

```
volcom@volcom-Dell-System-XPS-L502X:~/workspace/scala-book/functional-design-pat
terns$ java -cp target/functional-design-patterns-1.0.0-SNAPSHOT.jar com.ivan.ni
kolov.implicits.ImplicitExamples
The integer value for 7.6 is 8
HELLO!
```

There are a lot of useful things which we might need implicit conversions for. They could help in separating our code nicely, but we should be careful not to overuse them because debugging could be problematic and the code's readability might suffer.

Dependency injection using implicits

When we showed dependency injection using the cake design pattern, we also mentioned that it is possible to achieve it using implicits. The idea is that services are created in one place and then we can write methods that implicitly require what the services need. By now, you should have acquired enough knowledge to be able to get to the right solution alone, so here we will just show a subset of the big example we had previously:

```scala
case class Person(name: String, age: Int)
```

After we have a model defined, we can create a `DatabaseService` as follows:

```
trait DatabaseService {
  def getPeople(): List[Person]
}

class DatabaseServiceImpl extends DatabaseService {
  override def getPeople(): List[Person] = List(
    Person("Ivan", 26),
    Person("Maria", 26),
    Person("John", 25)
  )
}
```

Our database service does not depend on anything. It simply simulates that it reads something from a database. Now, let's create a `UserService`, which will depend on the `DatabaseService`:

```
trait UserService {
  def getAverageAgeOfPeople()(implicit ds: DatabaseService): Double
}

class UserServiceImpl extends UserService {
  override def getAverageAgeOfPeople()(implicit ds: DatabaseService):
Double = {
    val (s, c) = ds.getPeople().foldLeft((0, 0)) {
      case ((sum, count), person) =>
        (sum + person.age, count + 1)
    }
    s.toDouble / c.toDouble
  }
}
```

As you can see from the signature of the only method the user service provides, it requires an instance of `DatabaseService` to be implicitly available. We can also explicitly pass one and override the one we have for the purpose of testing. Now that we have these services, we can wire them up:

```
package object di {
  implicit val databaseService = new DatabaseServiceImpl
  implicit val userService = new UserServiceImpl
}
```

We have chosen to use a package object, but any object or class is fine, as long as we can import it wherever we need the object. Now, the use of our application is easy:

```
object ImplicitDIExample {
  def main(args: Array[String]): Unit = {
    System.out.println(s"The average age of the people is:
    ${userService.getAverageAgeOfPeople()}")
  }
}
```

The output will be the following:

```
volcom@volcom-Dell-System-XPS-L502X:~/workspace/scala-book/functional-design-pa
terns$ java -cp target/functional-design-patterns-1.0.0-SNAPSHOT.jar com.ivan.n
kolov.implicits.di.ImplicitDIExample
The average age of the people is: 25.666666666666668
```

As you can see, now we have used less boilerplate code than in the cake design pattern. A drawback of this approach is the method signatures, which can get more complex when we have more dependencies. In real-world applications, there could be a huge amount of dependencies, and also code readability will be affected due to the implicit variables. A possible solution to this could be wrapping dependencies in objects and implicitly passing them instead. In the end, it's mostly a matter of personal preference as to which dependency injection strategy will be used, as the same things can be achieved with both.

Testing with implicit dependency injection

Testing with implicit dependency injection is similar to testing with the cake design pattern. We can have a new object that creates mocks of the services and then makes them available to the test classes. When we want to use a concrete implementation of a service, we can just override it. We could also pass a dependency explicitly here.

Duck typing

A significant part of the work of a developer is to minimize the amount of code duplication. There are multiple different approaches to do this, including inheritance, abstraction, generics, type classes, and so on. There are cases, however, where strongly typed languages will require some extra work in order to minimize some of the duplication. Let's imagine that we have a method that can read and print the contents of a file. If we have two different libraries that allow us to read a file, in order to use our method, we will have to make sure the methods that read the file somehow become the same type. One way would be by wrapping them in a class that implements a specific interface. Provided that in both the libraries the read method has the same signature, which could easily happen, Scala can use duck typing instead, and this way it will minimize the extra work we will have to do.

 Duck typing is a term that comes from dynamic languages and it allows us to treat different types of objects in a similar manner based on a common method they have.

Another name for duck typing is **structural typing**.

Duck typing example

Everything becomes clearer with an example. Let's imagine that we want to have a method which can take a parser and print every word that the parser detects. Our parsers will have a method with the following signature:

```
def parse(sentence: String): Array[String]
```

A good way of doing this would be to have a common interface and make all the parsers implement it. However, let's set a condition that we cannot do this. The parsers could be coming from two different libraries where we cannot modify or connect in any way.

We have defined two different parser implementations for this example. The first one is as follows:

```
import java.util.StringTokenizer

class SentenceParserTokenize {
  def parse(sentence: String): Array[String] = {
    val tokenizer = new StringTokenizer(sentence)
    Iterator.continually({
      val hasMore = tokenizer.hasMoreTokens
      if (hasMore) {
```

```
          (hasMore, tokenizer.nextToken())
       } else {
          (hasMore, null)
       }
    }).takeWhile(_._1).map(_._2).toArray
  }
}
```

This parser makes use of the StringTokenizer class and returns an array of all the words separated by spaces. Another implementation that does exactly the same is shown here:

```
class SentenceParserSplit {
  def parse(sentence: String): Array[String] = sentence.split("\\s")
}
```

Here, we just split the sentence using a regular expression for space.

As you can see, both the classes have a parse method with the same signature, but they have no connection with each other. We, however, want to be able to use them in a method and avoid code duplication. Here is how we can do this:

```
object DuckTypingExample {
  def printSentenceParts(sentence: String, parser: {
    def parse(sentence: String): Array[String]
  }) = parser.parse(sentence).foreach(println)

  def main(args: Array[String]): Unit = {
    val tokenizerParser = new SentenceParserTokenize
    val splitParser = new SentenceParserSplit
    val sentence = "This is the sentence we will be splitting."
    System.out.println("Using the tokenize parser: ")
    printSentenceParts(sentence, tokenizerParser)
    System.out.println("Using the split parser: ")
    printSentenceParts(sentence, splitParser)
  }
}
```

In the preceding code, we passed both the parsers to the printSentenceParts method and everything compiles and works fine. The reason things work is because of duck typing and this can be seen in the highlighted part of our example. The output of our application is the following:

```
volcom@volcom-Dell-System-XPS-L502X:~/workspace/scala-book/functional-design-pat
terns$ java -cp target/functional-design-patterns-1.0.0-SNAPSHOT.jar com.ivan.ni
kolov.duck.DuckTypingExample
Using the tokenize parser:
This
is
the
sentence
we
will
be
splitting.
Using the split parser:
This
is
the
sentence
we
will
be
splitting.
```

We can use duck typing for requiring even more methods to be available for an object by just expanding the parameter signature.

Duck typing alternatives

As you can see from the preceding code, duck typing saves us from some extra code writing and the need to define common interfaces. Other ways to achieve the same would involve creating wrappers, which implement a common interface.

When to use duck typing

Overusing duck typing can negatively affect code quality and application performance. You should not avoid creating common interfaces in favor of duck typing. It should be really only used in cases when we cannot implement a common interface between different types. The argument about limiting the use of duck typing is further enhanced by the fact that, under the hood, they use reflection, which is slower and negatively impacts performance.

Memoization

Writing high-performance programs is usually a mixture of using good algorithms and the smart usage of computer processing power. Caching is one mechanism that can help us, especially when a method takes time to calculate or it's called a lot of times in our application.

 Memoization is a mechanism of recording a function result based on its arguments in order to reduce computation in consecutive calls.

Along with saving CPU cycles, memoization can also be useful to minimize the application memory footprint by only having one instance of each result. Of course, for this entire mechanism to work, we need to have a function that always returns the same result when the same arguments are passed.

Memoization example

There are different ways to achieve memoization. Some of them use imperative programming styles and it's pretty straightforward to get to them. Here, we will show an approach which is more suitable for Scala.

Let's imagine that we will need to hash strings millions of times. Each hashing takes some time, depending on the underlying algorithm, but if we store some results and reuse them for repeated strings, we can save some computation at the expense of having a table of results.

We will start with something as simple as this:

```
import org.apache.commons.codec.binary.Hex

class Hasher extends Memoizer {
  def md5(input: String) = {
    System.out.println(s"Calling md5 for $input.")
    new
String(Hex.encodeHex(MessageDigest.getInstance("MD5").digest(input.getBytes
)))
  }
}
```

The preceding code is of a class that has a method called `md5`, which returns a hash of the string we pass to it. We have mixed in a trait called `Memoizer`, which has the following representation:

```
import scala.collection.mutable.Map

trait Memoizer {
  def memo[X, Y](f: X => Y): (X => Y) = {
    val cache = Map[X, Y]()
    (x: X) => cache.getOrElseUpdate(x, f(x))
  }
}
```

The preceding trait has a method called `memo`, which uses a mutable map to retrieve the result of a function based on its input parameters, or calls the actual function passed to it if the result is not already in the map. This method returns a new function, which actually uses the aforementioned map and has its results memoized.

> The preceding memoizer example is potentially not thread safe. Multiple threads could access the map in parallel and cause the function to be executed twice. It's up to the developer to make sure thread safety is in place, if it's needed.

The fact that we have used generics means that we can actually use this method to create a memoized version of any one-parameter function. Now, we can go back to our `Hasher` class and add the following line:

```
val memoMd5 = memo(md5)
```

This makes `memoMd5` a function that does exactly what `md5` does, but uses a map internally to try and retrieve results that we have already calculated. We can now use our `Hasher` in the following way:

```
object MemoizationExample {
  def main(args: Array[String]): Unit = {
    val hasher = new Hasher
    System.out.println(s"MD5 for 'hello' is '${hasher.memoMd5("hello")}'.")
    System.out.println(s"MD5 for 'bye' is '${hasher.memoMd5("bye")}'.")
    System.out.println(s"MD5 for 'hello' is '${hasher.memoMd5("hello")}'.")
    System.out.println(s"MD5 for 'bye1' is '${hasher.memoMd5("bye1")}'.")
    System.out.println(s"MD5 for 'bye' is '${hasher.memoMd5("bye")}'.")
  }
}
```

The output of this example will be as follows:

```
volcom@volcom-Dell-System-XPS-L502X:~/workspace/scala-book/functional-design-pat
terns$ java -cp target/functional-design-patterns-1.0.0-SNAPSHOT.jar com.ivan.ni
kolov.memo.MemoizationExample
Calling md5 for hello.
MD5 for 'hello' is '5d41402abc4b2a76b9719d911017c592'.
Calling md5 for bye.
MD5 for 'bye' is 'bfa99df33b137bc8fb5f5407d7e58da8'.
MD5 for 'hello' is '5d41402abc4b2a76b9719d911017c592'.
Calling md5 for bye1.
MD5 for 'bye1' is 'cbaba8e623612f9c913bad9d7ac31dd0'.
MD5 for 'bye' is 'bfa99df33b137bc8fb5f5407d7e58da8'.
```

The preceding output proves that calling our memoized function for the same inputs actually retrieves the result from the map, instead of calling the part that processes the result again.

Memoization alternatives

The memo method that we showed previously is quite neat and easy to use, but it's limiting. We can only get memoized versions of functions with one parameter (or we have to represent multiple parameters as a tuple). However, the Scalaz library already has support for memoization using the Memo object. We can simply do the following:

```
val memoMd5Scalaz: String => String = Memo.immutableHashMapMemo {
  md5
}
```

The preceding code can go into our Hasher class and then we can instead call memoMd5Scalaz in our example. This would not require us to write the extra Memoizer trait and it will produce absolutely the same result as what we showed previously. Moreover, the Scalaz version gives us much more flexibility in terms of the way we cache and so on.

Summary

In this chapter, we saw how to apply some of the advanced concepts of the Scala programming language in order to tackle problems that commonly emerge in actual software projects. We looked at the lens design pattern, where we also had our first encounter with the brilliant Scalaz library. We saw how to implement dependency injection without any extra libraries in Scala, and what it is used for. We also learned how we can write extensions to the libraries which we don't have any modification access for. Last but not least, we looked at the type class design pattern, lazy evaluation in Scala, partial functions (also known as function currying), duck typing, memoization, and implicit injection. By now, you should have quite an extensive knowledge of the language possibilities of Scala as well as design patterns, which can be used together to write exceptional software.

In the next and last chapter of this book, we will focus a bit more on the Scalaz library, and we will show its support for some of the concepts we have already seen. We will also go through a final project that will combine our knowledge into something that can be used as production code. Finally, we will briefly summarize the content covered in this book and give useful pointers.

12
Real-Life Applications

We have come a long way in the world of design patterns in Scala. We saw some classical *Gang of Four* design patterns from the point of view of Scala, as well as features that are applicable specifically to this programming language. By now, you should have enough knowledge in order to build high-quality, extendible, efficient, and elegant applications. Everything we have covered until now, if taken into consideration, should have a really positive impact on any application you will create.

Many of the things you saw in this book we wrote from scratch. This is really helpful in terms of understanding a given concept, but it takes time, and in real-world applications, using a library that gives us some functionalities is usually preferred. There are a number of different libraries available that are accessible through a simple Google search and address just about anything you can think of. Apart from the fact that this could save a lot of time, it also means that we integrate into our code thoroughly tested components that are trusted by many others. This, of course, depends on the library we are trying to incorporate, but as long as it brings something useful to the community, it will most likely be reliable. Having said all that, our main focus of this chapter will include the following:

- The Scalaz library
- Writing a complete application
- Summarizing what we have learned so far

There are a lot of libraries for Scala out there and some might consider other libraries to be much more important to the language than Scalaz is. There are alternatives as well, which have spun up due to various reasons. We will, however, focus on Scalaz here, as it is generally used when someone wants to implement concepts such as monoids, functors, and monads in their application. And these concepts are really important in functional programming, as we saw earlier. We will also write a complete application that uses some of the techniques and design patterns we became familiar with in the previous chapters. This chapter will give some insights into how applications should be structured and how to understand our requirements and then build the solutions for them properly. Finally, we will summarize everything we have learned here.

Reasons to use libraries

Writing software applications will inevitably bring developers to the point where they will have to implement something that already exists. Reinventing the wheel is generally a bad idea unless we have some extremely specific and strict requirements that no library in the world satisfies, or if there is good reason not to include a specific dependency in our project.

People write libraries to deal with all kinds of problems in software. In a community such as the open source community, libraries are shared and everyone can use or contribute to them. This brings a lot of benefits, and the main benefit is that code becomes more mature, better tested, and more reliable. However, sometimes this also makes things harder—many people will create the same library and it becomes difficult to understand which one is the most suitable.

Despite the fact that there could be multiple implementations of the same library, using one is the way to go when we write enterprise applications. Filtering out the bad ones from the good ones is easy nowadays—if a library is good, many people will use it. If it's bad, people will avoid it. If there are multiple good ones, developers will have to spend some time investigating which one is the most suitable for their use case.

The Scalaz library

Scala is a functional programming language and, as such, it supports design patterns based on concepts such as monoids, monads, and others. We already saw these in Chapter 10, *Functional Design Patterns - the Deep Theory*, and we know the rules they follow and the structure they have. We wrote everything ourselves, but a library already exists that does this for us—Scalaz (https://github.com/scalaz/scalaz). This library is used when we need purely functional data structures.

 Another library that has a similar popularity to Scalaz in the community is Cats (https://github.com/typelevel/cats). They should both be able to help developers achieve the same functional programming concepts. In most cases, the choice between the two is based on personal preference, local community culture or company policies.

We have already encountered Scalaz in the previous chapter when we talked about lenses. In the following subsections, we will look at the library from the point of view of monoids, functors, and monads.

Monoids in Scalaz

One of the concepts we looked at in Chapter 10, *Functional Design Patterns - the Deep Theory*, was monoids. We defined a trait and some rules for them and then showed examples of how to use them and what they are good for. In these examples, we defined monoids for integer addition and multiplication as well as string concatenation. Scalaz already has a Monoid trait that we can use to write our own monoids. Also, this trait has a few monoids that we have defined before already implemented:

```
import scalaz.Monoid

package object monoids {
  // Int addition and int multiplication exist already,
  // so we will show them in an example.
  val stringConcatenation = new Monoid[String] {
    override def zero: String = ""

    override def append(f1: String, f2: => String): String = f1 + f2
  }
}
```

In the preceding code, we just showed how you can implement a custom monoid.

> The stringConcatenation monoid is defined in a package object. This means that it will be available to any code in the same package without the need to import anything. We take advantage of this in some of the following examples.

There also exists a string concatenation monoid, but here we just showed how you can opt for implementing the custom monoid if it doesn't exist. It is quite similar to what we had earlier. The difference is only in the name for the operation method (append) and its signature. However, this is just a minor difference.

Using monoids

Using Scalaz monoids is pretty straightforward. Here is an example program:

```
import scalaz._
import Scalaz._

object MonoidsExample {

  def main(args: Array[String]): Unit = {
    val numbers = List(1, 2, 3, 4, 5, 6)
```

```
        System.out.println(s"The sum is: ${numbers.foldMap(identity)}")
        System.out.println(s"The product (6!) is:
         ${numbers.foldMap(Tags.Multiplication.apply)}")
        val strings = List("This is\n", "a list of\n", "strings!")
        System.out.println(strings.foldMap(identity)(stringConcatenation))
    }
}
```

The imports in our code make sure that we can call `foldMap` on our list of numbers. If we run this example, we will get the following output:

```
volcom@volcom-Dell-System-XPS-L502X:~/workspace/scala-book/real-life-applicatio
ns$ java -cp target/real-life-applications-1.0.0-SNAPSHOT.jar com.ivan.nikolov.
monoids.MonoidsExample
The sum is: 21
The product (6!) is: 720
This is
a list of
strings!
```

Looking at the output and the code, you can see that for integer addition and multiplication, we have used the built-in monoids of Scalaz. The `sum` monoid takes precedence and is actually passed to `foldMap` implicitly. For the multiplication to work, we have to pass `Tags.Multiplication.apply` in order to make things work as expected. We have explicitly passed our string concatenation monoid to make the last statement work correctly.

Testing monoids

We know that monoids have to satisfy some specific laws. Our examples are simple enough to see that the laws are actually in place, but sometimes it might not be that obvious. In Scalaz, you can actually test your monoids:

```
import org.scalacheck.Arbitrary
import org.scalatest.prop.Checkers
import org.scalatest.{FlatSpec, Matchers}

import scalaz._

import scalaz.scalacheck.ScalazProperties._

class MonoidsTest extends FlatSpec with Matchers with Checkers {

  implicit def arbString(implicit ev: Arbitrary[String]):
  Arbitrary[String] =
```

```
        Arbitrary { ev.arbitrary.map(identity) }
    "stringConcatenation monoid" should "satisfy the identity rule." in {
        monoid.laws[String](stringConcatenation, Equal.equalA[String],
        arbString).check()
    }
}
```

In order to be able to compile and run the preceding example, we will need to have the following dependencies added to our `pom.xml` file:

```
<dependency>
    <groupId>org.scalcheck</groupId>
    <artifactId>scalacheck_2.12</artifactId>
    <version>${scalacheck.version}</version>
    <scope>test</scope>
</dependency>
<dependency>
    <groupId>org.scalaz</groupId>
    <artifactId>scalaz-scalacheck-binding_2.12</artifactId>
    <version>${scalaz.version}</version>
    <scope>test</scope>
</dependency>
```

The equivalent `build.sbt` file will need to have the following dependencies added:

```
"org.scalacheck" %% "scalacheck" % scalacheckVersion % "test",
"org.scalaz" %% "scalaz-scalacheck-binding" % scalazVersion % "test",
```

The preceding code sections are just fragments of the code examples coming with this book. These dependencies add bindings to ScalaCheck (`https://www.scalacheck.org/`)—a property-based testing framework. The preceding code will test our custom monoid for all the laws and fail if it doesn't satisfy them. Writing tests for our custom classes will require us to have an `Arbitrary` implementation as well as have our monoid implicitly available in the test scope.

Monads in Scalaz

In `Chapter 10`, *Functional Design Patterns - the Deep Theory*, we also looked at monads. If you remember, we had to define a functor trait first and then extend it in the monad trait. Similar to monoids, monads also follow some specific rules that have to be in place.

Using monads

Scalaz defines quite a lot of different methods that can be applied directly to any monad we have. There are multiple examples that show lists and options. The library also has a `Monad` trait that can be extended. It is similar to the `Monoid` trait.

We don't want to dig into list examples that show how to use monads, though. To make things interesting, let's look at the `IO` monad in Scalaz that can be used to perform I/O in a monadic way. What this basically means is that we can describe and compose those actions without actually performing them. This will lead to better code reuse as well. Let's see an example:

```scala
import java.io.{PrintWriter, File}

import scala.io.Source

package object monads {
  def readFile(path: String) = {
    System.out.println(s"Reading file ${path}")
    Source.fromFile(path).getLines()
  }

  def writeFile(path: String, lines: Iterator[String]) = {
    System.out.println(s"Writing file ${path}")
    val file = new File(path)
    printToFile(file) { p => lines.foreach(p.println) }
  }

  private def printToFile(file: File)(writeOp: PrintWriter => Unit): Unit =
  {
    val writer = new PrintWriter(file)
    try {
      writeOp(writer)
    } finally {
      writer.close()
    }
  }
}
```

First of all, we defined some methods in a package object that can manipulate files. There is absolutely nothing special about them. They seem pretty similar to what we did in Chapter 10, *Functional Design Patterns - the Deep Theory*, when we showed our custom `IO` monad. In the `readFile` and the `writeFile`, we added prints to help in debugging and show exactly what is going on. This will be really useful later.

We will make our application read a tab-separated file of data of people, parse it, and write it either to a file or the console. The example file will have the following content:

```
Ivan    26
Maria   26
John    25
```

Of course, we have a model that will reflect this file and it will be as simple as this:

```
case class Person(name: String, age: Int)

object Person {
  def fromArray(arr: Array[String]): Option[Person] =
    arr match {
      case Array(name, age) => Some(Person(name, age.toInt))
      case _ => None
    }
}
```

Together with the model, we've shown its companion object. It has one method that returns an optional `Person` object given an array of strings.

Now it's time to see our application and explain what is going on:

```
import com.ivan.nikolov.monads.model.Person

import scalaz._
import effect._
import Scalaz._
import IO._

object IOMonadExample {

  def main(args: Array[String]): Unit = {
    args match {
      case Array(inputFile, isWriteToFile) =>
        val people = {
          for {
            line <- readFile(inputFile)
            person <- Person.fromArray(line.split("\t"))
          } yield person
        }.pure[IO]

        System.out.println("Still haven't done any IO!")
        System.out.println("About to do some...")
        if (isWriteToFile.toBoolean) {
          val writePeople = for {
```

```
            _ <- putStrLn("Read people successfully.
             Where to write them down?")
            outputFile <- readLn
            p <- people
            _ <- writeFile(outputFile, p.map(_.toString)).pure[IO]
          } yield ()
          System.out.println("Writing to file using toString.")
          writePeople.unsafePerformIO
        } else {
          System.out.println(s"Just got the following people:
           ${people.unsafePerformIO.toList}")
        }
      case _ =>
        System.err.println("Please provide input file and true/false
         whether to write to file.")
        System.exit(-1)
    }
  }
}
```

Let's now see what exactly is going on in the previous listing. The actual code is in the first pattern matching case. The rest is some validation to run a console application and the parameters passed to it.

The first thing to pay attention to is the calls to .pure[IO], which is there for the people variable and when we write to the file. This method takes the value given to it and lifts it into a monad. Another important thing is that the value passed to the method is lazily evaluated. In our example, the monad is the IO monad.

Secondly, we can see some references to the putStrLn and readLn methods. Their names should be enough to explain what they do. They come from the scalaz.effect.IO object, that we have imported into our application. And this import requires another dependency in our pom.xml file:

```
<dependency>
    <groupId>org.scalaz</groupId>
    <artifactId>scalaz-effect_2.12</artifactId>
    <version>${scalaz.version}</version>
</dependency>
```

The equivalent dependency in the build.sbt file will be the following:

```
"org.scalaz" %% "scalaz-effect" % scalazVersion
```

The `putStrLn` and `readLn` methods also return an instance of the `IO` monad and they are just helpers.

Now, because our application is monadic and we use the `IO` monad, nothing will happen unless we do something about it. To trigger the actual actions, we must call `unsafePerformIO` on an `IO` instance. We've added some `print` statements that will prove that the code works as we expected it to.

Since we have two branches for our application, we will make two runs here. One that prints and another one that writes to a file. The example outputs are in the following screenshots:

```
volcom@volcom-Dell-System-XPS-L502X:~/workspace/scala-book/real-life-applicatio
ns$ java -cp target/real-life-applications-1.0.0-SNAPSHOT.jar com.ivan.nikolov.
monads.IOMonadExample people.tsv false
Still haven't done any IO!
About to do some...
Reading file people.tsv
Just got the following people: List(Person(Ivan,26), Person(Maria,26), Person(J
ohn,25))
```

The preceding screenshot shows the run that prints to the console. We can see that the reading from the file log comes after the initial logs from our application, even though we called the method earlier. This proves that indeed the `.pure[IO]` call lifts our function without evaluating it.

Similarly to the previous output, the following output shows that nothing happens until the very last moment when we write the output filename and hit *Enter*:

```
volcom@volcom-Dell-System-XPS-L502X:~/workspace/scala-book/real-life-applicatio
ns$ java -cp target/real-life-applications-1.0.0-SNAPSHOT.jar com.ivan.nikolov.
monads.IOMonadExample people.tsv true
Still haven't done any IO!
About to do some...
Writing to file using toString.
Read people successfully. Where to write them down?
people.out
Reading file people.tsv
Writing file people.out
```

Our example shows that the IO monad helps us to build a computation and execute it at the very last moment. Here, we've decided to surround it with a for comprehension and call pure[IO] on it so that we can actually use the read and write methods without monads if we want to. In other cases, you can make sure to return an IO monad from the read and write methods and then define mapping methods, which also return the IO monads and use them inside the for comprehensions. This would look like something similar to this:

```
val people = for {
  lines <- readFile(inputFile).pure[IO]
  p <- lines.map(i => Person("a", 1)).pure[IO]
} yield p
```

This version actually looks more monadical. We have enclosed smaller entities in the IO monad that we have combined and probably there will be more examples available online that follow this approach. This version actually also leaves the read method intact. The only thing in this case is that the for comprehension behaves differently than usual.

Which approach is used will probably depend on personal preferences and what someone wants to achieve.

The preceding example is similar to what we did in Chapter 10, *Functional Design Patterns - the Deep Theory*, with our custom I/O monad. Here, however, we can see that there is much less extra code than before.

Testing monads

Scalaz provides facilities to test monads as well. The tests look no different than what we saw for monoids, but here we simply have to use monad.laws instead.

The possibilities of Scalaz

We only looked at a handful of concepts covered by the Scalaz library. It contains much more than just that. You can think of Scalaz as an addition to Scala that makes it even more functional. It provides various type classes, data types, pimp my library instances for standard collections, out-of-the-box functionality for various standard types, and so on. The purposes also vary—from writing purely functional applications to making your code more readable. Scalaz is so vast that we can write a separate book about it.

It seems that people find it difficult to use Scalaz at first and only later do they get to know the possibilities it provides. We would like to encourage you to become familiar with the documentation and everything the library provides. There are also various blog posts for all levels of difficulty, which can be a real eye-opener for the first time user of Scalaz.

Writing a complete application

So far in the book, we've seen a lot of examples. Some of them were quite complete, while others were meant to demonstrate only a specific part of what we were looking at. In real applications, it is most likely that you will have to combine multiple design patterns that we went through. In order to do so properly, it is important that the requirements are well understood. In the following subsections, we will provide the application specifications and then we will go step by step through actually writing the application. The amount of code we write will be a lot, so we will focus on the more important parts of our application and we might skip others.

Application specifications

Before doing anything, we must always have some specifications. Sometimes, these specifications are not entirely clear and it is our responsibility to make sure everything is detailed enough for us to understand and achieve them. However, in an actual software engineering process, it will likely be the case that we start doing something when the requirements are not 100% clear and things change halfway through the project. It could be frustrating at times, but that is life and we have to deal with it. It also makes things interesting and dynamic and makes developers think of even more possibilities and problems that could arise when users use a given application. Some developers might refuse to even start working on an application that is not completely defined. They might have a valid point and this depends on how critical the tasks are, but generally, this kind of attitude doesn't take projects far.

Luckily, here we can come up with our own tasks, so everything will be well defined and we will not change requirements halfway through. So let's do this and get our hands dirty.

 Create a scheduler application that can run console commands or SQL queries against a database. The user should be able to schedule any command or query using configuration files, and they should be able to choose a granularity—hourly or daily, at a specific time.

So far, we have only given a top-level explanation of what we want to achieve. As we said earlier, some people might even refuse to go further until they have a complete definition with every single detail mentioned. This is a valid point; however, it is interesting to get your head around different use cases, edge cases, and possible improvements. It is the job of product managers to actually come up with all these specifications; but here, we are not learning how to be one. We are learning how to write nice code. So let's take what we have and try to come up with something usable, efficient, testable, and extendable.

Implementation

Let's start writing some code. No! This is wrong. Before we even start to write, we should answer all our questions and be clear with where we are going. Some people like drawing diagrams, others like writing things down, and so on. Everyone has their own techniques. Let's try and come up with a diagram first. It will show the top-level components that we will use, how they communicate with each other, and so on. A visual representation of our application will be extremely valuable to see any issues early and will also help us to implement the application easily:

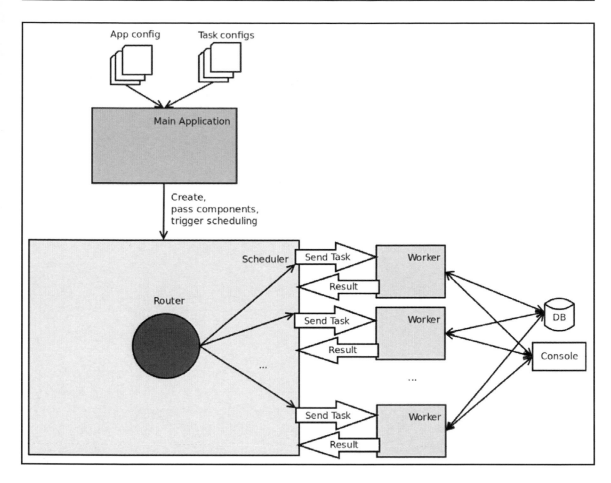

The preceding diagram shows our future application from a really high level. It is, however, enough to identify a few core components:

- The main application
- The scheduler
- The router
- The workers

By looking at the connections between the components, we can also see what dependencies they will have and what functionalities they will support.

Now that we have this diagram and a view of what we should eventually end up with, we can start thinking of how to structure the application.

The libraries to use

You can always take the approach of implementing everything from scratch on your own. This, however, would slow you down and would require some deep domain knowledge in a lot of other parallel disciplines. We have always encouraged the use of libraries in the examples in this book, and this is the case here too.

Looking at the preceding diagram, we can see that we will need to do the following operations:

- Read an application configuration
- Read scheduler configuration files
- Schedule tasks
- Exchange messages
- Access a database
- Execute console commands

Sometimes, while coming up with which libraries to use, it requires testing of the different alternatives and seeing which one is useful for our purposes. We won't be doing this here, and we will just use the libraries we have already seen or know about.

Reading the application configuration

To read the application configuration files, we have decided to use Typesafe config: https:/ /github.com/typesafehub/config. It is a mature and well-maintained library, supports various configuration formats, and is quite easy to use. We have included it in our pom.xml file using the following statement:

```
<dependency>
    <groupId>com.typesafe</groupId>
    <artifactId>config</artifactId>
    <version>${typesafe.config.version}</version>
</dependency>
```

The same dependency is added to build.sbt using the following line:

```
"com.typesafe" % "config" % typesafeConfigVersion
```

Reading the scheduler configuration

Our application will be reading configuration files for schedulers. There are different formats we can force our users to use. We've decided our format of choice to be JSON. It is easy to write our models based on it and we have already used libraries to parse the JSON format in the previous chapters of this book. We will be using json4s: `https://github.com/json4s/json4s`. We have included it using the following lines in our `pom.xml` file:

```
<dependency>
    <groupId>org.json4s</groupId>
    <artifactId>json4s-native_2.12</artifactId>
    <version>${json4s.version}</version>
</dependency>
<dependency>
    <groupId>org.json4s</groupId>
    <artifactId>json4s-jackson_2.12</artifactId>
    <version>${json4s.version}</version>
</dependency>
```

The same dependencies if you decide to use `build.sbt` will be added as follows:

```
"org.json4s" %% "json4s-native" % json4sVersion,
"org.json4s" %% "json4s-jackson" % json4sVersion,
```

Scheduling tasks

There are various scheduling libraries and programs. Some are more mature, others less. In this application, we decided to use Akka: `https://akka.io/`. First of all, it is a good library to be familiar with. Secondly, we have already talked about it in the earlier chapters of this book. Using Akka can be useful to you to see how to write applications using reactive programming. Akka can be included in our project by adding the following lines to our `pom.xml` file:

```
<dependency>
    <groupId>com.typesafe.akka</groupId>
    <artifactId>akka-actor_2.12</artifactId>
    <version>${akka.version}</version>
</dependency>
```

The same dependency, but in your `build.sbt` file, will look like this:

```
"com.typesafe.akka" %% "akka-actor" % akkaVersion
```

Akka uses messages to send tasks to workers, and we will see how this entire procedure is handled elegantly.

Accessing a database

In the previous chapter, we already saw how to write the code to access databases. Here, we will be using the H2 database engine again, as it doesn't require you to do anything extra in order to execute the example. The related `pom.xml` entry is as follows:

```xml
<dependency>
    <groupId>com.h2database</groupId>
    <artifactId>h2</artifactId>
    <version>1.4.197</version>
</dependency>
```

For `sbt`, the `build.sbt` file will need to have the following:

```
"com.h2database" % "h2" % "1.4.197"
```

Executing console commands

To execute console commands, we will be using the built-in functionalities of Scala. We will also use some extra dependencies that we have used in the other projects as well—a logging library (slf4j) and test dependencies—ScalaTest and Mockito.

Writing some code

Now that we know what we will be doing and what libraries we will be relying on, it's time to write some code. It is logical to start with things that don't have other internal dependencies.

One of these things is the application configuration. It is something that doesn't depend on anything, but many things depend on it. We decided to use the `.conf` files because they are simple, hierarchical, and similar to JSON. An example configuration file looks like the following code:

```
job-scheduler {
  config-path="/etc/scheduler/conf.d"
  config-extension="json"
  workers=4
  db {
    connection-string="jdbc:h2:mem:test;DB_CLOSE_DELAY=-1"
    username=""
```

```
        password=""
   }
}
```

The options are clear and anyone can easily provide a new config that suits their needs.

Coming up with our configuration options

Of course, we didn't come up with this file straight away. It evolved as we kept adding functionalities to our application. Start small and don't try to think about everything at once.

With this expected format, we can now write a component:

```
package com.ivan.nikolov.scheduler.config.app

import com.typesafe.config.ConfigFactory

trait AppConfigComponent {
  val appConfigService: AppConfigService

  class AppConfigService() {
    //-Dconfig.resource-production.conf for overriding
    private val conf = ConfigFactory.load()
    private val appConf = conf.getConfig("job-scheduler")
    private val db = appConf.getConfig("db")
    val configPath = appConf.getString("config-path")
    val configExtension = appConf.getString("config-extension")
    val workers = appConf.getInt("workers")
    val dbConnectionString = db.getString("connection-string")
    val dbUsername = db.getString("username")
    val dbPassword = db.getString("password")
  }
}
```

The highlighted line in the preceding code shows how easy it is to read our configuration file. It gets the application.conf from our resources folder. The user can easily override it by passing a -Dconfig.resource=path.conf when starting our application.

Our configuration file specifies a number of properties. Two of them are `config-path` and `config-extension`. We have basically taken the decision to provide a folder and an extension, and our program will read all the files with the given extension and use them as job configuration files. We have written a component that supports reading from a folder and returns all the files with the given extension:

```
package com.ivan.nikolov.scheduler.io

import java.io.File

trait IOServiceComponent {
  val ioService: IOService

  class IOService {
    def getAllFilesWithExtension(basePath: String, extension: String):
    List[String] = {
      val dir = new File(basePath)
      if (dir.exists() && dir.isDirectory) {
        dir.listFiles()
          .filter(f => f.isFile &&
          f.getPath.toLowerCase.endsWith(s".${extension}"))
          .map {
            case f => f.getAbsolutePath
          }.toList
      } else {
        List.empty
      }
    }
  }

}
```

This component doesn't do anything special. We haven't used monads or anything fancy for the I/O here because we actually want to eagerly evaluate things in this case.

Now that we know how to find all the job configuration files, we need to read them and parse them. We said that they will be JSON files and this means that we will have to define a model. Let's first see an example of a job configuration and then define the model:

```
{
  "name": "Ping Command",
  "command": "ping google.com -c 10",
  "frequency": "Hourly",
  "type": "Console",
  "time_options": {
    "hours": 21,
```

```
    "minutes": 10
  }
}
```

It is quite easy to start with a file that has everything we need and then define the models, rather than the other way around. According to the preceding code, we can define the following model for our job configuration:

```
case class JobConfig(name: String, command: String, jobType: JobType,
frequency: JobFrequency, timeOptions: TimeOptions)
```

The `JobType` and `JobFrequency` will be defined as ADTs. When we use json4s, some special care needs to be taken while serializing and deserializing these types, so we have defined some extra `CustomSerializer` implementations along with them:

```
import org.json4s.CustomSerializer
import org.json4s.JsonAST.{JNull, JString}

sealed trait JobType
case object Console extends JobType
case object Sql extends JobType

object JobTypeSerializer extends CustomSerializer[JobType](format -> (
  {
    case JString(jobType) => jobType match {
      case "Console" => Console
      case "Sql" => Sql
    }
    case JNull => null
  },
  {
    case jobType: JobType =>
     JString(jobType.getClass.getSimpleName.replace("$", ""))
  }
))
```

The `JobFrequency` is quite similar to the preceding code:

```
import org.json4s.CustomSerializer
import org.json4s.JsonAST.{JNull, JString}

sealed trait JobFrequency
case object Daily extends JobFrequency
case object Hourly extends JobFrequency

case object JobFrequencySerializer extends
CustomSerializer[JobFrequency](format => (
```

```
    {
      case JString(frequency) => frequency match {
        case "Daily" => Daily
        case "Hourly" => Hourly
      }
      case JNull => null
    },
    {
      case frequency: JobFrequency =>
        JString(frequency.getClass.getSimpleName.replace("$", ""))
    }
  ))
```

Our `JobConfig` class needs one more model to be defined, and it is shown as follows:

```scala
import java.time.LocalDateTime
import java.time.temporal.ChronoUnit
import java.util.concurrent.TimeUnit

import scala.concurrent.duration.{Duration, FiniteDuration}

case class TimeOptions(hours: Int, minutes: Int) {
  if (hours < 0 || hours > 23) {
    throw new IllegalArgumentException("Hours must be between 0 and 23:
      " + hours)
  } else if (minutes < 0 || minutes > 59) {
    throw new IllegalArgumentException("Minutes must be between 0 and
      59: " + minutes)
  }

  def getInitialDelay(now: LocalDateTime, frequency: JobFrequency):
  FiniteDuration = {
    val firstRun = now.withHour(hours).withMinute(minutes)
    val isBefore = firstRun.isBefore(now)
    val actualFirstRun = frequency match {
      case Hourly =>
        var tmp = firstRun
        Iterator.continually({
          tmp = tmp.plusHours(1); tmp
        })
          .takeWhile(d => d.isBefore(now))
          .toList.lastOption.getOrElse(
          if (isBefore)
            firstRun
          else
            firstRun.minusHours(1)
        ).plusHours(1)
      case Daily =>
```

```
        var tmp = firstRun
        Iterator.continually({
          tmp = tmp.plusDays(1); tmp
        })
          .takeWhile(d => d.isBefore(now))
          .toList.lastOption
          .getOrElse(
            if (isBefore)
              firstRun
            else
              firstRun.minusDays(1)
          ).plusDays(1)
    }
    val secondsUntilRun = now.until(actualFirstRun, ChronoUnit.SECONDS)
    Duration.create(secondsUntilRun, TimeUnit.SECONDS)
  }
}
```

The `TimeOptions` class has some validation during creation and a `getInitialDelay` method. The purpose of this method is to get the initial delay while scheduling a task, depending on its options.

After we have defined our models for the job configuration, we can write a service that reads and parses the configurations:

```
import java.io.File
import com.ivan.nikolov.scheduler.config.app.AppConfigComponent
import com.ivan.nikolov.scheduler.config.job.{JobTypeSerializer,
JobFrequencySerializer, JobConfig}
import com.ivan.nikolov.scheduler.io.IOServiceComponent
import com.typesafe.scalalogging.LazyLogging
import org.json4s._
import org.json4s.jackson.JsonMethods._

trait JobConfigReaderServiceComponent {
  this: AppConfigComponent with IOServiceComponent =>

  val jobConfigReaderService: JobConfigReaderService

  class JobConfigReaderService() extends LazyLogging {

    private val customSerializers = List(
      JobFrequencySerializer,
      JobTypeSerializer
    )

    implicit val formats = DefaultFormats ++ customSerializers +
```

`JobConfig.jobConfigFieldSerializer`

```
def readJobConfigs(): List[JobConfig] =
  ioService.getAllFilesWithExtension(
    appConfigService.configPath,
    appConfigService.configExtension
  ).flatMap {
    case path => try {
      val config = parse(FileInput(new File(path))).extract[JobConfig]
      Some(config)
    } catch {
      case ex: Throwable =>
        logger.error("Error reading config: {}", path, ex)
        None
    }
  }
}
```

It depends on the two components we already showed in the preceding code. There is nothing special about this component, except the highlighted part. The first statement takes the custom serializers we have for the frequency and job type. The second statement adds them to the default formats so that json4s knows how to handle them. If you observe carefully, you will notice the `JobConfig.jobConfigFieldSerializer` call as well. Let's see what it looks like:

```
import org.json4s.FieldSerializer
import org.json4s.JsonAST.JField

case class JobConfig(name: String, command: String, jobType: JobType,
frequency: JobFrequency, timeOptions: TimeOptions)

object JobConfig {
  val jobConfigFieldSerializer = FieldSerializer[JobConfig](
    {
      case ("timeOptions", x) => Some("time_options", x)
      case ("jobType", x) => Some("type", x)
    },
    {
      case JField("time_options", x) => JField("timeOptions", x)
      case JField("type", x) => JField("jobType", x)
    }
  )
}
```

We need it because the Scala field names that we have used are different from what is in our JSON files, and json4s needs to know how to translate them.

Now that we have all the required mechanisms to read the job configurations, we can go deeper and see how they will be used to execute our jobs. We already said that we will be implementing our scheduler and workers using Akka. One thing about Akka is that it communicates using messages. We had to come up with some messages that our application will need:

```
sealed trait SchedulerMessage
case class Work(name: String, command: String, jobType: JobType)
case class Done(name: String, command: String, jobType: JobType, success:
Boolean)
case class Schedule(configs: List[JobConfig])
```

These messages are quite descriptive, so let's not waste time on them. Let's go straight to the point and see what our scheduler will look like:

```
class Master(numWorkers: Int, actorFactory: ActorFactory) extends Actor
with LazyLogging {
  val cancelables = ListBuffer[Cancellable]()
  val router = context.actorOf(
    Props(actorFactory.createWorkerActor()).withRouter(
    RoundRobinPool(numWorkers)), "scheduler-master-worker-router"
  )
  override def receive: Receive = {
    case Done(name, command, jobType, success) =>
      if (success) {
        logger.info("Successfully completed {} ({}).", name, command)
      } else {
        logger.error("Failure! Command {} ({}) returned a non-zero
        result code.", name, command)
      }
    case Schedule(configs) =>
      configs.foreach {
        case config =>
          val cancellable = this.context.system.scheduler.schedule(
            config.timeOptions.getInitialDelay(LocalDateTime.now(),
             config.frequency),
            config.frequency match {
              case Hourly => Duration.create(1, TimeUnit.HOURS)
              case Daily => Duration.create(1, TimeUnit.DAYS)
            },
            router,
            Work(config.name, config.command, config.jobType)
          )
          cancellable +: cancelables
```

```
            logger.info("Scheduled: {}", config)
      }
    }
    override def postStop(): Unit = {
      cancelables.foreach(_.cancel())
    }
  }
```

We have called our scheduler `Master`, as it is the master actor in the actor system we will implement. We have skipped the imports in favor of saving some space. There are two places that deserve more attention in this actor—the `receive` method and the `router`. The former is essentially how actors work—the developer implements this method, which is simply a partially defined function, and if a message that we know about is received, it is handled. Our master actor can schedule a list of jobs by creating work items and sending them to the router. The router, on the other hand, is just a round-robin pool of workers, so every task we schedule will go to a different worker.

All workers will be running the same code, as follows:

```
import sys.process._

class Worker(daoService: DaoService) extends Actor with LazyLogging {
  private def doWork(work: Work): Unit = {
    work.jobType match {
      case Console =>
        val result = work.command.! // note - the ! are different methods
        sender ! Done(work.name, work.command, work.jobType, result == 0)
      case Sql =>
        val connection = daoService.getConnection()
        try {
          val statement = connection.prepareStatement(work.command)
          val result: List[String] = daoService.executeSelect(statement) {
            case rs =>
              val metadata = rs.getMetaData
              val numColumns = metadata.getColumnCount
              daoService.readResultSet(rs) {
                case row =>
                  (1 to numColumns).map {
                    case i =>
                      row.getObject(i)
                  }.mkString("\t")
              }
          }
          logger.info("Sql query results: ")
          result.foreach(r => logger.info(r))
          sender ! Done(work.name, work.command, work.jobType, true)
```

```
      } finally {
        connection.close()
      }
    }
  }
  override def receive: Receive = {
    case w @ Work(name, command, jobType) => doWork(w)
  }
}
```

They can only accept one message type (`Work`) and process it accordingly. For example, to run console tasks, we have used the built-in Scala functionality. Then the highlighted line makes sure a message is sent back to the sender (`Master` in our case) and, as you can see, it will handle it.

We have already seen a bunch of components that look a lot like how you would implement dependency injection using Scala—the cake design pattern. However, the general pattern that is followed with our actors isn't the way the cake design pattern is set up. That's why we've created a factory—`ActorFactory`,which can inject objects into our actors:

```
package com.ivan.nikolov.scheduler.actors

import com.ivan.nikolov.scheduler.config.app.AppConfigComponent
import com.ivan.nikolov.scheduler.dao.DaoServiceComponent

trait ActorFactory {
  def createMasterActor(): Master
  def createWorkerActor(): Worker
}

trait ActorFactoryComponent {
  this: AppConfigComponent
    with DaoServiceComponent =>
  val actorFactory: ActorFactory
  class ActorFactoryImpl extends ActorFactory {
    override def createMasterActor(): Master =
      new Master(appConfigService.workers, this)

    override def createWorkerActor(): Worker = new Worker(daoService)
  }
}
```

You can see how the preceding factory is passed (using the `this` reference) and used in the `Master` actor for creating `Worker` instances.

We have already seen everything we need in order to run console jobs with our scheduler. Now we have to implement things in order to support database access. We will skip the database code here, as it is pretty much the same as the one we saw in Chapter 11, *Applying What We Have Learned*, it is based on the cake design pattern. We have only skipped some convenience methods that we don't need here. However, the database our scheduler can query still has the same schema:

```
CREATE TABLE people(
  id INT PRIMARY KEY,
  name VARCHAR(255) NOT NULL,
  age INT NOT NULL
);

CREATE TABLE classes(
  id INT PRIMARY KEY,
  name VARCHAR(255) NOT NULL,
);

CREATE TABLE people_classes(
  person_id INT NOT NULL,
  class_id INT NOT NULL,
  PRIMARY KEY(person_id, class_id),
  FOREIGN KEY(person_id) REFERENCES people(id) ON DELETE CASCADE ON UPDATE
CASCADE,
  FOREIGN KEY(class_id) REFERENCES classes(id) ON DELETE CASCADE ON UPDATE
CASCADE
);
```

We have also added some extra database statements to aid us in unit testing but they are minor, and not putting them here will not affect anything.

Wiring it all up

It seems like we already have all the components our application will be using. Now we just need to wire things together and fire it up. We are using the cake design pattern for dependency injection; so, as you have already seen, we can create one component registry with everything we need:

```
package com.ivan.nikolov.scheduler.registry

import com.ivan.nikolov.scheduler.actors.{ActorFactory,
ActorFactoryComponent}
import com.ivan.nikolov.scheduler.config.app.AppConfigComponent
import com.ivan.nikolov.scheduler.dao._
import com.ivan.nikolov.scheduler.io.IOServiceComponent
```

```
import com.ivan.nikolov.scheduler.services.JobConfigReaderServiceComponent

object ComponentRegistry extends AppConfigComponent
  with IOServiceComponent
  with JobConfigReaderServiceComponent
  with DatabaseServiceComponent
  with MigrationComponent
  with DaoServiceComponent
  with ActorFactoryComponent {

  override val appConfigService: ComponentRegistry.AppConfigService = new
AppConfigService
  override val ioService: ComponentRegistry.IOService = new IOService
  override val jobConfigReaderService:
ComponentRegistry.JobConfigReaderService = new JobConfigReaderService
  override val databaseService: DatabaseService = new H2DatabaseService
  override val migrationService: ComponentRegistry.MigrationService = new
MigrationService
  override val daoService: DaoService = new DaoServiceImpl
  override val actorFactory: ActorFactory = new ActorFactoryImpl
}
```

Now that we have a component registry, we can use it and write the main application class:

```
package com.ivan.nikolov.scheduler

import akka.actor.{Props, ActorSystem}
import com.ivan.nikolov.scheduler.actors.messages.Schedule
import com.typesafe.scalalogging.LazyLogging

import scala.concurrent.Await
import scala.concurrent.duration.Duration

object Scheduler extends LazyLogging {
  import com.ivan.nikolov.scheduler.registry.ComponentRegistry._
  def main(args: Array[String]): Unit = {
    logger.info("Running migrations before doing anything else.")
    migrationService.runMigrations()
    logger.info("Migrations done!")
    val system = ActorSystem("scheduler")
    val master = system.actorOf(
      Props(actorFactory.createMasterActor()),
      "scheduler-master"
    )
    sys.addShutdownHook({
      logger.info("Awaiting actor system termination.")
      // not great...
      Await.result(system.terminate(), Duration.Inf)
```

```
      logger.info("Actor system terminated. Bye!")
    })
    master ! Schedule(jobConfigReaderService.readJobConfigs())
    logger.info("Started! Use CTRL+C to exit.")
  }
}
```

Our application has some very simple Akka wiring up and then everything is triggered when we execute the highlighted line. We send a `Schedule` message to the master with all the job configurations and then it will schedule them to run periodically according to their definitions.

The end result

After all this code is written, we will end up with the following tree in our IDE:

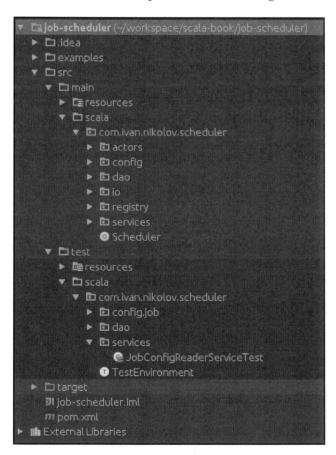

You can see that our code also contains unit tests. We will spend some time on them in the next subsection.

Testing our application

Testing is a really important part of every application. Using TDD is really good, as we can write and test our applications simultaneously instead of coming back to something that is already done. We used this approach while writing the application, but separated the code and the tests in favor of explaining things better and not mixing them up.

Unit testing

As you have already seen earlier, testing applications that rely on the cake design pattern is simple. We have defined the following test environment:

```
package com.ivan.nikolov.scheduler

import com.ivan.nikolov.scheduler.actors.{ActorFactory,
ActorFactoryComponent}
import com.ivan.nikolov.scheduler.config.app.AppConfigComponent
import com.ivan.nikolov.scheduler.dao._
import com.ivan.nikolov.scheduler.io.IOServiceComponent
import com.ivan.nikolov.scheduler.services.JobConfigReaderServiceComponent
import org.mockito.Mockito._
import org.scalatest.mockito.MockitoSugar

trait TestEnvironment
  extends AppConfigComponent
  with IOServiceComponent
  with JobConfigReaderServiceComponent
  with DatabaseServiceComponent
  with MigrationComponent
  with DaoServiceComponent
  with ActorFactoryComponent
  with MockitoSugar {

  // use the test configuration file.
  override val appConfigService: AppConfigService = spy(new
AppConfigService)
  // override the path here to use the test resources.
when(appConfigService.configPath).thenReturn(this.getClass.getResource("/")
.getPath)
  override val ioService: IOService = mock[IOService]
  override val jobConfigReaderService: JobConfigReaderService =
```

```
mock[JobConfigReaderService]
   override val databaseService: DatabaseService = mock[DatabaseService]
   override val migrationService: MigrationService = mock[MigrationService]
   override val daoService: DaoService = mock[DaoService]
   override val actorFactory: ActorFactory = mock[ActorFactory]
}
```

When we do testing, we use an actual application configuration file instead of working with mocks and can use any file inside our test resources folder. We have written quite extensive tests for the TimeOptions class, more specifically the part that calculates the initial delay. There are tests to read job configuration files as well as database access tests. They can all be seen in the projects provided with this book.

Application testing

No doubt, the part that everyone wanted to see the most is where we actually give our application an actual spin. However, because it is a scheduler, we first need to prepare some configurations. We will use the following application configuration file:

```
job-scheduler {
   config-path="/etc/scheduler/conf.d"
   config-extension="json"
   workers=4
   db {
      connection-string="jdbc:h2:mem:test;DB_CLOSE_DELAY=-1"
      username=""
      password=""
   }
}
```

We will name our file `production.conf` and we will put it in `/etc/scheduler/conf.d`. Now we need to create some actual job configurations. We will have to put them where the `config-path` property is pointing to:

```
// ping.json
{
  "name": "Ping Command",
  "command": "ping google.com -c 10",
  "frequency": "Hourly",
  "type": "Console",
  "time_options": {
    "hours": 21,
    "minutes": 10
  }
}
// ping1.json
{
  "name": "Ping1 Command",
  "command": "ping facebook.com -c 10",
  "frequency": "Hourly",
  "type": "Console",
  "time_options": {
    "hours": 21,
    "minutes": 15
  }
}
// query.json
{
  "name": "See all people",
  "command": "SELECT * FROM people",
  "frequency": "Hourly",
  "type": "Sql",
  "time_options": {
    "hours": 21,
    "minutes": 5
  }
}
```

The last job should have no issues running on any operating system. You may need to change the commands in the first two jobs if you are using Windows, for example. Also, time options might need to be changed, depending on when the application is being run and if you don't want to wait for hours before you see proof that it actually works.

If we run our application now with these configurations, we will get the following output:

```
volcom@volcom-Dell-System-XPS-L502X:~/workspace/scala-book/job-scheduler$ java
-cp target/job-scheduler-1.0.0-SNAPSHOT.jar com.ivan.nikolov.scheduler.Schedule
r -Dconfig.resource=/etc/scheduler/conf.d/production.conf
[main] INFO  com.ivan.nikolov.scheduler.Scheduler$  - Running migrations before
 doing anything else.
[main] INFO  com.ivan.nikolov.scheduler.Scheduler$  - Migrations done!
[main] INFO  com.ivan.nikolov.scheduler.Scheduler$  - Started! Use CTRL+C to ex
it.
[scheduler-akka.actor.default-dispatcher-4] INFO  com.ivan.nikolov.scheduler.ac
tors.Master   - Scheduled: JobConfig(Ping Command,ping google.com -c 2,Console,H
ourly,TimeOptions(1,33))
[scheduler-akka.actor.default-dispatcher-4] INFO  com.ivan.nikolov.scheduler.ac
tors.Master   - Scheduled: JobConfig(Ping1 Command,ping facebook.com -c 2,Consol
e,Hourly,TimeOptions(1,34))
[scheduler-akka.actor.default-dispatcher-4] INFO  com.ivan.nikolov.scheduler.ac
tors.Master   - Scheduled: JobConfig(See all people,SELECT * FROM people,Sql,Hou
rly,TimeOptions(1,33))
[scheduler-akka.actor.default-dispatcher-2] INFO  com.ivan.nikolov.scheduler.ac
tors.Worker   - Sql query results:
[scheduler-akka.actor.default-dispatcher-2] INFO  com.ivan.nikolov.scheduler.ac
tors.Worker   - 1        Ivan    26
[scheduler-akka.actor.default-dispatcher-2] INFO  com.ivan.nikolov.scheduler.ac
tors.Worker   - 2        Maria   25
[scheduler-akka.actor.default-dispatcher-2] INFO  com.ivan.nikolov.scheduler.ac
tors.Worker   - 3        John    27
[scheduler-akka.actor.default-dispatcher-6] INFO  com.ivan.nikolov.scheduler.ac
tors.Master   - Successfully completed See all people (SELECT * FROM people).
PING google.com (216.58.210.78) 56(84) bytes of data.
64 bytes from lhr14s24-in-f14.1e100.net (216.58.210.78): icmp_seq=1 ttl=56 time
=7.10 ms
64 bytes from lhr14s24-in-f14.1e100.net (216.58.210.78): icmp_seq=2 ttl=56 time
=6.94 ms

--- google.com ping statistics ---
2 packets transmitted, 2 received, 0% packet loss, time 1002ms
rtt min/avg/max/mdev = 6.948/7.026/7.104/0.078 ms
[scheduler-akka.actor.default-dispatcher-5] INFO  com.ivan.nikolov.scheduler.ac
tors.Master   - Successfully completed Ping Command (ping google.com -c 2).
PING facebook.com (66.220.158.68) 56(84) bytes of data.
64 bytes from edge-star-mini-shv-07-frc3.facebook.com (66.220.158.68): icmp_seq
=1 ttl=76 time=98.6 ms
64 bytes from edge-star-mini-shv-07-frc3.facebook.com (66.220.158.68): icmp_seq
=2 ttl=76 time=98.5 ms

--- facebook.com ping statistics ---
2 packets transmitted, 2 received, 0% packet loss, time 1001ms
rtt min/avg/max/mdev = 98.522/98.608/98.694/0.086 ms
[scheduler-akka.actor.default-dispatcher-2] INFO  com.ivan.nikolov.scheduler.ac
tors.Master   - Successfully completed Ping1 Command (ping facebook.com -c 2).
^C[shutdownHook1] INFO  com.ivan.nikolov.scheduler.Scheduler$  - Awaiting actor
 system termination.
[shutdownHook1] INFO  com.ivan.nikolov.scheduler.Scheduler$  - Actor system ter
minated. Bye!
```

We can leave the application and it will keep executing the tasks we had every one hour or day, depending on how the tasks are scheduled. Of course, we could add more meaningful jobs, allocate more workers, change other configurations, and so on.

The future of our application

We have used a number of techniques and concepts that we have learned throughout this book—dependency injection, factory design pattern, ADTs, and the Akka library, which can be used to implement the observer design pattern. This was a complete application that was designed to be testable and extendible.

We can easily add more granularity to the execution schedule of the jobs, the different types of tasks, and also have tasks trigger each other, different routing mechanisms, and so on. We showed that we have learned about a great number of useful concepts in this book, and now we can put everything to use in order to create great programs.

Summary

Here, we are at the end of our journey through the Scala design patterns. As you already know, design patterns exist in order to cope with a certain limitation of a language. They also help us to structure our code in a way that makes it easy to change, use, test, and maintain. Scala is an extremely rich language, and we focused on some of its features that make it capable of achieving things that other languages might not be able to do without any extra effort and knowledge.

We looked at the different *Gang of Four* design patterns from the point of view of Scala—creational, structural, and behavioral design patterns. We saw that some of them are not even applicable in functional languages and that others can be approached differently. We also saw that some design patterns still remain valid and knowing them is really important for any developer.

We can't talk about Scala without dealing with concepts such as monoids and monads. At first, they could be pretty scary and abstract and manage to put people off. So, we spent some time with them and showed their value. They can be used to write powerful applications in a purely functional way. They can be used to abstract and reuse functionality. By minimizing the dry theory and focusing on understandable examples, we hopefully made them much more approachable and usable for those of you who don't have a deep mathematical background.

Using the rich features of Scala opens up another large group of design patterns. We spent some time on design patterns that are possible just because of the way Scala works and the different features it provides.

Throughout the book, we have tried to provide meaningful examples that can be used as a reference to find specific patterns and applications of the techniques we learned here. In this last chapter, we even implemented a complete application. On many occasions, we have tried to showcase how different design patterns can be combined. Of course, in some cases, the concepts could be pretty complicated by themselves, so we simplified the examples.

We've given some advice about when to use certain design patterns and when to avoid them. These points should be extremely helpful to you in terms of what details to focus on.

The use of libraries has been encouraged throughout the book. Especially in the last few chapters, you have been exposed to quite a large number of interesting libraries that can be easily added to your arsenal. We have hopefully also sparked an interest and a habit to always do checks before trying something *new*.

Finally, all the examples found in this book can also be found online at `https://github.com/nikolovivan/scala-design-patterns`.

Other Books You May Enjoy

If you enjoyed this book, you may be interested in these other books by Packt:

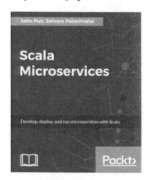

Scala Microservices
Jatin Puri, Selvam Palanimalai

ISBN: 978-1-78646-934-2

- Learn the essentials behind Microservices, the advantages and perils associated with them
- Build low latency, high throughput applications using Play and Lagom
- Dive deeper with being asynchronous and understand the superiority it provides
- Model your complex domain data for scale and simplicity with CQRS and Event Sourcing
- Be resilient to failures by using message passing
- Look at best practices of version control workflow, testing, continuous integration and deployments
- Understand operating system level virtualization using Linux Containers. Docker is used to explain how containers work
- Automate your infrastructure with kubernetes

Scala for Machine Learning - Second Edition
Patrick R. Nicolas

ISBN: 978-1-78712-238-3

- Build dynamic workflows for scientific computing
- Leverage open source libraries to extract patterns from time series
- Write your own classification, clustering, or evolutionary algorithm
- Perform relative performance tuning and evaluation of Spark
- Master probabilistic models for sequential data
- Experiment with advanced techniques such as regularization and kernelization
- Dive into neural networks and some deep learning architecture
- Apply some basic multiarm-bandit algorithms
- Solve big data problems with Scala parallel collections, Akka actors, and Apache Spark clusters
- Apply key learning strategies to a technical analysis of financial markets

Leave a review - let other readers know what you think

Please share your thoughts on this book with others by leaving a review on the site that you bought it from. If you purchased the book from Amazon, please leave us an honest review on this book's Amazon page. This is vital so that other potential readers can see and use your unbiased opinion to make purchasing decisions, we can understand what our customers think about our products, and our authors can see your feedback on the title that they have worked with Packt to create. It will only take a few minutes of your time, but is valuable to other potential customers, our authors, and Packt. Thank you!

Index

Made in United States
North Haven, CT
22 May 2022

19411343R00217